Tourism and Archaeology

Sustainable Meeting Grounds

Edited by

Cameron Walker
Neil Carr

Walnut Creek, California

LEFT COAST PRESS, INC.
1630 North Main Street, #400
Walnut Creek, CA 94596
http://www.LCoastPress.com

ISBN 978-1-61132-988-9 hardback
ISBN 978-1-61132-989-6 paperback
ISBN 978-1-61132-990-2 institutional eBook
ISBN 978-1-61132-748-9 consumer eBook

Library of Congress Cataloging-in-Publication Data:

Tourism and archaeology: sustainable meeting grounds/[edited by] Cameron Walker, Neil Carr.
    pages cm
    Summary: "The global popularity and lucrative potential of tourism has made sustainability a major concern for archaeologists, site managers, politicians, local communities, tourism officials, and other stakeholders. This book establishes new, interdisciplinary ground for tourism and archaeology that will foster a new generation of sustainable thinking and practice. First, three teams of co-authors from both disciplines tackle key conceptual dilemmas: exploration vs. exploitation, education vs. entertainment, and cultural sensitivity vs. embeddedness. Then, international case studies examine site development, marketing, community relations, and other on-the-ground examples of heritage work. The volume launches an important new era of collaboration in this growing field" — Provided by publisher.
    Includes bibliographical references and index.
    ISBN 978-1-61132-988-9 (hardback) — ISBN 978-1-61132-989-6 (paperback) — ISBN 978-1-61132-990-2 (institutional eBook) — ISBN 978-1-61132-748-9 (consumer eBook)
    1. Heritage tourism. 2. Archaeology—Social aspects. 3. Culture and tourism. I. Walker, Cameron Jean, editor of compilation. II. Carr, Neil, 1972-editor of compilation.
    G156.5.H47T67 2013
    338.4'791—dc23

                          2013022662

Printed in the United States of America

⊚™ The paper used in this publication meets the minimum requirements of American National Standard for Information Sciences—Permanence of Paper for Printed Library Materials, ANSI/NISO Z39.48–1992.

Tourism and Archaeology

Contents

Illustrations

Part ONE

Concepts

Chapter 1
Tourism and Archaeology: An Introduction

Cameron Walker and Neil Carr

> The study of tourism, and the management of it, demands that it be seen as an extended field of relationships not readily disentangled from one another, not easily sorted . . . into clear-cut and exclusive, opposing categories: host and visitor, local and global, we and they, here and there. (Geertz 1997:20)

Introduction

For many, the appeal of anthropology lies in the tradition of looking at the world as a complex, interconnected system. Rather than looking at human culture as isolated blocks of information, it is in the myriad ways that certain bits of information are associated with other bits of information that makes human beings and their cultures so enormously fascinating. To better understand various aspects of human behavior, it is necessary for the academic world to sort them

Tourism and Archaeology: Sustainable Meeting Grounds, edited by Cameron Walker and Neil Carr, 11–36. ©2013 Left Coast Press, Inc. All rights reserved.

into subcategories that, in the context of this book, have to do with tourism, heritage, archaeology, and sustainable conservation as the focus of research, analysis, and discussion. Unfortunately, focusing on separate subcategories actually takes the spotlight away from the systemic connections. With this approach, scholars often spend their careers analyzing similar subjects from different perspectives, and then they publish their conclusions as separate collections of information.

To get around this academic compartmentalization, this book has brought together assorted scholars from many different parts of the world and from various areas of scholarship to discuss topics that are of mutual concern. For many of us, this book marks the first time there is a sharing of knowledge and perspectives, which serves to deepen our overall understanding. This dialog also allows us to look for solutions to mutual concerns that make sense in the present and are sustainable into the future. For scholars interested in the issues of anthropological archaeology, those interests inevitably shift toward the complexities involved with opening an archaeological site for tourism. Those interests include relationships with local communities, the surrounding ecosystem, the myriad sociopolitical scenarios, and the need to provide interpretation for visitors.

In the late 1990s, archaeologists were just beginning to write about the subject of archaeological tourism; so it was necessary to turn to tourism literature as a way to expand into theory, methods, and other perspectives. It is still somewhat unusual for an article on archaeological tourism to be intended for an interdisciplinary audience or for the literature to incorporate other fields. Increased communication between the disciplines of archaeology and tourism studies seem to benefit both disciplines; so the idea for collaboration led to a partnership between Cameron Walker, an anthropological archaeologist based in California, and Neil Carr, a prolific tourism scholar in New Zealand. The plan for this book gradually developed a format that includes three conceptual chapters which address some of the more crucial issues that challenge archaeologists and tourism scholars. In order to produce a meaningful dialogue on each of these three concepts, we partnered an archaeologist or anthropologist with a tourism scholar whose experience included archaeological tourism. We asked the three teams to discuss their individual perspectives and, in particular, we asked each team to discuss one of the following issues: exploration versus exploitation; education versus infotainment; and cultural sensitivity versus embeddedness. To round out the book and provide a variety of on-the-ground, applied viewpoints, we also sought out a variety of case study experiences with archaeological tourism.

Perhaps unsurprisingly, the result was quite a complicated endeavor because, as it turned out, we had launched several multinational and multidisciplinary dialogues that became ever more complex as different perspectives were voiced. We had expected an intricate exchange of ideas, of course, but there were other additional hurdles from within the disciplines of archaeology and tourism studies, as well as from the many different national perspectives.

Ultimately, we have produced a book with more than 20 internationally diverse authors discussing their own experiences with archaeological tourism along with the challenges and lessons learned. In order to place the book within the realm of contemporary scholarship, we begin with a description of the world of archaeological tourism as it straddles the parallel academic arenas of archaeology and tourism studies.

Tourism and Heritage

Tourism is an immensely popular global social phenomenon, and it appears to be growing despite the otherwise daunting factors of global economic and political instability that are so much a feature of the early 21st century. As a topic, tourism has been separated into many different subtypes, many of which overlap one another. Our discussion of tourism sticks close to the theme of tourism at archaeological sites; although, the topic is also discussed in broader terms of heritage tourism, cultural tourism, ecotourism, and volunteer tourism, to name only a few examples.

Timothy (2011:341) provides one example of the overlap between many types of tourism:

> Much of the world's knowledge of the human past has come to light through the labors of amateur archaeologists or of volunteers undertaking archaeology experiences during their vacations, especially in the early years of archaeological exploration.

While recognizing the broader settings of archaeology and tourism, this discussion focuses on tourism of archaeological sites and adopts a definition of tourism that says it is part of "human exploratory behavior" that serves as a diversion from the ordinary and helps to make life more interesting and "worth living" (Berlyne 1962; Graburn 1989:21–22).[1]

Clearly, archaeological remains (artifacts and sites), and archaelogy as an academic discipline, can be situated within the broader field of heritage. At the same time, archaeology and heritage are not the same thing; so while debates about heritage and heritage tourism can and should inform our understanding of archaeological tourism, they should not be used as a substitute for focusing more specifically on the phenomenon of tourism of archaeological sites. The significant amount of work that has been published on heritage tourism has in general been implicit, and on occasion, explicit, when discussing issues associated with archaeology. This has certainly helped to inform much of the work thrashed out in this book; and while the focus of the book is on archaeological tourism, it is clear that any implications that are highlighted here will also have relevance for the fields of heritage studies and heritage management. Therefore, it is hoped that by putting archaeology in the spotlight, this book will also add to the literature on heritage studies and heritage tourism.

Archaeology is a fascinating, sometimes misinterpreted, discipline that is often romanticized in fictional (e.g., Indiana Jones and Lara Croft) and documentary media (e.g., the British TV program *Time Team*; Holtorf 2007; Walker 2009). Actually, the earliest archaeologists were themselves tourists (Russell 2006) who had the gumption and wherewithal to search for mysterious cities and lost artifacts. Archaeology remains a romantic pursuit for the public; although, it has also become an academic discipline that adheres to the rigors of scientific and humanistic scholarship. Archaeologists do not work in isolation, and an archaeological site is not merely a pile of ruins or a collection of ancient things. Rather, there is a more complex setting that includes the present-day ecosystem, local communities, and the sociopolitical networks that must also be considered.

By its very nature, archaeology is a destructive process, so it is necessary to predetermine how to protect a site after it has been excavated. Where will the excavated artifacts be placed? Who will study them? Will the analysis be published? What are the potential effects of excavation research on local communities and the surrounding environment? If the site entices the interest of tourists, what are the ramifications for bringing visitors into and out of the area? What are the presumed benefits of tourism, and what can be done to insure that negative impacts are mitigated? Which practices are sustainable, and how do we project them into the future? These are only a few of the many important considerations that are connected with tourism of archaeological sites, and no one, not even the tourists, are spared responsibility for their choices and their actions.

Tourism and heritage scholars are well aware of the detrimental effects of poorly planned tourism and have offered up recommendations that include the responsibilities of tourists. In the *8th Draft of the International Cultural Tourism Charter, Managing Tourism at Places of Heritage Significance*, as adopted by ICOMOS (International Council on Monuments and Sites) at the 12th General Assembly in Mexico in October, 1999, tourism responsibilities were made explicit:

> Tourism should bring benefits to host communities and provide an important means and motivation for them to care for and maintain their heritage and cultural practices. The involvement and co-operation of local and/or indigenous community representatives, conservationists, tourism operators, property owners, policy makers, those preparing national development plans and site managers is necessary to achieve a sustainable tourism industry and enhance the protection of heritage resources for future generations. (http://www.icomos.org/tourism/charter.html)

While tourism and archaeology are, without a doubt separate disciplines, they share a significant number of interests, such as the educational and financial responsibilities of archaeologists and those who manage archaeological sites and museums. The archaeological tourism market, as a vital part of a larger heritage tourism market, involves the interaction of archaeologists, tourism experts, and heritage site managers throughout the world. A growing trend highlights publishing articles about archaeological tourism in such widely varied disciplines as the *National Association for the Practice of Anthropology* (NAPA), *World Archaeology, The International Journal of Tourism Research, Sustainable Development*, and *Conservation and Management of Archaeological Sites*. Additionally, related articles can be found in such diverse academic publications as *Museum Management, Heritage and Society, Journal of Tourism Studies, Pasos,* and the *Journal of Interpretation Research.* In concurrence with the premise of this book, *The Journal of Heritage Tourism* has this to say about the need for particular scholarly collaborations:

> During the past 20 years, the study of tourism has become highly fragmented and specialized into various theme areas, or concentrations. Within this context, heritage tourism is one of the most commonly investigated forms of tourism, and hundreds of scholars and industry workers are involved in researching its dynamics and concepts. This academic attention has resulted in the publication of hundreds of refereed articles in various scholarly media, yet, until now there has been no journal devoted specifically to heritage tourism; *Journal of Heritage Tourism* was launched to fill this gap. (http://www.tandfonline.com/action/aboutThisJournal?show=aimsScopeandjournalCode=rjht20)

This book aims to establish another type of forum for promoting the discussion of at least some of the issues that are so critical to archaeologists, anthropologists, and tourism scholars. Prior to this book, it has been relatively rare for articles and books on tourism to cross over into the realm of archaeological research, site management, and the public interpretation at archaeological sites; just as the perspectives of site managers, anthropologists, and archaeologists have had little influence on tourism scholars.

The discussion of issues at the core of archaeological tourism has been framed within a social, cultural, environmental, and economic ideal of sustainable development. The needs of archaeologists, tourists, local communities, the tourism industry, and the wider society must be recognized and considered while ensuring the viability of archaeological sites for the benefit of future generations. Ultimately, this book emphasizes specific areas where the demands of managing archaeological sites within a sustainable framework have become explicit to those who are involved at both the scholarly and entrepreneurial levels. In this way, the book represents an intellectual, yet applied, "reach across the gap" for tourism and archaeological literature.

Where Does Heritage Fit In?

Ashworth (1997) has described heritage as almost anything inherited from the past or destined for the future. Another perspective is provided by Harrison (2005) and Herbert (1995b:14), who suggest that "heritage" is a concept that "encapsulates notions of history, politics and identity," which are often wrapped around historical artifacts and sites. This view of heritage is taken further by Franquesa and Morell (2007:171), who have noted that heritage and heritage-making is "inseparable from questions of influence, politics, interests, and authority – in short, power."

According to the International Tourism Charter, adopted by ICOMOS in 1989:

> Heritage is a broad concept and includes the natural as well as the cultural environment. It encompasses landscapes, historic places, sites and built environments, as well as biodiversity, collections, past and continuing cultural practices, knowledge and living experiences. It records and expresses the long processes of historic development, forming the essence of diverse national, regional, indigenous and local identities and is an integral part of modern life. It is a dynamic reference point and positive instrument for growth and change. The particular heritage and collective memory of each locality or community is irreplaceable and an important foundation for development, both now and into the future. (http://www.icomos.org)

The "meaning" given to an archaeological site or an artifact does not simply derive from what it is, but from those who present it to the public (Beeho and Prentice 1997). It is, therefore, essential to recognize that heritage is not merely a passive presentation of history, but an active agent in the formulation of how information is presented to the public. Given the interpretative nature of heritage, its meaning is not fixed either temporally or geographically but is employed to service a diverse global population (Ashworth 1997; Hodder 1991).

It must also be noted that heritage is often a flexible economic tool, which is separate from the ideological dilemmas discussed in the tourism and heritage literature (McMorran 2008). A multivocal approach is a key component of Ian Hodder's archaeological excavation project at Catalhoyuk, Turkey, where they employ an ongoing and reflexive research plan. Their work demonstrates that it is both possible and necessary to collaborate with all of the stakeholder groups in a manner that determines which questions, answers, and interpretations will eventually emerge (Hodder 2003:180).

The recognition by humankind of the fundamental obligation to preserve heritage sites has been demonstrated by the presence of such influential institutions as UNESCO (United Nations Educational, Scientific, and Cultural Organization), which maintains lists of sites that have been deemed to be of critical importance to the world's heritage. Some of the designated sites are natural, others are cultural, and a few are recognized because they embody both cultural and natural components. The lists comprise sites that are considered to be unique and significant to the world – including underwater sites – and the need to protect them and to prevent the illicit traffic of antiquities is made explicit. The World Monuments Fund and ICOMOS function as international, non-governmental organizations dedicated to the conservation of monuments and sites around the world (www.icomos.org; www.wmf.org).

Even more specific to archaeology are organizations such as ICAHM (International Scientific Committee on Archaeological Heritage Management), which advises ICOMOS and the World Heritage Sites Committee on matters that relate to the management of archaeological sites and landscapes, including formulating standards and best practices for archaeological research and cultural resource management (http://www.icomos.org).

A more recent plan initiated by the Archaeological Institute of America involves the SPI (Sustainable Preservation Initiative). The plan offers funding and advisory expertise "to save and preserve some of the world's cultural heritage by providing transformative and sustainable economic opportunities" for communities adjacent to cultural heritage sites. The SPI motto, "Saving Sites by Transforming Lives," is demonstrated by providing funding and guidance for communities near archaeological sites in such diverse locations as Peru, Easter Island, and Jordan (http://www.archaeological.org/sitepreservation/spi).

Individual archaeologists working in the field have also been instrumental to site preservation. A number of applied examples come from archaeologists working in Mexico and Central America, where for example, Anabel Ford of the University of California at Santa Barbara has received acclaim for her years of work at El Pilar in Belize (Bawaya 2005; Ford 1999). With funding sources from the Ford and MacArthur Foundations, among others, Dr. Ford has built a cultural center, a caretaker house, organized a women's collective to sell crafts, and fostered an annual festival to cultivate community involvement and celebrate local cultural traditions (Bawaya 2005).

According to archaeologist Arthur Demarest of Vanderbilt University, "archaeology transforms a region," and the days of excavating a site, then leaving it without further regard for the site or the local community are long gone. To avert destruction of the site of Cancuen, Guatemala, by looters and other human activities, Demarest and his team have enlisted the cooperation of local communities who have come to see it as part of their cultural heritage and are prepared to act as on-the-ground stewards. Over the last few years, Demarest has helped to establish a visitor center, an inn, a guide service, and a campground for the site, which is now a national park. Three nearby villages collaborate to manage the operations, and their profits now pay for the water systems, school expansions, and medical supplies (Bawaya 2005).

While the concept of heritage certainly includes material sites and objects, it also encompasses a wider range of less tangible aspects such as literature, music, and art and can exist across broad landscapes, as well as at specific sites (Beeho and Prentice 1997). Such a clear link between heritage and culture helps to explain why political parties and movements have a history of using heritage sites and artifacts to create and/or reinforce images of nationality that fit their own agendas (Rowan and Baram 2004). It is important, therefore, to recognize that archaeological sites and artifacts are often presented to the public through lenses other than those of the excavating archaeologists.

Clearly, archaeology has a role to play in the construction of heritage through the discovery of sites and the analysis and interpretation of their meanings (Slick 2002). More than ever before, archaeologists must now incorporate the issues of preservation and interpretation for the public and considerations of local and regional heritage as key components of their work. One of the well-documented, ongoing excavation research and conservation measures that Hodder developed at Catalhoyuk, Turkey, (Hodder 1991, 2003, 2010) further exemplifies such dedication. The scientific foundation of archaeology directs the research, but it is later filtered through the social construction of heritage. In the United States, this principle is a primary component of the CRM (Cultural Resource Management) field that now employs the vast majority of archaeologists working in the US today. The responsibilities for stewardship, interpretation, and sustainability represent an applied approach in anthropological archaeology and are as necessary for modern research as permits and trowels. Even as an applied approach (which means taking lessons learned from past research to help solve today's problems), scholars debate about who the relevant stakeholders are and who gets to decide about the big questions (Pinter 2005; Pyburn 2009).

At this point, every aspect of heritage can be said to have been "marketed" (with a small "m" that encompasses the social constructions of history and a capital "M", which stems from corporate representations of history). For many archaeologists, the tourism industry represents yet another group that may appropriate and manipulate their work; and the tourism industry often views archaeologists as prone to interfering or further complicating plans for tourism promotion. The tourism industry and politicians have long utilized archaeological finds to create an abstracted heritage to sell to the public, especially when there are significant numbers of tourists visiting an archaeological site long after the archaeologists' research has wrapped up. It is against this background that a lack of communication between tourism and archaeology has developed despite the many shared interests and concerns.

Tourism: An Overview

The characteristics of the tourists who visit archaeological sites represent one point where the interests of tourism and archaeology overlap and a definition may help to understand where some archaeologists' concerns about tourism have emerged and why tourists have so often been seen as either the death knell or the economic savior for troubled destinations and nearby communities. Perhaps the definition of tourism offered by Valene Smith (1989:1) is particularly useful for this discussion: "Tourism = leisure time + discretionary income + positive local sanctions" (and where the positive local sanctions reinforce the curiosity, intellectual interests, or other motivations for visiting an archaeological site). This last component of the definition of a tourist is important because it stresses that tourists are primarily interested in fulfilling their own desires and gaining social capital from their experiences. By going on holiday, tourists have specifically chosen to escape their ordinary lives and the work associated with it. As such, tourism has been likened to a liminal experience (Hall 2007) where at least the "perception" of freedom is of central importance to the tourist's satisfaction and enjoyment.

An enormously diverse tourism industry's economic prosperity depends upon its ability to ensure consumer satisfaction and any failure to do so will not only reduce the levels of income received from visitors but may also lead to negative word-of-mouth recommendations from visitors. As the most influential of marketing tools, personal recommendations have the potential to significantly influence the income potential of tourist attractions and destinations (Carr 1997; Laing 1987).

As a mass phenomenon, tourism is a modern entity that emerged from the technological advancements in transportation that occurred during the Second World War and the economic boom that followed the war, especially in North America and Western Europe. Figure 1.1 shows the extent of the growth of international tourism since 1950, which the World Tourism Organization (2006b) predicted would

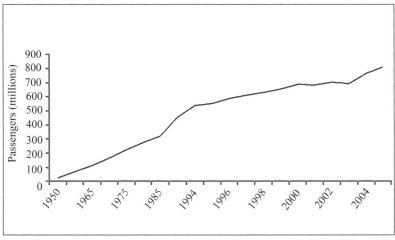

Figure 1.1   International tourist arrivals worldwide between 1950 and 2005.

continue with 1.56 billion people taking international holidays by the year 2020. Yet, these numbers pale in significance when compared to the scale of domestic tourism. While identifying accurate figures for domestic tourism is notoriously difficult, in 1994 the World Tourism Organization estimated that 70% of the total global demand for commercial accommodation was driven by domestic tourists (Weaver and Oppermann 2000). Indications of the scale of domestic tourism have been reinforced by the suggestion that up to 1 billion domestic vacation-related trips were undertaken annually in Europe in the early 1990s (Davidson 1998).

Over the last 50 years, the growth of tourism has been startling, but the phenomenon of tourism goes all the way back to ancient civilizations, where visitors wandered around the ruins of even more ancient settlements. Sometimes those ancient tourists brought home an actual artifact as a souvenir, which makes archaeological tourism one of the earliest forms of tourism (Timothy and Boyd 2006). Until the time of the Industrial Revolution, tourism was the preserve of the social/economic elite (i.e., those people with access to the free time and disposable income necessary to travel for pleasure; Holden 2008). With the emergence of the middle class in the modern era, the majority of the Western world's populations gained access to some disposable income; tourism was no longer solely the domain of the "elite" but instead became a mass phenomenon. Given the scale of tourism today, it is not surprising that there is the potential to generate a huge income for places attracting tourists, which can also have a significant impact on local, regional, and national economies. Indeed, in 2005, international tourism generated approximately $680 billion around the world (World Tourism Organization 2006b).

Today, opportunities for tourism experiences are offered virtually everywhere in the world, both catering to and aiding in the development of the desires of tourists. After all, tourism is an enormous, lucrative business, and governments, public officials, individuals, and private enterprises are all keen to benefit from it. Holidays that are dominated by relaxation and sunbathing on a beach continue to be the most popular type of vacation experience (Weaver and Oppermann 2000; Wickens . . . ; although, the variety of attractions and services offered to tourists has greatly diversified over the last 60 years. In general, tourism opportunities incorporate everything from sexual services, mega-events, and snow-capped mountains to idyllic rural landscapes and thrill-seeking adventure experiences.

Today, archaeological and heritage tourism are recognized as increasingly important segments of the tourism industry (Carr 1994; Fyall and Garrod 1998; Herbert 1995; Lovata 2007). Among others, Poria et al. (2005) have noted heritage as one of the fastest growing components of tourism. The increasing popularity of both heritage and archaeology as a tourism experience reflects the changing patterns in the nature of the tourist population. The decline of the traditional nuclear family may be linked to a drop in the relative popularity of the family beach holiday. The increasing number of adults without dependent children has also coincided with an increased level of education in the world's general population and the rise in the levels and utilization of paid, free time in many countries of the world, especially in Western Europe. In contrast, the United States is a notable exception to the trend in levels of annual leave (Burke 2006; Robinson 2006). These changing trends reflect a growing tendency among tourists to take multiple short vacations in increasingly diverse types of locales that allow them to experience activities other than relaxing on the beach. Archaeological sites represent one type of destination that has proven to be increasingly popular with a wider variety of tourists than has traditionally been the case. Although there is nothing new in the concept of archaeological tourism, it has historically been the preserve of a minority population, whereas today it reflects the enormous growth of tourism in general (Russell 2006).

Traditional visitors to archaeological sites were mainly an educated minority who are comparable in many ways to archaeologists and historians. They were often content to visit sites unadorned by visitor centers, cafes, or gift shops and to explore sites where minimal or no information was provided. Today, while traditional visitors still exist, the average visitor to an archaeological site is often just as concerned with the provision of shops and cafes on the site as with the archaeological ruins and artifacts on display (Gazin-Schwartz 2004). It may not, therefore, be surprising to note that entertainment, rather than "other motivations such as personal education, education of children, authenticity, or helping support historic preservation efforts" is the number one reason for visiting archaeological and heritage sites

(Slick 2002:223). It is also important to mention that the presence of souvenir shops and cafes may actually detract from the quality of the tourism experience for the traditional visitor to archaeological sites (Gazin-Schwartz 2004). This highlights the importance of understanding even visitors to single sites as heterogeneous with widely divergent and potentially conflicting desires rather than homogeneous populations.

So significant is the demand for archaeological tourism today that Tracy Ardren (2004:103) has noted that:

> One of the strongest factors in the commercialization of the archaeological record is the growing role of tourism in world economies. Archaeological sites and symbols are often used by national tourism agencies to promote their countries.

This, of course, emphasizes how tourism may encourage the morphing of archaeological sites and artifacts into heritage, and in the process, potentially setting archaeologists at odds with tourism developers and tourists. This problem may be further exacerbated by the realization that:

> For archaeological stories to acquire wider relevance they have to be billed as something other than what archaeologists think they are about. It means that few people are interested in archaeology in the same way archaeologists are interested in it. (Holtorf 2006:20)

The potential for economic benefits accruing from tourism became the primary focus of early research within the tourism discipline, but significant research has since brought to light the various potential impacts associated with tourism development. This research has recognized that tourism can have simultaneously negative and positive economic, environmental, social, and cultural impacts (Hall and Lew 2009). Furthermore, research has shown how the nature of these impacts is location-specific, and the perception of them may vary across populations within a given place. Despite recognizing the potential harm tourism development can inflict upon a location and its society, there is still a wildly held perception among the general population that tourism, as a leisure activity, must be "harmless," and as a huge economic phenomenon, it is often assumed to be a "white knight" capable of risk-free solutions for local financial woes.

In comparison to archaeology, tourism as an academic discipline is a young upstart that has rapidly developed over the last 30 years. Scholars within the discipline have gravitated to tourism from a wide range of disciplines that have historically included anthropology, geography, sociology, and psychology among others. More recently, tourism has begun to produce its own researchers and other emerging disciplines. Marketing and management studies, for instance, have also been increasingly influential in the discipline. While the discipline of tourism studies is most commonly situated within university business schools, the broad social science/humanities foundation of many of the early researchers in the field continues to be influential in ensuring, at least in an academic context, that tourism is perceived as both an industry and a social phenomenon. The social science foundation of tourism is, of course, sometimes at odds with the more scientific aspects of archaeology and is something that can hinder the debate between tourism academics and archaeologists. At the same time, the social science roots of tourism may appeal more to the field of heritage studies.

Tourism and Archaeology: A Sustainable Meeting Ground

An archaeologist's portfolio now includes not only the preservation of buildings and artifacts but also the hidden or lost histories of a place. Among their numerous responsibilities, they must also wear the hats of public educators and guardians of authenticity, as well as the myth busters of inauthenticities (Lovata 2007). As such, archaeologists are keenly aware of the potential for visitors to archaeological sites to damage the buildings that have been unearthed, and in general, archaeologists have also been wary of the potential for the tourism industry to appropriate the archaeological data to market to tourists. Herbert (1995:xi) has stated that, "for those committed to preservation as the overriding priority, heritage tourism is a threat." Robb (1998) claims that archaeologists are often concerned about visitor access and an inherent commercialization of sites by the tourism industry echoes this view. It feeds into the notion that many of those charged with managing heritage sites do not wish to see themselves as part of the tourism industry. The result is that, "the notion has even been advanced that some of these managers, particularly those in the museums and galleries sector, actually resent tourists for distracting them from their curatorial goals" (Garrod and Fyall 2000:684). The result, according to McKercher and du Cros (2002:2), is that the tourism industry and heritage management sector, largely, "still operate in parallel, with little real evidence being shown of true partnerships forming between them."

Images of the potential threat to archaeological sites posed by tourism abound. An example can be seen with the site of Stonehenge, depicted in Figure 1.2, which shows the site not as a place of scientific research and a measured understanding of history, but rather of mass tourism where visitors view the monument on hard surface walkways behind rope barriers while listening to prerecorded overviews of the site's history. Such negative images of tourism at archaeological sites are perpetuated, as Bender suggests (1998 in Gazin-Schwartz 2004), that visitors to Stonehenge spend more time in the gift shop and café than actively studying and learning about the monument. Based on the concerns of some archaeologists, it is important to ask whether there is room for tourism and archaeology to coexist at some sites.

Part of any answer to the question of coexistence must be based on the recognition that although archaeologists may be suspicious of

Figure 1.2 Stonehenge, UK.

the potential of tourism to destroy archaeological remains, they are increasingly aware of the importance of public interest in archaeology and the value of public understanding and support for the work of archaeologists. If they do not understand why it is important, why would they support it? Leaving aside "treasure hunters," who are looters of sites, the archaeological fraternity is often dependent on governmental funding to conduct archaeological excavations, analyze their finds, preserve them, and make the information public. As such, public appreciation of the value of archaeological research is vital for ensuring funding avenues from governments and public authorities. Young (2006:240) clearly highlights this by stating that, "it goes without saying that in these days of diminishing federal funds for archaeology, the public's understanding of the mission of archaeology is essential if the discipline is to survive." This is not new; indeed as far back as 1975, archaeologist Goran Burenhult observed, "in final analysis, archaeology is dependent on the general public attitude towards it" (Holtorf 2006:114). Unfortunately, by focusing on the academic importance of sites and artifacts, archaeologists have often failed to adequately engage the general public, as affirmed by Holtorf (2006:61):

> Professional archaeology has long been a field that defined and legitimized itself nearly exclusively in narrow academic terms. Even today, the benefits of archaeology are seldom discussed in relation to the evident fascination of many people with the subjects of archaeology, the archaeological past, and archaeological heritage.

Consequently, as far as Little (2002:3) is concerned "there is no question that archaeologists need to do a better job at identifying and communicating the public benefits of archaeology." One way of developing the interest and appreciation of the public in all things archaeological is to provide them with access to archaeological materials in a manner that is simultaneously engaging and educational. Doing this accurately and with the active participation of archaeologists helps to overcome the perception of being "fundamentally misrepresented [in the eyes of the general public] regarding the depiction of both the existing knowledge about the past and their own occupation" (Holtorf 2006:105).

Opening archaeological sites to visitors also offers site managers with a potential income through the levying of entry fees and the provision of refreshments and souvenirs. Income generated in this manner could be utilized to aid the preservation of sites and artifacts and fund further archaeological investigations. Since opening in 1984, the reconstructed Viking settlement in York, UK, known as Jorvik, had attracted 14 million paying visitors by 2006, which demonstrates the significant economic potential of archaeological tourism. Visitors have helped fund archaeological research through their entrance fees and have boosted York's economy through the money they have spent during their visit. It is arguable that without Jorvik, a significant number of the people who have visited the site would not have taken a holiday in the city and, consequently, had a positive impact on the local economy (Holtorf 2006). This demonstrates the importance of archaeological tourism not just for archaeological sites but also for local economies, and it helps to explain why public authorities are so keen to exploit their archaeological resources to increase visitor numbers in their regions. The importance of funds from tourism to archaeological sites is noted by Herbert (1995b:10), who, when talking about heritage tourism states, "there is a need to generate funds to allow preservation and conservation; the state will not assume the whole mantle of responsibility."

Accordingly, tourism professionals and scholars have argued that the industry can make a substantial contribution to the preservation of archaeological sites through the education of visitors and direct financial support (Weaver and Oppermann 2000). Furthermore, Hall (1998:237) has suggested that "tourism has meant that many buildings have been restored and has ensured that Australia's [and elsewhere] architectural heritage has been preserved not as a 'museum' but as something which is alive and pertinent to modern society." While this may be seen in a very positive light in terms of engaging people with the past, it potentially distorts the evidence of archaeological sites forcing the evidence to conform with modern perceptions of history in a manner that will appeal to a consumer, which is something the archaeological community takes great effort to avoid.

Unfortunately, at least from the archaeological perspective, tourism and tourists are not a passive phenomenon that only provides archaeologists with a source of research funds and a willing and supportive audience. Instead, the tourism industry is, in the modern capitalistic world, profit-oriented, and tourists, while potentially interested in archaeological sites, are not necessarily in tune with the mindset of archaeologists. The tourism industry is interested in the development and exploitation of archaeological sites and artifacts to satisfy the apparently insatiable desire among tourists for experiences that make connections with the past. In order to ensure sufficient visitors to make it profitable, the tourism industry must make certain that archaeological attractions have a high novelty value and provide satisfactory experiences. Recognizing the huge potential for archaeological tourism to not only generate funds for archaeological research, but also to develop regional economies through direct tourist spending and indirect multiplier effects, local, regional, national, and even multinational authorities are increasingly seeking to develop archaeological sites. Archaeologists and others interested in the preservation and authenticity of archaeological sites voice concerns when economic returns on investments and the satisfaction of tourists are ranked higher than other interests.

Archaeologists are not the only ones concerned with the preservation of sites, and the tourism industry itself has become increasingly aware of the potential to inflict harm on the very things it profits from. Now, there is widespread recognition of the need to preserve a site and its authenticity in the face of an ever more educated and demanding public audience. It is fair to say that both sides of the tourism-archaeology debate are increasingly interested in preservation, although for different reasons. Now it is necessary to collaborate to find ways for the two sides to work together in a mutually productive manner. The need for cooperation is supported by Slick (2002:221), who suggests archaeologists "must consider the tourism industry our partner, rather than an adversary, if we want to increase our ability to enhance public awareness about the importance of archaeology." The concept of sustainable development offers the potential for a meeting ground where archaeologists, the tourism industry, and tourists can come together in ways that enable the continuation of archaeological research and preservation efforts, while meeting the needs for economic development and the desires of tourists.

Sustainable development is a concept that can be traced back to works, such as *The Waste Maker*, by Vance Packard in 1960, which critiqued the throw-away society of the Western world at the time. The ideas of Packard were, indirectly, further developed in the book, *Limits of Growth* (Meadows et al. 1972).

In 1987, concerns about the exploitation of the planet and its resources by modern-day humanity culminated in the production of the Brundtland Report, entitled *Our Common Future*, by the World Commission on Environment and Development. This report crystallized the definition of "sustainable development" as "development which meets our needs today without compromising the ability of people in the future to meet their needs" (Swarbrooke 1999:3). Sustainable development recognizes the need to ensure that all parties interested in the utilization and preservation of a site should have an active voice in discussions about the process (Rees 1989). Ensuring the agency of all parties interested in archaeological sites provides a basis for generating their support in processes that allow for preservation and development in a balanced and sustainable manner.

In order to utilize the concept of sustainable development (which is grounded in an awareness of the need to preserve the natural environment) in the context of archaeological tourism, the definition must be refined to encompass the past as well as the present and future. Refining the definition of sustainable development also includes the importance of authenticity by recognizing the fact that physical preservation does not necessarily entail preservation of the meaning of sites and artifacts. Changes to the meaning of sites and artifacts may result in historical artifacts losing their presumed "meaning," which people are then unable to identify with; or it may result in artifact having their meaning redefined as something that is only pertinent to the present day. The trick is figuring out how to ensure that the meanings of sites will retain "authenticity" while making our understanding of the past accessible and relevant to the current population. Additionally, it is essential to ensure that preservation and utilization of archaeological sites does not endanger a site's authenticity. An example of a site where authenticity may be under duress is demonstrated by the Great Wall of China as shown in Figure 1.3. Here the scale of visitors and restoration efforts on the Wall threaten to undermine the authenticity of the site, which has been further compromised by the positioning of billboards near the Wall to advertise the 2008 Olympic Games.

Figure 1.3   Great Wall of China.

Any definition of sustainable development must be sufficiently flexible to recognize the validity of multiple representations of archaeological sites and artifacts and to guard against what has been called "Disneyfication." Furthermore, reorientation is necessary to include the realization that "development" is not always a necessary component of sustainability. Rather, the decision not to develop a site for tourism, or indeed the decision not to excavate a site, can be seen as a step toward both the preservation of archaeology and the continued sustainability of existing archaeological tourism sites by preventing a flood on the market with too many competing rather than complementary attractions. Finally, any viable definition of sustainable development needs to take into account the individual uniqueness of the needs of the archaeological site as well as the needs of the tourists. This is crucial to guard against oversimplifying any problems that may exist at the meeting ground between tourism and archaeology and the creation of ill-fitting homogenized solutions to them.

Book Structure

After the introduction, the book is divided into two sections. The first section is divided into three chapters and focuses on the analysis of the macro-conceptual issues that are central to the importance of sustainable utilization of archaeological sites by tourists and the tourism industry. Tourism must not detract from the cornerstones of archaeology (i.e., exploration, analysis, understanding, education, and preservation). As such, these issues represent the "meeting grounds" for archaeologists, researchers, managers, and scholars on the one hand, and tourism scholars, tourism industry entrepreneurs, and tourists on the other. The discussion of these issues is set within the concept of sustainability as outlined in the introduction and covers areas of agreement and disagreement between the two disciplines. To facilitate discussion of relevant issues in a manner that encompasses the viewpoints of both the archaeological and tourism organizations, the chapters in this section are written by a combination of people either who are situated within one of these two camps or who straddle them both.

The first of the conceptual chapters, "Archaeology Meccas of Tourrism: Exploration, Protection, and Exploitation," by Quetzil E. Castañeda and Jennifer P. Mathews, provides an informative discussion of the historical relationships between exploration, protection, and exploitation in the thinking of archaeologists. This situates contemporary presentations and representations of archaeology and tourism and charts the interconnected histories of these two social phenomena and fields of academic research. Castañeda and Mathews identify how archaeology and the tourism attractions associated with archaeological activities are inherently intertwined with myriad social, cultural, and political issues that shape and are shaped by tourism and archaeology in a process of exploration and exploitation. Consequently, within this chapter the theoretical rights of people to access and "possess" archaeological materials and of entrepreneurs to cater to visitors are debated within contemporary considerations of the value of archaeological explorations and the importance and nature of cultural preservation and representation. This is set against the economic real-ities that at least partially govern archaeological explorations and attempts at preservation. As such, this chapter provides a critical examination of issues that underlie decision-making processes about whether and in what manner to open archaeological sites to visitors.

Following the discussion provided by Castañeda and Mathews, the Chapter 3, "Integrating Education and Entertainment in Archaeological Tourism: Complementary Concepts or Opposite Ends of the Spectrum?" by Karen Hughes, Barbara J. Little, and Roy Ballantyne, is focused on the theoretical and actual nature, position, and roles of education at archaeological sites and with archaeological tourism in general. They examine the potential tension between the perceived need for educating visitors at archaeological sites and the preferences of both the tourism industry and tourists regarding what, if any, educational component should be included in archaeological tourism. This debate is situated within the potentially conflicting worlds of visitor satisfaction and the scholarly value of archaeology. Consequently, this chapter touches on what is meant by "education" and questions the extent to which education can be transformed until it becomes mere amusement. The perception of authenticity, from both a tourism and archaeological perspective, forms a central theme of the debate within this chapter.

The book's third and final conceptual chapter, "Cultural Sensitivity and Embeddedness" by Tim Wallace and Kevin Hannam, is based on the recognition of the potential for most archaeological sites to "tell" multiple and potentially conflicting stories that relate both to previous periods and contemporary subcultures. Wallace and Hannam discuss how the construction and presentation of these stories is an exercise in power that incorporates the potentially competing voices of various sociocultural groups, archaeologists, members of the tourism industry, and governments. The discussion of power and the exercising of it in archaeological tourism draws links with the various issues discussed in the two previous chapters in this section of the book. Central to the chapter by Wallace and Hannam is the notion that the sustainable development of archaeological tourism demands that all participants act in a culturally sensitive manner that takes into account all the potentially competing contemporary and historical cultures that have a claim to an archaeological site.

The second and more applied section of the book contains nine case studies that contextualize the issues raised within the previous conceptual section. These case studies cover a broad range of cultures and nationalities and demonstrate the complex meeting ground of archaeological and tourism-related issues. The first case study focuses on Hadrian's Wall and is by Gary Warnaby, David Bennison, and Dominic Medway; it concentrates on the management and market-ing of the wall for tourism and community experiences. This is followed by a case study by Andrew Birley who concentrates on Vindolanda, a Roman site on Hadrian's Wall in the United Kingdom.

Birley provides an informative analysis of the potential benefits of archaeological investigation to be gained from tourism juxtaposed with the sometimes critical views of Vindolanda espoused by archaeologists. The third case study, by Teresa L. Pinter, tells the story of attempts to develop an archaeological site as a tourism attraction in the American state of Arizona and illustrates the various reasons behind these attempts. Perhaps, most significant is that Pinter's case study also highlights how the development of an archaeological site for tourism does not automatically guarantee that it will become a successful tourism attraction.

In the fourth case study, then graduate student Emilie Sibbesson provides a personal account of her experience of her combined role as an archaeologist and tour guide at an archaeological dig in Dilston, UK. The fifth case study, by Scott Hamilton, provides an informative discussion of the nature of the relationship between tourism and archaeology in Western Canada and incorporates issues of power, cultural sensitivity, representation, and economics. The sixth case study is by Julie Tate-Libby, who examines the complex social and cultural issues that surround the proposed tourism development of Punaluʻu Black Sands Beach on the Big Island of Hawaii. This case study highlights the potential for specific sites to be claimed as important to different interest groups.

The seventh case study is by Ming-chun Ku, who relates her perceptions through interviews and participant-observation research on tourism to the Mogao Caves, a World Heritage Site, in Northern China. Ancila Nhamo, in the eighth case study, writes about the archaeological sites of Great Zimbabwe and how political and economic realities have impacted a once-flourishing tourism business in this region of Africa. Finally, the ninth case study, written by Tricia Gabany-Guerrero and Narcizo Guerrero-Murillo, relates the often misguided attempts to attract tourists to the Phurépecha culture in Northern Mexico.

The concluding chapter, "Conclusion: Manifesting Sustainable Meeting Grounds," draws together the various discussions that have taken place throughout the book to identify the nature and extent of the meeting grounds between tourism and archaeology in the contemporary era. Continuing on from this, the chapter discusses potential future directions for scholars and practitioners (tourism and archaeological alike) to explore through research and in practice.

The often-held objective for designing archaeological and heritage tourism that is really sustainable has swiftly become a defining cause for archaeologists, site managers, politicians, local communities, and tourism officials – to mention only a few of the stakeholders involved. This book represents the launch of a much-needed collaboration between the disciplines of archaeology and tourism studies. It intends to strengthen the understanding and communication between both disciplines.

Note

1. It is not the purpose of this book to launch into debates of what exactly constitutes tourism. These debates may be encountered in works, such as Franklin and Crang (2001); Hall (2005); Williams and Hall (2002); Sheller and Urry (2006); Weaver and Oppermann (2000); Cooper et al. (1998); and Hall and Lew (2009).

Chapter 2

Archaeology Meccas of Tourism: Exploration, Protection, and Exploitation

Quetzil E. Castañeda and Jennifer P. Mathews

This chapter is divided into two distinct sections that are positioned in a point-counterpoint structure of dialogue. These two position statements invoke the etymological meanings of the word essay: to attempt, put to the test, trial, to act out, to explore, travel, or to travail. The first is an historical analysis written in the third person by an anthropologist whose expertise includes the ethnography of archaeology and the anthropology of tourism. The second is a counterpoint commentary written by an anthropologist whose specializations include Pre-Columbian and historical archaeology. Both of us have significant research experience in the same area of the Maya world in Yucatán, Mexico. From these two differing vantage points, we chart our perspectives on the relationship between archaeology and tourism in terms of the problems of exploration, protection, and exploitation.

Tourism and Archaeology: Sustainable Meeting Grounds, edited by Cameron Walker and Neil Carr, 37–64. ©2013 Left Coast Press, Inc. All rights reserved.

In the first section, Castañeda takes a historical approach to the emergence of archaeology in the institutional context of the modern museum. He essays an analytical and theoretical manifesto about the deep, intimate interconnections between tourism and archaeology as revealed through an understanding of the museum. In his historical analysis of the role of archaeological representation in the museum, he identifies the sociological creation of universal heritage. He theorizes a notion of the universal citizen-heir as the implied benefactor of this universal heritage. In the second section, Mathews elaborates a commentary on this historical analysis of archaeology, tourism, heritage, and the museum. Specifically, she counter-argues and assesses Castañeda's theoretical and analytical claims through the use of archaeology and tourism at sites that are not "postcard" worthy. Together these two "attempts" grapple with the historical and contemporary interconnections between archaeology and tourism. Together, we put to the test our typical assumptions about the ethics of archaeologists, tourists, and tourism promoters in the contemporary contexts in which we are now beginning to ask how and why archaeology and tourism are interwoven phenomena in today's world.

Exploration, Protection, and Exploitation: Historical Analysis of the Archaeology Museum

Quetzil E. Castañeda

As of the mid-19th century, archaeology and tourism have shared a hidden history of emergence that links them together with the figure of the tourist and the institutional space of the museum. Despite conflicts between the ideological positions and practices of tourism and archaeology, the increasingly entangled, reciprocal, even collaborative relationships, however fraught, between tourism and academic archaeology now allow us to question this shared genealogy and rethink their contemporary intersection. Since the second half of the 19th century, the two have had an intimate, if also somewhat secret, interdependence based on their relationships to the modern museum. Given the way these interconnections have been forgotten, obscured, or hidden, a statement made in 1930 by Alfred V. Kidder is an especially welcome antidote to our historical myopia even if what he suggests may assault our contemporary sensibilities and historical assumptions.

Upon becoming the chairman of the new Division of Historical Research of the Carnegie Institution of Washington (CIW), Kidder explained how the CIW-sponsored Maya archaeological program had pioneered a "new" approach to Mesoamerican and Maya archaeology, specifically at the site of Chichén Itzá, Mexico.[1] He argued that this new approach eschewed the collection of antiquities for metropolitan museums for its own sake. His reasoning held that collectionism is politically improper in terms of international relations and ethically problematic for archaeologists who might be viewed as robbing a nation's patrimony.[2] He further asserted that collectionism is unproductive in terms of the scientific agenda of knowledge production, but Kidder then unambiguously linked the scientific research agenda of archaeology, even its success, as an academic field with tourism as the means and method by which archaeology could progress.[3]

> In the first place, because of its outstanding scientific and artistic importance, Chichén Itzá deserves our best efforts. Second, it is thought that if the project is handled in a manner so obviously altruistic it cannot fail to produce a feeling on the part of the Mexican government and the Mexican people that American agencies can be trusted within their borders. And, third, if Chichén Itzá can be kept both interesting and beautiful, it will without question become *a Mecca of Travel*, and incidentally, a most valuable asset for archaeology which, like every other science, needs its "show-windows." Its more recondite aims the public can not, in the beginning, be expected to grasp; but public interest must be aroused and eventual public understanding must be achieved if archaeology is to go forward: *for from the public comes, in the last analysis, all support for scientific endeavor.* (Kidder 1930:99, emphasis added)

This statement is both mundane and scandalous, and the discussion in this chapter unpacks the implications of Kidder's reflections and elaborates the meanings that it has for contemporary relationships between archaeology and tourism. The statement, on the one hand, is mundane for pointing out an obvious economy of cause and effect; archaeology, like any science as science, requires public interest to create public support, which in turn motivates and translates into the funding of archaeology in general. This, in turn, stimulates the emergence of more practitioners who desire to make careers out of this science, which necessitates more venues for public dissemination of results. Therefore, there is an increased public audience for the entire scientific endeavor, including appreciation by the public for more "recondite aims" and rarified knowledge.

On the one hand, when archaeology does its scientific work effectively in terms of knowledge objectives, ethical imperatives, and aesthetic engagement, it creates sites of and for travel that we can call, following Kidder, "tourism meccas." These restored sites of the past are ideal show-windows – marketing and promotional venues for archaeology – in which tourists can have their interests aroused in the specific culture and understanding of archaeological science. Finally, public support can be further stimulated, thereby enabling the progress of archaeology and the advancement of archaeological science.

On the other hand, Kidder scandalously identifies a symbiotic relationship in which archaeology depends in a fundamental way on tourism, that is, the travel industry that creates and propagates tourist publics and consumers out of "travelers" (i.e., tourists). This insight is so understated that its scandalous implications have been overlooked; Kidder does not say, nor does the present chapter argue, that specific types, topics, or culture areas of research are supported by tourism. Rather, he proposed that the entire endeavor of archaeology is dependent upon tourism, albeit indirectly, for the creation of a public culture of appreciation of and for archaeology, which in turn is what motivates and models the economic, cultural, and ideological support for archaeology in the world. Archaeology must create tourism meccas as promotional show-windows and marketable products that public audiences consume. The scandal is that archaeologists, and more generally anthropologists, have historically denigrated tourism as something of a rapacious disease that permanently destroys "authentic" cultures, communities, and archaeological heritage. And yet, archaeology, according to Kidder, must actively participate in the creation and propitiation of tourism in order to survive! The deeply ironic logic of this positioning is that anthropology has historically been wedded to the Romanticist ideology that opposes intellectual and artistic work from the capitalistic perspectives of production, marketing, and consumption.

Closer inspection of the quote enlarges the irony. The tourist, that is, the consumer/producer of tourism, is the generalized and generic public that functions for archaeology as its consuming-producing audience. How is it that archaeology shares with tourism as an historical reliance upon an ideologically constructed figure of the tourist as consumer, audience, and thus, as producer of both tourism and archaeology? In order to make sense of the intertwined histories of archaeology and tourism, I introduce the concept of "universal citizen-heir" and chart out how this figure is the embodied link within the institutional space and ideological functions of the modern museum. The first section of this chapter is an historical account of the birth of these twins within the museum, while the second section explores the contemporary contexts of collaboration between postcolonial archaeology and postmodern tourism.

Archaeology, Tourism, and Museums

The emergence of the modern museum in the 19th century had many sources, including world's fairs and expos, which were important catalysts for tourism and the transformation of private, elite collections of art and cultural exotica into institutionalized public spaces of exhibition open to all classes of the nation.[4] The articulation of these two exhibitionary systems in the emergent modernist museum coalesced in the projection of a universal civilization. This is an imagined community in which all of humanity is located and differentiated in a stratified, totalizing hierarchy along the lines of nations, races, and cultures. Thus, within this representational space of the museum, the ideological function has been to create both a national imaginary that could interpellate visitors as citizens of specific nations and an imagined universal human civilization in which nations serve as the primary agents (see Althusser 1971 on interpellation; cf. Sawyer 2002). Archaeology was significant for the emergence of the modern museum not simply for providing aesthetically, politically, and socially worthy specimens from major archaeological sites from the global south, but for providing a logical visual discourse that presented a totalizing hierarchy of humanity within narratives of evolution and the progress of civilization (Donato 1979). Certainly, the critique of the evolutionary discourse of museum exhibitions (most evident in natural history, archaeology, art, and ethnographic museums) and the analysis of the interpellation of citizens in the museum is not new (e.g., see Bennett 1995), but these two understandings have not yet been conjoined. Thus, what I propose is a simple, new idea that has yet to be examined; the modern museum since its historical emergence operates to interpellate individuals in the position of citizen-subjects who are simultaneously interpellated as universal citizens. This corresponds to the museum's projection of an imagined community of universal humanity, and this projected vision of a totalized humanity is expressed in all varieties of social theory and philosophies of the era, from E. B. Tylor's 1874 notion of culture (in the singular, not Geertzian plural) and Hegelian philosophy.

The ideological interpellation of the individual visitor-tourist as proper national citizen is therefore simultaneously the creation of a subject position of *citizens of humanity* – that is, *citizens and heirs of civilization*, as portrayed and constructed in the exhibitionary narratives of universal human civilization.[5] The acknowledgement of this ideological constitution and interpellations of a latent universal citizen-subject of humanity within the subject position of national citizenship has profound implications. First, this understanding allows us to see the intimate history of collusion and interconnection between tourism and archaeology that has been otherwise concealed from analytical inspection. Second, it allows us to ask about the changing political economy of archaeology in relationship to the museum and tourism from the 19th to the 21st centuries. What becomes evident is that archaeology's increasing dependence on tourism turns into explicit and overt collaborations with tourism actors by the end of the 20th century.

Universal Heritage and Universal Citizen-Heir

Museums within metropolitan centers had two interconnected goals of representation. On the one hand, archaeological exploration designed for museum collections created national patrimony as one of its imagined "primordial origins" of the nation (Anderson 2001; Geertz 1997). Although this might be called heritage, it is not in the contemporary sense a resource subject to control or management and ownership by identity. A more accurate term is "patrimony," precisely because it works to construct and constitute national identity rather than being the target of struggles for control through identity rights and ownership (see Castañeda 2009b, 2009c). On the other hand, the national patrimony constructed by the archaeology-museum apparatus is not univocal. The national patrimony is also constructed as the social fiction of *universal heritage* belonging to *generalized humanity* and deriving from a *universal civilization*.

The exhibition of these patrimonies has always served the explicit social purpose of education from the initial mid-19th century reformulation of museums to the present day. This educational imperative has similarly aimed for two objectives. As noted above, the museum works to constitute proper citizens of the imagined nation and encourages the notion that we are citizens of the world. The significance here is that the subject position of "citizen of humanity" is therefore also the *proper heir* of this patrimony, regardless of whose specific culture or civilization *is that group's patrimony*. In and through the museum exhibitionary complex, therefore, all cultural, social, and historical past becomes "heritage" for the imagined citizen of universal civilization in a quite explicit expropriation of the past from minority and non-Western descendant groups. The museum interpellation, therefore, constituted not only citizen-heirs of the (metropolitan) nation but also projected these as citizens of humanity and *proper heirs of universal civilization*.

Heritage, by definition, is something that is passed on to someone, the heir, or the inheritor; sociologically speaking, heritage also interpellates (i.e., identifies, defines, and calls forth) the heir as the proper owner-recipient. Heritage requires an heir, which we tend to assume is defined by descent. However, the substantive nature of different kinds of heritage can restrict or expand who may be legitimately identified and designated as a "proper" inheritor. For example, the inheritance of DNA happens through a different process than that of cultural values and personal property, which underscores the notion that descent is not at all stable. It can range quite dramatically from blood, racial, and other biological diagnostics to abstract modes of ethnic, linguistic, religious, cultural, and social descent/lineage as well as affiliation. Further, the proper heir can always be ascribed outside the lines of descent, regardless of how "descent" may be legally and culturally defined. Thus, heritage not only requires heirs but also a broker/mediator and custodian/curator who negotiate claims among possible heirs to ensure the passage of patrimony *to the proper heir.* Thus, the identification of the proper heir is not a passive act, but it is rather an active, constitutive process that interpellates the proper heir.

Archaeology has functioned in this role of "inheritance lawyer" of the past that it also constructs. This sociopolitical function is ethically formalized in the concept of stewardship in modernist archaeology that in turn is prescribed by and legitimated through the moral values (and ideology) of science. Archaeology produces (knowledge and the materiality of) "the past" in the name of the universal citizen of humanity. This should not be surprising since all of science claims to be in the service of humanity, for the good of humanity. Thus, archaeological exploration is ultimately legitimized by the scientific rationality of protecting "the past" and the available material fragments that are imbued with the power to symbolize "the past" as its embodiment. The scientific mandate of "protection of the past" is laid out in ethical codes of archaeology and consciously serves to distinguish modernist, academic archaeology from its colonial ancestor. Protection, in this modernist, scientific mode of archaeology is constructed in practical terms as preservation/conservation methodologies and in moral terms as stewardship.

In turn, contemporary social archaeologies (see Castañeda 2008; Castañeda and Matthews 2008) also use this stewardship function as a crucial point to distinguish themselves from other modernist, science-oriented forms of archaeology. They do so by reformulating stewardship, not only by substituting the "universal citizen of humanity" with particular "descendents/stakeholders" in the place of the proper heir, but by drastically reducing (if not eliminating entirely) the "custodian/curator" function in favor of the "mediator/broker" capacity. In concrete terms, this shift can be expressed in a variety of ways, but one of the most prominent is the drive to do "public archaeology" as a means to "engage descendent-stakeholders." As well, the archaeology of some geographic-culture regions, such as the US Southwest, Australia, the Maya world, and Latin America, is driven by its new social (versus scientific) morality and the assumption of responsibility to foment collaborations with nearby stakeholder/descendent communities beyond simple outreach programs (Colwell-Chanthaphonh and Ferguson 2008; Zimmerman 2008). Pyburn

(2008), for example, has proposed that archaeology be reformulated as a mode of action research or participatory action research, and it is among this group (i.e., those involved in one or another form of indigenous, Marxist, postcolonial, feminist, social, public, or engaged/action archaeologies) that archaeologists are most likely to be proactive collaborators with tourism development.

México is an especially notable region where these postcolonial initiatives have led to collaborations that aim for the creation of *community museums*, as well as where the heritage content (always a mix of archaeological, historical, and ethnographic material) is therefore immediately and unambiguously "passed on" by the research project (in the name of the archaeological stewardship) to the *proper heirs* to protect, own, and manage. While this might be fine in contexts where the descendant-stakeholders are corporately organized and demanding repatriation (e.g., the US, Canada, and Australia), this moral-scientific agenda runs the risk of imposing an artificial conception of proper ownership if the local stakeholders have not been or are not yet properly interpellated as proper heirs of archaeological stewardship (see Ardren 2002; Breglia 2006; Castillo Cocom 2002; Castillo Cocom and Castañeda 2002; Watkins et al. 2000). Nonetheless, as discussed below, expertise based in academic training and institutions remains crucial to the new ways that socially oriented archaeologists articulate themselves with communities of citizen-heirs who are no longer "universal," but are particular heirs localized in and identified by specific geopolitical-cultural regions.

It is as "stewards of the past for all humanity" that archaeology has historically claimed the legitimacy of its existence, the basis for professional expertise, disciplinary practices, and an attempt at monopoly control of the archaeological past (Wylie 1999). As scientific steward, archaeology reclaims the past from the dead in order to pass it along to the rightful universal citizen-heir of humanity. Thus, archaeology – that is, all archaeologies whether colonial, modernist, or postcolonial – require legitimate heirs. The question of who counts as legitimate heir, however, is not and has never been determined by science; this is a domain of politics, especially in the case of political determinations resorting to "science" as the way to validate criteria for determining legitimate heirs. Archaeology has thus been historically dependent upon the museum (that is, the ideological functioning of the museum to interpellate citizens) for the construction of the proper heir in the discursive and exhibitionary constitution of citizen-subjects of nation, empire, and humanity. Modernist archaeology, since its emergence in the late 19th century, has been dependent upon the ideologically constructed subject position that circulated in the undercurrents of archaeological discourse as expressed in museum narratives and displays. This dependence also provides the ideological legitimization of the museum as the place where archaeology must deposit that which it has collected; for it is here where the universal citizen exists in tangible form and can receive the "inheritance of the past" that is due "him" (it is constructed as male and most often "white").

The professionalization of archaeology in the university institution in the first decades of the 20th century entailed a shift in the political economy of archaeology from dependency on the museum to dependency on the university. This economic break from the museum also entailed a shift in its ideological legitimization (from collectionism for museums to science and the scientific accumulation of knowledge of the past for all humanity). This shift also correlates with the rise of the archaeological construction of iconic sites of world civilizations as tourism meccas of travel, as was the case with Chichén Itzá in the 1920s and 1930s. Although the construction of Knossos was in the beginning of the 20th century, it perhaps marks the emergence of the modernist era of archaeological meccas (Duke 2007; Gere 2009). As in the case of all sciences, universities do not make massive financial investments in research except on a low scale as additional salary benefits. The overwhelming task of financing research corresponds with non-university governmental and private sectors and non-governmental public sectors. This role has been assumed by the emergent funding apparatus – which is a network of private, corporate, governmental, and non-profit funding agencies operating within the public sphere – as pioneered by Andrew Carnegie through his investment in diverse foundations.

It is important to note that Kidder was not only writing in this historical moment of the transition in the political economy of archaeology, but that he was also precisely located in this sphere of public funding at a private, non-profit, para-governmental research institution (the CIW). His observation – that archaeology needs show-windows to sway public opinion in its favor in order to progress – must have been based on his own awareness that CIW funding of archaeology was entirely in the hands of the Board of Trustees who had to be continually convinced that archaeology was not simply a recreational sport of wealthy men but actually a science. Indeed nine years later, the incoming CIW President determined that archaeology was a pseudo-science and all but eliminated it as a research practice (Castañeda 2004, 2009a). Thus, Kidder astutely recognized that archaeology needs tourists as its audience and as the means to create favorable public opinion. This in turn is necessary to motivate the funding agencies to believe that giving grant monies to archaeological research of any type is an important and valuable contribution to society. In this economic calculus, tourism is the social mechanism that would bring tourists to archaeology's restored sites of iconic cultures, and thus, transform these new, open-air museums of the past into meccas of travel. Indeed, archaeology has become increasingly connected to tourism in terms of popular imaginaries and representations of the past, if not also economically dependent upon it for the production of the ideological appreciation of the past. This is an area of investigation that has only begun to be studied in a sustained manner (see Castañeda 1996, 2008, 2010, 2012 n.d.; Castañeda and Matthews 2008; Holtorf 2005, 2007).

Tourism, Tourists, and Archaeology's Show-Windows

Archaeologically restored sites are science fictions, and as such, they are constructed copies of something that *never existed* in that way. Rather than a denial of the past, it is a denial of the constructed site that accurately, empirically represents a reality other than what corresponds to the archaeological images of the past in that place and time. At a methodological level, there is always a telescoping or collapsing of time and the selective elimination or addition of occupation periods, objects, and information in both the processes of excavation and restoration of a fictional past. Therefore, these restored sites do not become open-air, in situ museums that represent and symbolize a particular human settlement (city, village, cemetery, or sacred site). On this basis, they do the work of representing an entire civilization in a complex signifying chain. This is clearly evident with many iconic sites of the new and old worlds, such as Chichén Itzá, Monte Albán, Tiwanaku, Knossos, the Coliseum and the Forum, and the Parthenon, not to mention the landscape of European castles, and many historical sites related to the colonial period in the global south or the rise of capitalism in Europe. The logic and agenda of this "restoration," – which is always a construction and not a reconstruction – of the past is often explicitly, but always implicitly, to create tourism meccas of travel. Archaeology, then, is not only dependent upon tourist publics, but also the tourism industry that creates the flows of consumer audiences and tourism agents for their broader dissemination of archaeological interpretations via multiple promotional and on-site discourses.

The explicit goal of protection as practiced in and by museum collection and exhibition is to care for the materiality of the past as the means to guard knowledge *of* the past. But in so doing, the museum and its ancillary disciplines such as archaeology and art history, do not simply preserve or conserve but also actively produce a knowledge that is laden with the ideological meanings, messages, narratives, and imaginaries related to the subject position of self and other. In light of this, the key issues do not revolve around the methods, concepts, and practices of protection. They revolve around, for example, whether preservation or conservation is the goal, whether they are the same or different things, whether the past is actually selectively destroyed by protection, or what the methods of protection should be (Bernstein 1992; Drennan and Mora 2002; King and Lyneis 1978; Layton and Thomas 2003; Wilk 1999; Wylie 1999). Instead, the crucial question is: *for whom is this past protected* (see Greene 1999)? What this analysis illustrates is that, historically speaking, the archaeological objective of protection is *not for those minority peoples* of the global south to whom the material belongs in terms of cultural traditions and historical pasts. Rather, the tourist, that is, the subject position that is simultaneously nowhere and yet everywhere, has been increasingly privileged as the concrete representation and embodiment of the imagined citizen-heir of universal humanity.

The metropolitan museum was designed as a representational system. Similarly, archaeological sites constructed as restorations of the past that express, both explicitly and implicitly, specific narratives and meanings. These are ideologically driven discourses and messages of civilizational-cultural hierarchies, whether or not they are explicitly evolutionary narratives of progress (Castañeda 2012, 1996; Cobos 2006; Duke 2007; Gere 2009; Handler and Gable 1997; Jones 1995;

Molyneaux and Stone 1994; Stone and Planel 1999). Site restoration functions as the material embodiment of the archaeological imagery of the society-culture or the civilization in question, as well as a tangible manifestation of universal humanity in general. The question arises, therefore, for whom is the archaeological past exhibited? Archaeological restoration is inherently a practice that has as its goal and purpose the creation of fictional replicas of the past for tourism that is for tourists to see, experience, and identify with as descendant-heirs.

The Tourist-Citizen and the Rights of the Universal Citizen-Heir

The historical function of the museum is crucial to understand in order to assess the validity of the idea that any person, anywhere, has the inherent right to visit, learn about, consume, and otherwise experience the (archaeological or ethnographic) heritage of other peoples. The museum is a key locus in the historical genesis of the subject position of the tourist as citizen of the world, who is free to visit any place at any time regardless of legal, moral, and cultural ownership and rights of those in the global south. This general and generic citizen of humanity is the subject to whom modernist archaeology has at the same time always appealed as the proper heir of human civilization and as the proper citizen-stakeholder of the archaeological production of knowledge of humanity's past.

The tourist-citizen, then, is the proper heir, or descendent-stakeholder – of all human cultures. Archaeology is an apparatus that silently grants and legitimates the tourist's right to visit, consume, in addition to developing the patrimony and heritage of any society's past for tourism purposes. As the production of tourism commodities and markets grew in the 20th century, so did the importance of the tourist as the consumer of archaeological monuments, restored sites, and exhibitions.

Tourism Meccas of Travel and the Political Economy of Archaeology

The interconnections between archaeology and tourism have been obscured or expressly hidden throughout the 20th century, in part because of pervasive and still-enduring Romanticist ideals, which science borrowed to distinguish science/knowledge from capitalism/ commercialism. However, there has been a transformation in the political economy of science and scientific knowledge production that has necessarily revealed the fiction of this opposition and forced its radical reformulation. The ideological illusion that knowledge/ science is separate from capitalism (i.e., capitalist production and consumption) was possible only because science fixed its economy to the non-profit, para-governmental, public institution called the university.

However, by the end of the 20th century, it has become indisputable that the university is now thoroughly market driven (Bok 2004; Slaughter and Leslie 1999; Washburn 2005; Zemesky et al. 2005). Under neoliberalism, this university has increasingly had its "non-profit mode" of production transformed into capitalist relations of production. It is clearly the case for the majority of high-profile, hard-science fields that university-based research has shifted from being a para-governmental, public, non-profit to a para-corporate factory. This shift is not so clear in the soft sciences and humanities where the infiltration of market production does not happen as it does in the hard sciences. Archaeologists are not in the business of inventing products, much less "the past" or "heritage," that requires patents for their commercialization; nonetheless, see Holtorf (2005, 2007) who argues that archaeology is a "brand."

It is necessary to return to Kidder's insight and modify it. The funding of archaeology via traditional foundations and private funding relies upon a strong public desire to consume the past. This drive in turn is promulgated by what we can call an archaeological imaginary that is forged through tourism, edu-tainment and educational TV, and text-based media, which no doubt helps to feed enrollment in archaeology courses and thus create a potential labor market of future archaeologists. It is important to note that tourism can be understood in a narrow sense as a multi-faceted industry that transports and accommodates consumer-travelers and then provides them with various commodity products (experiences, souvenirs, etc.). In this sense, tourism is certainly fundamental to the new economy of archaeology that was initiated as it split off from its dependence on the museum. Historically speaking, tourism is the strategic mechanism by which audiences are created for the iconic show-windows of archaeological science. Tourism as an economic force of archaeology operates, however, in a different register than does CRM, which is already a part of archaeology and, thus, has a direct impact on the field as a major source of employment for archaeologists. Tourism can also be understood and theorized in an expanded sense beyond those industry networks of transportation, hotel, restaurant, and on-site businesses that give tourists something to do. Tourism in an expanded sense would also include the production and marketing of travel desires, images, commodities, and motivations that occur in "off-locations" of edutainment TV, the internet (blogs, YouTube, etc.), print media, education-based travel (e.g., study abroad, Peace Corps), Hollywood, and documentary film, for example. Thus, tourism in this expanded sense operates indirectly from outside of archaeology as an important ideological engine and, therefore, as an economic foundation of archaeology as a scientific enterprise. In other words, the media and tourism production of the *ideological desires for the past generally and of specific pasts that can be marketed, consumed, and identified with* is what creates the very need in and desire for archaeology in the first place, including the technical management of the past as cultural resource. Archaeology operates, as Holtorf (2005, 2007) notes, as a brand that is supported media-driven consumerism and, especially, tourism (Castañeda 2012, n.d.).

Neo-liberal Tourism: Collusion and Sustainability

Within the last two decades there has been a transformation in both global economy and culture. Although sociologists of various disciplinary stripes are concerned with globalization, this issue is not the most meaningful in the context of tourism studies. Tourism, that is modern, mass tourism has always been a global phenomenon. More significant processes have been underway that could be encompassed by the idea of the neoliberalization of tourism. To my mind, this first references the proliferation of new forms of alternative and niche tourism, such as ecotourism, culinary tourism, dark tourism, heritage tourism, adventure tourism, and so on. These new forms clearly correspond to a capitalist logic of market diversification of a product. Second, correlated to this has been an ever-increasing involvement of new tourism agents (i.e., social actors consciously involved in the creation and development of tourism commodities, markets, and experiences) beyond the traditional for-profit industry operators (i.e., in marketing, transportation, hospitality, recreation-leisure, and food industries). These now include non-profits, civil associations, NGOs, INGOs, and para-governmental agencies at all scales, as well as cultural communities that seek to gain or that have been targeted for, greater inclusion into tourism development projects via the dream of sustainability.

These two tendencies have created a unique situation. Whereas we have argued, from the shoulders of Kidder, that archaeology has always needed and has increasingly depended upon tourism for ideological and economic reasons, tourism has gone about its business with only a haphazard relationship with archaeology. The current market segmentation of tourism has created a few niche forms of travel commodities that require and, thus, are dependent upon archaeology and anthropology more generally.

An example can be found in Mexico where the federal agency devoted to the educational, social, and cultural welfare of Mexico's indigenous peoples, the *Instituto Nacional Indigenista* (INI), was terminated and replaced by the *Comisión Nacional para el Desarrollo de los Pueblos Indígenas* (CDI) in 2009. This organization is now devoted, at least in Yucatán, to giving grants to community associations in order to develop (or even create) local environmental or cultural resources into tourism destinations (the towns of Ek Balam, Yokdzonot, and Xcalacoop are just three examples). In turn, these communities become targets for partnerships and free assistance programs from a multitude of metropolitan actors that are not traditionally involved in tourism.

The Mexican examples can be characterized in general terms to define a common scenario: Metropolitan graduate students in a variety of sciences and fields of study avidly hunt for such sustainable community-based development around which to formulate thesis or dissertation projects. Metropolitan professors with international inter-active learning, internship, or field training programs also feverishly seek out such community organizations in the global south in order to send their students/participants and create long-term research opportunities. The latter gain their "global" culture course credits and international study-abroad experience. The professor creates an "active research program" that "involves students" and publications while gaining a wide variety of professional benefits from tenure, promotion, and grants to teaching assistants and course reductions; and, of course they accrue extra status and cultural capital as knowledge experts. Metropolitan I/NGOs partner up and provide additional subsidy support in terms of managerial expertise, infrastructure development, and ongoing training to locals.

This training is crucial as it grounds the transformation of the subject positioning of locals from unruly subjects to proper citizens and heirs of heritage. Meanwhile, the government provides welfare under a neoliberal façade of competitive grants that only pays for a portion of the cost even as it contributes to the legitimization of the political party in power and ultimately of the state itself. Finally, "the community" receives assistance that is sometimes helpful, sometimes harmful; regardless, it is always assistance that community members manipulate at the cost of staging themselves as the proper citizen-subject of the global south that is in need of non-profit sustainable development. In five or ten years, with luck, the site will become part of the standard network of destinations in the mass tourism region. But, it is certain that within a handful of years the majority of community members who participated in civil associations will be run out of the program by a cohort of leaders who convert sustainable community tourism development into their quasi-private business subsidized by both the national government and a series of metropolitan NGOs, non-profits, research foundations, academics, and volunteers (Taylor 2012). What is significant is that tourism existed there from the beginning in the non-traditional, non-mass form of educational and research tourism (study abroad, Peace Corps, Earthwatch), and "observers" organized by international rights and advocacy groups to be on-site, third-party, civilian peace keepers. Archaeological field schools, domestic or abroad, are in fact a niche mode of tourism; although not quite a direct descendant of the Grand Tour despite certain historical surface similarities, it does belong within that ever-expanding category of "educational tourism." Non-profits such as Earthwatch and the School of International Training have been pioneers of this educational tourism that has only recently become recognized and, thus, identified *as such*, but which nonetheless *has always operated to create tourism*.

The Romanticist ideology of sustainability, to give it a positive spin, is motivated by a neo-liberal morality in which self-interested profit making coincides with and thereby creates an increase in the greater good of others in a manner that can be endlessly maintained into the future. However, the negative characterization is that the latter value is simply a pretense for business with a softer edge and a browner face; this is tourism's version of social entrepreneurship.

In today's 21st century version of the high-modernist development project, there are additional levels of mid-range experts who broker tourism development for communities and, thus, maintain a social hierarchy of transnational scope. In this dream, not only do traditional tourism agents seek to find the oasis of sustainability, but an increasing number of academics of all types actively participate in, promote, and promulgate tourism. It would be revealing to gauge the extent to which the research projects of academics (from non-industry fields of study) are either overtly or inherently complicit with the grand, global venture of tourism. It is exceptionally clear for the field of applied anthropology in which an ever-increasing number of students and scholars are conducting projects that aim to assist communities or community groups to take greater control, boost participation, or augment profits from tourism. In archaeology, an increasing number of professionals reconvert mandates for a publicly engaged discipline committed to the heritage interests of *descendent-stakeholders* into a mandate to foment tourism to stakeholder communities by collaborating with them in the creation of tourism destinations based on in situ ruins or community heritage museums. This archaeological drive to create heritage tourism for communities is not expressed everywhere in the world. There is an uneven distribution of this type of ethical archaeology and the reason for this that is why it is strongly expressed in Mayanist archaeology and not in Greece for example is worth substantial analysis. Nonetheless, it points out that we are a long way, thankfully, from the days when everyone – academics generally and anthropologists especially – not only loathed tourists but disparaged tourism scholars and scholarship.

The collusion and complicity between academics and tourism takes many shapes. Despite its widespread frequency, it is still fraught with ideological anxiety over its morality. On the one hand, there is the incorporation of science experts into the info-tainment documentaries that proliferate on the National Geographic, Discovery, History, Food Network, and Travel Channels. While experts may pursue pure research in the most abstract mode of science, by participating in the media, they become incestuously involved in the production of tourism, the creation of tourist motives, and the legitimization of tourism consumerism. Their own academic career and funding politics are not only augmented but are increasingly intertwined and dependent upon such media publicity. Despite our commitment to this type of status game, we often hide from an implicit assumption about the inherent immorality of the scientific involvement with tourism – and in the commodification of scientific expertise by mass media, generally – which is nonetheless contradicted by our practices, goals, and motivations.

This process of shifting the university and the sciences away from the idealized context of public, non-profit, and para-governmental economies to an increasingly capitalist market-driven economy is now well known. Archaeology, perhaps more obviously than other social sciences and humanities, is also now connected to the commercial sector of markets and consumerism. It is a fair question to ask about the extent to which the political economy of archaeology, although still situated in the university, has become based in tourism in the sense that Kidder suggested in 1930. In turn, there is a major sector of the tourism industry that relies on archaeologists, among other expert-knowledge collaborators in and outside the university, to produce the past as heritage attractions and to create ideologies, practices, and projects marked by sustainability.

The Dream of Meccas of Travel in the Age of Sustainability

The "reconstructed" or "restored" sites of archaeology are effectively open-air, in situ archaeological museums "without walls." At the end of colonial archaeology, these sites came to be conceptualized as places that could be visited by commoner classes as well as by elites. Significantly, this follows some three or four decades of the "demo-cratization" or "modernization" of metropolitan museums of the 19th century. From the middle to the end of the 19th century, museums were increasingly opening up to common and working classes with the idea of both transforming them into proper citizens and installing the representational system of nation (Bennett 1995; Castañeda 1996;

Genoways and Andrei 2008; Hooper-Greenhill 1992; Horne 1984). Significantly, it is in this historical period of the latter half of the 19th century that "tourism" also began to develop based on the expansion of leisure travel for secular purposes (i.e., non-religious/pilgrimage) by the non-elite classes beyond recreational sites (such as Brighton Beach or the Parisian Arcades) to historic sites and landmarks. The intertwining of archaeology and tourism is evident in the last two decades of the 19th century by the commercial expansion of Cook Tours. This pioneering development of modern, mass tourism began to organize travel to the Middle East and Egypt in what can be anachronistically called "heritage tours" (see Campbell 1988; Feifer 1985; Turner and Ash 1976; Urry 1990; Walton 2005; Withey 1998). This no doubt could have inspired Kidder, who had already dreamed of archaeological Meccas of Travel, to advance science. In 1916, while still working in the American Southwest, he wrote a postcard in which he expressed his wish that the archaeological restoration of Pueblo and Hopi sites would stimulate tourism (document in CIW archives, "Kidder, Alfred V." file). The novelty of Kidder's dream of a Mecca of Travel is that it consolidated inherent motives, goals, and reasoning in an explicit agenda for archaeology.

Today, in fact, the effort of tourism and archaeology practitioners to create in situ archaeological museums (i.e., restored archaeological sites) and community-stakeholder museums (in which heritage collections use a variable mix of contemporary ethnographic, historical, and recently excavated archaeological materials from nearby ancient sites) is overtly and irreducibly ideological. These community museums express the ideologies of contemporary, postcolonial ethics! For contemporary postcolonial archaeologists, the ethical mandates to engage publics and stakeholders often turns into attempts to develop collaborations with locals that aim to create community museums. Significantly, this ethic functions to have archaeology assume the role as "inheritance lawyer" by brokering the transfer of the past heritage to ideologically preconceived proper heirs. Trouble may arise for archaeologists, however, when the *descendent-stakeholders* refuse to be contained by the archaeologists' conception of what it is to be a good citizen-heir of archaeological heritage (see, for example, Ardren 2002; Breglia 2006; Castillo Cocom 2002; Castillo Cocom and Castañeda 2002).

The specific ideology may vary – as well as design style of the "community museum" – but the meta-trope that governs these ideologies is "sustainability." Within this framework, the goal of what I call "heritage knowledge" is the hegemonic logic and agenda of archaeological restoration in the contemporary postcolonial situation. The ideology of sustainability and the agenda of heritage knowledge also operate to rule over the domain of archaeological exploration of sites where it competes with and ultimately subordinates the goals and logic of scientific knowledge production. Today, archaeology could not exist except for the transformation of the institutional-economic bases that has made archaeology into a global, transnational industry and neoliberal market. Professional varieties of archaeology (based in the university, museum, government, and private/semiprivate CRM sectors) are dependent upon and intertwined with tourism and media-communications. This dependency is based on the latter's creation of universal citizen-stakeholders (and consumers) of "the archaeological past" via the dissemination of the archaeological imagery/knowledge produced through archaeological exploration and restoration. This, in turn, not only generates consumer subjects as the proper heirs of the past in whose name scientific archaeology always claims to be serving; but it also generates the driving motivation of private, public, and governmental consumer-stakeholders to invest in and finance archaeological exploration and protection (of all types). This then, provides tourism, media-communications, and educational industries the content from which to manufacture "the past" into commodities that feed and satisfy the multiple and diverse consumer markets.

In his dream of archaeological meccas for tourism, Kidder may not have ever imagined the substantive and reciprocal interdependence of archaeology, tourism, and mass-media, but he had nonetheless already anticipated the motives for how things would develop. The "advancement" of archaeology as a science is fully dependent upon "public understanding" or appreciation which in turn feeds all funding. Today, however, the in situ museum-meccas for tourism are not archaeology's only show-windows. The news media, popular literatures, Hollywood film, education industry, internet, and wireless technologies are the driving economic engine and exhibitionary mode of consuming and reproducing archaeology.

Life on the "B List:" Archaeology and Tourism at Sites that Aren't Postcard Worthy

Jennifer P. Mathews

As Castañeda argues above, the historical interconnections that developed between archaeology and tourism in the 19th century continue to be important today. He therefore examines how academic archaeology is still informed and shaped by the relationship between museums and tourism. This argument is based on his understanding of large archaeological sites that are iconic of major civilizations, which is extrapolated from the case of Chichén Itzá where he has worked for over two decades. However, while these "primary" sites garner the attention of the media, major archaeological projects, and the majority of tourists, the reality is that most sites are second or third tier, as defined by their overall size, political power, and influence in antiquity. Thus, as archaeologists, it is important that we raise the issue of what role these smaller sites play in tourism development to and critically examine the ways in which tourism directly or indirectly impacts our aims to produce knowledge, as well as the costs and benefits of integrating issues related to tourism within the research agendas of contemporary archaeological projects.

Most archaeologists would quietly admit that they were originally drawn to archaeology because of the romance and glamor of these show-window sites as portrayed in glossy magazines and televisions shows. *National Geographic* seduces many children to want to search for mummies in Egypt and study giant heads on Easter Island. However, not every archaeologist can focus on these grand sites, nor should they want to, as they represent only one very small part of the story. In some cases, archaeologists have intentionally taken research paths as a kind of reaction against the large-scale projects to be able to say how the rest of the population lived. For example, beginning in the 1970s, many Maya archaeologists explicitly began studying settlements outside of the major sites' centers, trying to understand agricultural practices of how populations fed themselves. In the last decade especially, household archaeology and the study of commoners has become a central focus in the field. However, there are also practical reasons why project directors may choose to develop smaller, less complicated projects. In Mexico and in other parts of the world, government agencies (like the National Institute of Anthropology and History, or INAH) dictate research access to archaeological sites. Particularly, as a foreigner, attempting to do research at a "primary" site can be complicated because these governing agencies understandably want their own people to head up the work. Research at a secondary or tertiary site can also be more modest in terms of costs, as survey, mapping, and small-scale excavation generally require smaller budgets and crews and less intricate infrastructure.

As a discipline, we all can directly benefit from the research conducted at primary sites, as it is these high-profile projects that keep the general public interested in archaeology and gets students excited about taking classes. In reality, the majority of archaeologists that conduct research focus on smaller sites never seen on a postcard or that might appeal, at best, to "ecotourists" who are interested in visiting sites "off the beaten path." And yet, it remains important to examine what role the museum and tourism play today in shaping our research agendas at these kinds of sites.

Museums, Tourism, and Tourists in Small-Scale Archaeology

In general, the relationship between museums and archaeology as a whole has declined dramatically, and presently in the US, fewer than 5% of archaeologists report being employed in museums (SAA Salary Survey 2005). Museums have had even less influence on archaeologists working at smaller or lesser-known sites as they have produced fewer picturesque artifacts, and they rarely encounter objects that would make it into a museum collection.[6]

Similarly, at smaller and more remote sites, few people, tourists, or otherwise will ever visit because they are difficult to find or are simply unknown to outsiders. While archaeologists working at secondary or tertiary sites still "restore" the past through their interpretations, with rare exception, this is not done with tourists in mind. Rather, this research is influenced by the requirements of academic institutions, funders, and publications, which often have a narrower focus. But is this wise? Do we not have the responsibility to engage in outreach to the general public about the research that we produce? Is not small-scale tourism, at least at some level, an extension of public outreach, and would it not contribute to the agenda of public archaeology to educate the general public about the questions that we are asking about the past?

In thinking of future and potential collaborations between tourism and archaeology, it is important to grasp the typical attitude of an archaeologist. Most express concern about the damage that tourism development can cause at archaeological sites, and they might also view tourists themselves as disruptive to their research project. At smaller or more isolated sites in particular, visitors, whether tourists in the general sense of the word, or curious locals who arrive unannounced, archaeological work is more likely to be interrupted. The arrival of visitors often brings fieldwork to a stop while team members provide tours, give background on the site, and explain the goals of the project. In some cases, groups may enjoy a meal with the researchers, or even be housed for an overnight visit and, thus, disrupt tightly regulated schedules and work regimens. Although such visits are likely to be infrequent, they can consume significant amounts of project members' time in a context where time is essential for the successful completion of each season's research agenda.

Nonetheless, not only are there ways to incorporate these kinds of interactions directly into a project's research agenda, there can be great benefits from these face-to-face interactions with an interested public. Project directors may actively recruit students or researchers whose interests focus on ecotourism, community engagement, and/or educational outreach to become project members at archaeological sites. These specialists can then take on the responsibility of organizing these visits, as well as arranging for the creation of educational materials, signage, and other mechanisms for the public dissemination of knowledge. Additionally, they might lead discussions and focus groups among the project researchers about the inherent value and difficulties of sharing research results beyond academic venues. Archaeologists might also lead tours of visitors outside of the regular field season and focus on visits to lesser-known sites and lead discussions about research related to the lives of every-day peoples, archaeological stakeholders, and descendent communities.

This outreach can also extend to local communities, including meetings with community leaders, educational materials in the local language, as well as site tours. A good example of this is the Paxil Kiwi Project in Yucatán. This project, codirected by George Bey,

Tomas Gallareta, and Bill Ringle, is based on a private preserve that employs local peoples, protects the archaeological materials of the Maya site, and has created an ecological program of preservation of the surrounding forest. Paxil Kiwi provides detailed signage at the site, maintains an educational website, and provides private tours to a limited number of ecotourists, visiting researchers, and local school groups who are allowed to interact directly with archaeological fieldworkers (http://www.kiuic.org).

Archaeologists might also be helpful to communities that have chosen to develop ecotourism projects and assist communities in reaching target audiences of ecotourists. As individuals who have participated as tourists, archaeologists can help local peoples develop materials that would be of use to foreign tourists, such as bilingual brochures or informational posters that explain local history. Archaeologists can also act as intermediaries, providing feedback about "what tourists want" – perhaps helping them to avoid spending money on things that might ultimately detract from a site from the tourist perspective.

Despite these benefits, the incorporation of small-scale tourism as part of the research agenda at these smaller, more isolated B-list archaeological sites is fraught with complications. As to Castañeda's question about "to whom the past belongs," even at a smaller scale, tourists are ultimately the focus of our efforts. Increasingly, there are more archaeological scholars who engage in outreach with indigenous communities; this is certainly the case in Mexico where various projects have provided teaching materials about local history, helped to develop small-scale tourism projects, or worked to develop community museums (see, for example, Ardén 2002; Canny 2010; Glover et al. 2012). However, even these small-scale efforts are saturated by politics of different scales that revolve around the control of how projects are to be developed. This may or may not involve the politics between foreign academic archaeologists and governmental archaeology agencies, such as exists in México, but it certainly involves nearby stakeholder communities and groups who must not only negotiate with these distinct types of archaeologists but also among themselves. For example, in the case of community-museum development, key issues are often deeply meaningful to locals, including who determines the content that is presented and how the profits are to be distributed. This was certainly the case at the site of Chunchucmil for the archaeologists who wanted to help the local communities develop a "living museum" (Ardren 2002). Despite the efforts of the archaeologists, this museum never came to fruition in part because of the difficulty of working with five different *ejidos* and five different agendas (Traci Ardren, personal communication 2010; see also Breglia 2006).

Similarly, in my own research in a small village located within the boundaries of an ancient Maya site in Yucatán, I have witnessed the community leaders debate the development of a community museum and small-scale tourism. Although they had an opportunity to work with a successful local tourism cooperative, the leaders of the community chose not to because of their perception and concern that they would not be able to control the development and distribution of profits. This likely stems from a long history of empty promises from both political parties in control of the state and from transnational NGOs dedicated to helping third world communities. These include half-constructed bathrooms that the PRI political party started before an election and never came back to finish; the mailbox that was installed but that never received actual postal service; and the compost bathrooms that an environmental group started but never finished. Furthermore, there are long and complicated relationships between neighbors and family members within any community that will always have a bearing on how decisions are made. Archaeologists who attempt partnering with village leaders in developing small-scale tourism need to understand these complicated histories, as well as Castañeda's excellent suggestion (2008, 2010) that archaeological projects would be wise to incorporate a staff ethnographer.

Conclusions

As the discipline of archaeology has shifted from a rich man's leisurely pastime to an academic field, research has been shaped by scholarly expectations for garnering tenure and promotion, an ever-shrinking grant pool, and the fiercely competitive process of publishing in academic journals and books. While we might criticize those who "sell their soul" to make the cover of a popular archaeological magazine, the reality is that we all have to sell our projects and our research and make them "sexy" in order to compete for funding and publication space. This is particularly true for those working in the tenure-track world of academia who must prioritize their time and resources by calculating the cost-benefits of how to get the most "bang for the buck." Too often, archaeologists don't have time to dedicate to working with local communities in the field to help develop small scale tourism due to other numerous commitments during the field season, and because this behavior is not rewarded on the academic track. The time that it takes to engage with community members or to help in putting educational materials together can be considerable; and frankly, it takes away from not only field and lab time, but time for writing and publishing. At this point, few academic institutions would reward a faculty member for this endeavor nor acknowledge such work as a product that counts toward tenure or promotion (Glover et al. 2012).

With the reality that academic archaeology and tourism will continue to intersect, I believe that it would be in our best interest to forge an academic culture that rewards professionals for developing these kinds of community partnerships, and putting time into developing materials for small-scale tourism. We need to go beyond Jeremy Sabloff's (1999) original call for public outreach in archaeology and recognize that this service can extend to small-scale tourism at secondary and tertiary, or any out-of-the-way sites, as well as to the local communities in which we work. This means changing our academic culture by arguing to tenure committees that public engagement is a valuable use of time and resources.

Notes

1. The program began in 1915 as archaeological reconnaissance throughout southern México, Guatemala, Honduras, and Nicaragua. In 1923, the CIW shifted into a program of excavation-based research at various sites, including Chichén Itzá (1923–1938), that lasted until 1956. Although not a focus of this chapter, it is important to note that this research was used with the approval of the CIW as a cloak for covert Naval Intelligence work conducted by the CIW archaeologist Sylvanus G. Morley (see Castañeda 2003, 2004, 2010; Harris and Sadler 2003; Maca 2010).
2. In fact Kidder's text functions in part as a camouflage for the fact that Morley was an unknowing participant when a colleague smuggled an Aztec artifact out Mexico. Morley later participated in its return, which

thereby allowed for Kidder and the CIW to adopt a posture of moral good will.

3. The classic assessments of the Carnegie paradigm of archaeological research are by Kluckhohn et al. (1940) and Taylor (1948). These are significantly expanded by Maca (2010).

4. The literature on museums is extensive. The following works are among those that have informed the present analysis: Anderson 2001; Bennett 1995; Buntinx and Karp (2007); Castañeda (1996); Corsane (2005); Genoways and Andrei (2008); Handler and Gable (1997); Hooper-Greenhill (1992); Horne (1984); Karp et al. (2006); Kirshenblatt-Gimblett (1998); Lavine (1991); Rydell (1993); and Tenorio-Trillo (1996).

5. The editorial need to qualify "civilization" with universal and human or to capitalize the word as a way to insist upon the older, inclusive meaning indicates a thick history of concepts that is very pertinent to this discussion and to the politics of heritage.

6. In fact, excavating massive quantities of artifacts can become a major issue for a small project. In a country like Mexico where artifacts cannot be removed from the country, it is the archaeologist's responsibility to provide a permanent storage facility for their materials. This has prompted some archaeologists to excavate more sparingly. Additionally, there is an increasing focus on materials like soil samples and ethnobotanical remains that can be brought back to our home institutions to be analyzed.

Chapter 3

Integrating Education and Entertainment in Archaeological Tourism: Complementary Concepts or Opposite Ends of the Spectrum?

Karen Hughes, Barbara J. Little, and Roy Ballantyne

> There is the challenge! To put your visitor in possession of at least one disturbing idea that may grow into a fruitful interest. (Tilden 1977:91)

The editors of this volume raise the question of how far can entertainment go and still be educational. In examining how education and entertainment are compatible within the context of archaeological tourism, it is argued that they are indeed compatible and that entertaining experiences can be designed to have maximum educational impact. "Education" is often thought of as formal classroom-teaching

Tourism and Archaeology: Sustainable Meeting Grounds, edited by Cameron Walker and Neil Carr, 65–90. ©2013 Left Coast Press, Inc. All rights reserved.

of children, but we also use the term more broadly to include adult free-choice learning and all types of opportunities to learn for any age group. "Entertainment" is often thought of as enjoyable and voluntary. However, experiences designed to be entertaining can also be vacant and boring if a viewer can find no content or learning opportunity in them. The learning can be quite variable from new interpretive technology (the gee whiz factor), to new facts (I didn't know people back then did that), provocative inquiries, and new conceptual questions (e.g., I never thought about it that way before). There will be differing perspectives on the meeting grounds of tourism, archaeology, and education; and for this reason, the definitions for education and entertainment are left loose and flexible.

Archaeological tourism includes a variety of possible experiences, including physically passive viewing of a museum display to active participation in an archaeological investigation. Tourists might make a destination out of an archaeological region such as the island of Crete, the Yucatán, or the Four Corners area of the US Southwest to visit spectacular archaeological ruins. An archaeological attraction might be a side trip, such as visiting Tulum while on a beach trip to Cancun in Mexico. Travelers may find themselves unexpectedly in a position to visit an archaeological investigation in progress. Such opportunities can occur in the field in settings as varied as national parks and city centers, particularly as more cultural heritage management firms open their excavations for public education. "Accidental" visits may also involve laboratory investigations. For example, tourists on a trip to Washington DC visiting the shops and studios in the renovated Old Torpedo Factory in Alexandria, Virginia, will find themselves viewing artifact analyses through the window of Alexandria Archaeology's city-managed archaeology laboratory. Whether on recreational or cultural trips, whether by design or by accident, travelers can find themselves being archaeological tourists.

The Concept of Learning from the Tourism Scholar's Perspective

Now, what I want is, Facts. Teach these boys and girls nothing but Facts. Facts alone are wanted in life. Plant nothing else, and root out everything else. You can only form the minds of reasoning animals upon Facts: nothing else will ever be of any service to them. This is the principle on which I bring up my own children, and this is the principle on which I bring up these children. Stick to Facts, sir! (Dickens 1995:9)

Ask people to describe their concept of learning, and many will automatically reflect upon their school days – the tedium of listening to teachers drone on; the challenge of converting facts, figures, and dates into something useful; the mind-numbing drudgery of revising for exams, and so on. Do their recollections include descriptors such as "fun," "entertaining," or "interesting?" Very rarely! Why not? Are learning and entertainment mutually exclusive terms? Is it not possible to have fun and learn at the same time? Learning and entertainment can, and probably should, occur simultaneously if archaeological sites are to attract and educate a broad range of visitors.

Free-Choice Learning Environments

While learning is traditionally associated with schools and tertiary institutions, almost all our adult learning experiences take place outside these formal learning environments. Such non-formal learning environments include places such as libraries, museums, parks, wildlife centers, aquariums, heritage sites, and art galleries. The learning that occurs in such settings is known as "free-choice learning" because people are free to choose what, where, when, and with whom they learn (Falk 2001; Packer 2006). In other words, learning is voluntary and is often guided by the motives and interests of the individual. The type of learning experience also varies – some visitors have specific learning goals in mind (to discover more about the Inca civilization, to view a particular style of art, or to identify a historical artifact) while others have more general interests such as being out with family or friends. For many, the key attraction of free-choice learning environments is that they offer opportunities for discovery, exploration, adventure, and enjoyment (Packer 2006).

As highlighted in the introduction to this book, heritage experiences are attracting increasing numbers of visitors worldwide. This phenomenon has been attributed to a range of factors, including a growing public awareness of heritage; more flexibility in terms of leisure, mobility, and disposable income; the desire to escape from "everyday" routines; and the psychological fulfillment of learning about personal family history (Waitt 2000). The popularity of television programs such as the BBC's *Time Team*, which documents a three-day archaeological dig, is further testament to the popularity of such experiences. What implications does this growing public interest in archaeology have for the type of educational experiences offered at heritage and archaeological sites?

Perhaps most importantly, the widespread popularity of heritage sites and attractions suggests that visitors are no longer likely to be people with specialist knowledge of, or interest in, history or archaeology. Indeed, it is widely documented and accepted that visitors to tourism attractions (including heritage and archaeological sites) are heterogeneous, comprising tour groups, independent travelers, grey nomads, backpackers, historians, archaeologists, families with young children, community groups, and school groups with a wide range of interests, experiences, needs, and expectations (Falk and Dierking 2000; Ham 1992; Moscardo 1999; Orams 1994). Thus, any discussion of what should and should not be offered to visitors must first consider who actually visits archaeological sites and why. As Beeho and Prentice (1997) caution, tourist attractions that fail to understand, anticipate, and satisfy their visitors' motives and needs are unlikely to flourish in the current competitive marketplace. This is important to remain economically viable. Historic and archaeological sites are under considerable pressure to develop experiences and attractions that appeal to wider audiences, both physically and intellectually (Malcolm-Davies 2004).

Visitor Motivation

Common motives identified in studies of heritage and archaeological sites include viewing works of art, learning about architecture, worshiping, visiting attractive settings, absorbing the site's "atmosphere," experiencing a pleasant day out, connecting to one's ancestors, and paying homage (Poria et al. 2005). Gaining educational and nostalgic insights into past cultures and civilizations has also been identified as a motive for visitation (Chhabra 2007). These motives are relatively general in nature and rarely reflect a specific interest in history or archaeology. Studies of ancient monuments in Wales conducted in the mid-1980s revealed that although the majority of visitors were interested in learning about the site, the emphasis was on informal rather than formal learning – visitors wanted to be informed, but few wanted to be "educated" per se (Light 1995). A more recent study of 12 historic sites variously located in Sweden, the UK, Canada, and the US found that visitors' top three priorities were to learn, to gain a sense of the past, *and* to have fun (Light 1995). Beeho and Prentice (1997) also found that fun was an important motive for heritage visitation. They interviewed 40 visitors to New Lanark World Conservation Village in Wales, a restored industrial village that was historically significant during the British industrial revolution. Respondents' motives for visitation generally related to the desire to spend the day with family and/or friends. The researchers noted that respondents did not cite a specific interest in history, further supporting the notion that visitors are searching for general rather than specific historical experiences.

These general "pleasant-day-out" motives are not unique to heritage sites. A recent comparative study by Ballantyne et al. (2008) compared motives of visitors who attended nine types of tourism sites in Australia (museum, art gallery, wildlife center, aquarium, heritage site, national park, marine park, botanic garden, and whale watching). Analysis revealed that museum and art gallery visitors were predominantly motivated by goals related to "learning and discovery" and "enjoyment." For all the other sites (including the heritage site), enjoyment was the most important motive. Similar research in wild-life tourism settings, such as zoos and aquariums, also indicates that visitors are largely motivated by non-educational goals, and these attractions are often regarded as places of entertainment and recreation rather than sites for serious learning. To illustrate, Reade and Waran (1996) found that the most common reasons for visiting Edinburgh Zoo were: somewhere to go with friends and relatives for fun and entertainment. Only 4% of the sample claimed their visit was based on the desire to learn about animals. Likewise, Shackley (1996) found that in 1992, 48% of visitors to UK zoos came "for a day out" and a further 40% visited "to entertain their children." Again, only a small proportion (6%) stated their visit was motivated by a desire to learn more about animals and conservation. Similar findings have been reported by researchers in New Zealand (Coll et al. 2003; Ryan and Saward 2004) and the US (Dunlap and Kellert 1989; Holzer et al. 1998). In such cases, learning is likely to be regarded as an optional extra rather than the *raison d'etre* of the visit.

These studies all suggest that visitors are largely motivated by the desire to have an interesting, pleasant, and/or entertaining experience. Learning appears to be secondary, but does that actually matter? If visitors only learn one or two interesting things, is that not better than nothing at all? As Lowenthal states, is it not better to have "a light-hearted dalliance with the past than a wholesale rejection of it"? (1981:232). The tourism perspective in this chapter argues in the affirmative, presenting research and examples for support.

Most heritage attractions regard their primary purpose as one of education (Malcolm-Davies 2004). The provision of entertainment is often seen as detracting from this goal, and indeed, the role and suitability of entertainment at such sites is a hotly debated topic. Fundamental to these arguments is the notion that education and entertainment are mutually exclusive constructs. Experiences that are perceived and marketed as strictly educational may have limited appeal and are unlikely to attract the visitor numbers needed to ensure the ongoing viability of the site. For most visitors, the promise of entertainment, fun, and engagement are essential to attract customers. This argument will be explored further in the sections below.

Heritage tourism is in direct competition with a wide range of other leisure and tourism activities and experiences. Modern society is accustomed to accessing information from a wide variety of sources: television, Internet, and pod casts are commonplace, and information is delivered and absorbed in bite-size chunks. The challenge for visitor attractions, therefore, is to design products and experiences that complement or "fit in" with what consumers are accustomed to. It is granted that the development of high-tech presentation techniques is unlikely to sit comfortably in many heritage and archaeological sites, but there needs to be some element of entertainment to appeal to the mass audiences that are visiting these sites in increasing numbers.

Visitor Experiences

Visits to tourist attractions are often regarded as experiences, ones that involve and evoke emotional reactions, feelings, expressive behaviors, and activities. Gilmore and Pine (2007) posit that rather than simply focusing on goods and services, modern consumers (tourists, travelers, and visitors) also search for memorable experiences that are engaging and personal. Thus when making purchasing decisions, visitors consider what benefits will accrue from the experience. It is, therefore, important to stimulate interest, to appeal to visitors' emotions, and to offer benefits or rewards for participation or visitation.

As an example, Beeho and Prentice's (1997) survey of visitors to New Lanark World Heritage Village found that the most satisfying aspect of the attraction was the Annie McLeod Experience, a simulated ride through a recreated village complete with the sounds and smells of 1820s. The narration is provided by the "ghost" of Annie, a ten-year-old mill girl who is portrayed via a hologram. Visitors reported that they particularly enjoyed this experience because it brought history to life and presented information in a different and interesting way. They also found it emotive and engaging, and they were prompted to reflect on how different their lives are from the ones portrayed. Thus, although the narration and models are based on facts, the method of presentation taps into visitors' emotions and helps them to view the site from the perspective of one of its past inhabitants. In this way, visitors learn through *experiential* insight into history rather than from facts and figures (Beeho and Prentice 1997).

Another popular tourist attraction that has made full use of this approach is Jorvik Viking Center in York, England. One of the UK's most popular tourism attractions outside London (Jones 1999), the center allows visitors to travel in "time cars" through a reconstruction of the actual Viking-Age streets that once stood on this site. The houses and shops are laid out in exactly the same pattern as they were at 5.30 p.m., October 25th, AD 975, and are presented complete with the sounds and smells of the time. The faces of the models have also been reconstructed from Viking skulls, further adding to the sense of realness. The experience includes an activity area where visitors are allowed to handle and sort replicas of actual finds from the archaeological dig.

Researchers argue that experiences that envelop visitors in the sounds, smells, textures, and tastes of a place or event are particularly popular as they give visitors a feel for belonging in another time/place (Falk and Dierking 2000; Knudson et al. 1995). Indeed, if carefully designed, multi-sensory exhibits can give visitors a reasonably realistic impression of what it must have been like to have been a slave in ancient Egypt, a Crusader in the Holy Land, a farm laborer in the Middle

Ages, a priestess in the Inca civilization, and so on. This approach is both entertaining *and* educational. However, there is a view among some tourism and educational scholars (Jordanova 1989; Sorensen 1989) that these experiences tend to ignore the less pleasant aspects of history. It is true that the "seedier" side of heritage sites (e.g., poverty, disease, crime, or human suffering) are often "glossed over" to make the experience more palatable for tourists (Waitt 2000). From the interpreter's point of view, selective interpretation is often necessary as some aspects of history are difficult or impossible for visitors to visualize or experience. This primarily occurs because visitors have different knowledge, attitudes, and beliefs to their ancestors, and may be unable (or unwilling) to fully transport themselves back to a time when hardship, extreme poverty, disease, and brutality were an accepted part of life (Moscardo et al. 2007). (Also see the case study for western Canada in which Hamilton [Chapter 9] discusses tensions between telling tourists the often-grim realities of colonialism for Aboriginal peoples vs. the more celebratory story of Canada's origins as a nation.)

Although interpretive experiences enable us to illustrate aspects of other times and locations, they rarely provide total simulation (Robertshaw n.d.). Nevertheless, with careful planning and attention to detail, these experiences can provide visitors with an unparalleled insight into the topic, site, or event being interpreted. Whether these experiences are authentic is a related and hotly debated issue.

Messages in Archaeological Tourism from the Archaeological Perspective

Archaeologists are familiar with the ways in which the past is constructed to support certain contemporary understandings, particularly those deeply embedded in a sense of how the world works (e.g., Kehoe 1998; Shackel 2003; Shanks and Tilley 1987). It continues to be important for archaeologists and descendant communities to research and critique how cultural assumptions about such concepts as race, gender, and social hierarchies are reified in archaeological interpretations in museums and tourism sites.

The American Southwest has hosted archaeological tourism for generations. A combination of adventure travel and reassuring (to colonizers) messages about the place of Native peoples in the United States fueled this tourism. Thompson (1989:222) observes that:

> The idea that archaeology in this country must have something to do with prehistoric southwestern Indians is still deeply rooted in the public mind. Early attitudes about the Southwest and its Indian populations, both past and present, helped get this persistent idea started.

These early attitudes are deeply embedded in both tourism and national identity. Chambers (2000:17) explains how modern tourism found justification in its relationship to nation building:

> Travelers to the southwestern United States were encouraged to indulge their interests in Native American and Hispanic cultures in association with ideals of social and political conquest. The Indian peoples of the region were interpreted for tourists not only in respect to their cultural uniqueness, but also as symbols of Western expansion.

Hotelier Fred Harvey and the Atchison, Topeka, and Santa Fe Railroad shaped tourism in the southwestern US until the end of World War I when the automobile opened the region to mass tourism. With the advent of automobile tourism, Harvey promoted "Indian Detours" that embedded places like Taos Pueblo and Mesa Verde firmly into the American consciousness (Chambers 2000:24). As a result, tourist expectations of timeless authenticity still haunt Native American people (Little and McManamon 2005).

Some tribes are developing their own tourism agendas, in part to counter this legacy. Welch and his colleagues (2005) discuss intersections among Native nation building, heritage tourism, and archaeology. The White Mountain Apache Tribe in eastern Arizona in the United States is using the economy of tourism to link self-governance, self-determination, and self-representation. They explain that heritage tourism gives the Tribe the opportunity to integrate both their history and contemporary issues into tourism products. So they can more fully appreciate Apache perspectives, tourists are encouraged to examine the "ambiguous and occasionally hostile sentiments relating to events, places, memories, and the links among these and the imagined frontier" (2005:19).

Archaeological tourism inevitably intersects with the interests of local descendant communities. In her study of archaeological tourism in the Yucatán region of Mexico, Walker indicts the short-term view and economic choices that endanger both ecology and archaeological sites as well as the host communities. She writes (2009:2):

> The Maya Riviera's sanitized resorts have now effectively erased most of the previous cultural markers and replaced them with an implausibly generic tourist destination. Scratch the carefully burnished veneer and you will find the dark underbelly formed out of greed, neglect, antipathy, and carelessness.

Walker advocates changes in tourism to combat these destructive forces, suggesting that one of the tools would be education for tourists so that they learn about the host culture while increasing their appreciation for other cultures and encouraging responsible behavior toward the hosts and the resources.

The case studies in this book raise the necessity of including Indigenous perspectives, not only by including Native histories, but also by involving Native people as decision makers in tourism strategies. The Hawaiian case study of competing uses for an attractive beach (Chapter 10) highlights a clash between Native spiritual values and tourism's profit motive within a broader state-wide context of ongoing struggles between local and "outsider" control. The case of Casa Malpais (Chapter 7) demonstrates that the most effective preservation and presentation of heritage may not be for tourism but for effective support of local and regional community cohesion. Similarly, the wilderness tourism projects in western Canada (Chapter 9) point to multiple values of documenting heritage. One the one hand, such documentation provides essential information for authentic tourism experiences; on the other hand, it provides educational materials for youth in projects designed to reduce intergenerational stress and misunderstanding.

Because the stories told at archaeological places are tangled in the relationships between Indigenous populations and descendants of colonizing populations, there is an opportunity to challenge such stories in those places far more directly than elsewhere. Silverman (2002, 2005) analyzes the complex ways in which Peru's archaeological past is presented and contested. She contrasts the very different visions of two archaeological museums in Cusco, Peru. The Museo Inka, administered by the underfunded National University since 1919, has modest displays and includes sections on the devastation caused by Spanish invasion, Indigenous resistance, *Incanismo* movements of the 19th and 20th centuries, and contemporary Andean culture. As Silverman (2005:30) states, "this is an anthropological museum with an overt political message. Its coherent, didactic script makes the museum effective and important in its local context, especially as narrated by local guides and local school teachers." One block away, the Museo de Arte Precolombino (MAP), opened in 2003, presents a different viewpoint. Privately owned and financed as a tourist attraction, "MAP is a traditional – indeed reactionary – art museum. So decontextualized and retrograde is the MAP exhibition that quotes about 'primitivism' by renowned international artists (Gaugin, Kandinsky, Klee, Matisse, Moore, among others) are placed in the various galleries to validate the 'universal' greatness and appeal of the hyper-aestheticized art on display" (Silverman 2005:31).

Silverman (2005:32) contrasts the messages of these museums. The messages conveyed by Museo Inka explicitly expose the roots and current realities of poverty and disenfranchisement of Native people. Acknowledging and describing oppression and resistance are themselves methods of resisting structural inequalities. However, MAP ignores the social and political context of Indigenous culture. Its messages reinforce those inequities. In addition to reinforcing ethnic inequalities, or perhaps as part of the disenfranchisement, it is worth noting that the objects displayed at MAP are from the collection of a well-known collector, further encouraging the marketing of antiquities and perhaps the looting of sites to obtain objects for sale (e.g., Brodie et al. 2006; Renfrew 2000).

The looting of artifacts and the antiquities trade is an issue that cannot be disconnected from archaeological tourism. Saving Antiquities for Everyone, founded in 2003, offers museum tours of the Metropolitan and Boston Museum of Fine Arts to alert people to items of dubious origins. Professionals involved in combating the antiquities trade have found that there is a connection between pervasive messages about the meanings of artifacts and looting. Paula Lazrus (2006:275) describes her experience of giving museum tours to demonstrate how context is essential for learning from archaeological objects. She explains how public interpretation matters:

> Unless it is explained otherwise, people never seem to realize that there is anything to be learned from ancient objects aside from their being old and attractive. This issue of communication is a critical aspect of the problem, and it appears to have been overlooked by scholars, who continue to talk in general terms about helping people understand cultures of the past.

Museums as institutions and archaeologists as individual scholars are in positions to offer appropriate education to place the archaeological record in context, both to protect sites and to clarify the significant contributions of people and cultures that created the archaeological heritage.

Deep ideological foundations of modern society are often presented as timeless truths. The erasure via aesthetics of Indigenous heritage at archaeological sites is one symptom. Colonial relationships are not the only deeply embedded ideology, however, that could be questioned. Philip Duke (2007:14) summarizes his insight from studying tourists of the Minoan Bronze Age on Crete:

> My claim is that public archaeology on Crete, manifested in sites and museums and the vast array of tourism information media, produces a virtually monolithic message about a particular past and therefore about a particular present; namely that social inequality is the essential metanarrative of the Minoan past and thus abets in the legitimization and naturalization of this same social inequality as the primary organizational structure of the modern West.

Uncovering such deeply embedded messages requires intentional analysis of the interpretations that tourists are presented, something far too few professional archaeologists have done.

The studies described above support the view that tourists do not necessarily form their own opinions but easily accept the authority of the interpretations that are presented to them. Unless there is some incentive to pay enough attention or to care enough to question, there is no reason for a tourist (or a student in a classroom) to engage sufficiently to form opinions. Duke (2007:26) bemoans this missed opportunity on Crete:

> The sites and museums do not offer anything to offend or indeed to make the tourist think of anything beyond their antiquity and their wondrousness. The past is simplified and sterilized. What could be an engaging dialog with a dynamic an ever-changing past becomes a synchronic moment, a fetish to be commoditized, used and then cast away. The site becomes dead, inert.

In her analysis of visitor comments collected at each of Cuzco's museums, Silverman also found that while tourists appreciate the museums, most do not question the content or messages, even if they have gone to both of the diametrically opposed museums in Cuzco. These findings highlight the importance of providing experiences, messages, and stories that help visitors link new information to their current store of knowledge and experiences. The interpretive imperative is to anticipate and respond to the unspoken "so what?" question. In particular, archaeologists and educators need to design thought-provoking messages and innovative "frameworks" that enable individuals to make meaningful connections and inferences. Such skills are the foundation of effective interpretation.

Authenticity at Heritage Sites from the Tourism Perspective

One of the main challenges facing archaeologists is to design experiences that are interesting and engaging but that do not detract from the educational messages and artifacts of the site itself. In particular, sites need to retain an element of authenticity to ensure that visitors can place educational messages and experiences into some sort of context. Conventional definitions of "authenticity" include concepts such as accuracy, genuineness, and truthfulness (Waitt 2000). MacCannell (1976) claims that tourists seek authentic experiences and are frustrated by settings and experiences that are inauthentic. Cohen (1988) disagrees, arguing that tourists seek different levels of authenticity and that some are willing to accept experiences and products that others would reject as being too contrived or fake. Both researchers agree, however, that heritage events and attractions are rarely authentic but rather are predominantly "staged" to suit the needs and interests of guests and residents. In other words, the site and/or experiences are reconstructed to meet the needs of modern visitors. As Chhabra et al. (2003:705) explain, "heritage is thus created and re-created from surviving memories, artifacts, and sites of the past to serve contemporary demand."

Some sites and experiences could be criticized for presenting just one version of the truth, a version that in some cases has only a passing resemblance to the original. Indeed, in many communities, local customs and heritage sites have become tourist commodities with little substance or meaning for locals or visitors (Cohen 1988). In such cases, the authenticity of the tourist experience becomes secondary to the "performance" itself. This raises the question of whether visitors notice or even care if experiences are strictly authentic. Furthermore, do perceptions of authenticity impact satisfaction with the visit, and if so, what implications does this have for the design of visitor experiences at these sites?

There have been a number of studies exploring visitors' conceptions and perceptions of authenticity in heritage tourism settings. In 2000, Chhabra et al. (2003) used self-administered questionnaires to explore visitors' perceptions of authenticity at the Flora MacDonald Highland Games held in North Carolina in the US. Five hundred visitors were asked to rate the authenticity of events and activities on a five-point Likert scale with five being most authentic. Overall, the mean rating of the event's authenticity was four. Interestingly, respondents rated Highland dancing as the most authentic aspect of the experience, even though it has been progressively modified over the years. These responses suggest that although the events and activities are staged, they are nevertheless perceived to be authentic.

Similarly, Moscardo and Pearce (1986) asked 562 visitors at a historical theme park in Australia what they had most enjoyed about their visit. Thirty-nine percent responded that the overall authenticity of the experience had been the best feature. This is despite the fact that the park is a recreated gold-mining town that offers staged re-enactments designed for the entertainment and education of visitors. The researchers repeated their study at a second historic theme park, this time specifically exploring the concept of authenticity and its relation to visitor satisfaction. Ninety-five percent of the 502 visitors questioned agreed with the statement that these attractions should "strive to be as genuine and historically accurate as possible even if some modern facilities for visitors are lacking" (Moscardo and Pearce 1986:474). Further analysis suggested perceived authenticity is the best predictor of visitor satisfaction. In addition, it seems that respondents believe their visit has provided them with an insight into the lives of those who lived in the area, despite the fact that the entire setting is what MacCannell (1976) would classify as "staged" authenticity.

Waitt's (2000) survey of 372 visitors to The Rocks historical area in Sydney, Australia, found that the built environment (stone steps, cobbled streets, and sandstone buildings) was particularly important in contributing to the area's perceived authenticity. This is despite the fact that the area has been extensively demolished and "beautified" to the extent that it bears little resemblance to the squalid crowded streets of the past. Interestingly, features such as pubs that would have been part of the original landscape were seen to detract from the perceived authenticity of the area. Waitt (2000) argues that these responses probably stem from visitors seeing pubs as modern "entertainment" venues rather than part of the heritage scene. These responses indicate that perceptions of authenticity may be founded on misinformation that features with little historic value can sometimes be perceived as authentic, and that those with historic integrity can be regarded as inauthentic.

The key term throughout these studies is *perceived* authenticity – that is, authenticity as perceived by the visitor. Researchers such as Chhabra et al. (2003) have suggested that the important feature of heritage sites is that even if they are not strictly authentic, they are perceived to be. Thus, satisfaction depends "not only on [the site's] authenticity in the literal sense of whether or not it is an accurate recreation of some past condition, but rather on its perceived authenticity (consistency with nostalgia for some real or imagined past)" (705). Likewise, Worsley (2004) contends that the illusion of authenticity is fundamental if sites are to meet the needs of visitors and that this may change in response to visitors' changing needs and interests.

In a similar vein, Cohen (1988:378) argues that the majority of visitors are willing to accept experiences that are not completely authentic.

They will be prepared to accept a cultural product as authentic, insofar as traits, which they consider to be diacritical, are judged by them to be authentic. These traits are then considered sufficient for the authentication of the product as a whole.

Cohen (1988) goes further to suggest that tourists he describes as "recreational tourists" are willing to participate in experiences that are obviously staged because it enables them to pretend or play act. Thus, in many cases authenticity has been commoditized for mass consumption (McIntosh and Prentice 1999). Provided there is some semblance of reality, however, visitors are likely to be more than satisfied with the experience. In other words, entertainment needs to be relevant to the topic/event/objects being described and should be grounded in reality. As Goldberg (1983) states, even though most tourists are not seeking fully authentic experiences, neither are they content with the provision of entertainment merely for the sake of it.

Attractions such as medieval festivals are a case in point. These are obviously staged events with many activities. Generally, there are far more knights, lords, and ladies than serfs and beggars. Is this authentic? Certainly not. Do visitors get a sense of what it would have been like to live in medieval times? Research suggests that yes, they do. As an example, Robinson and Clifford (2007) explored tourists' perceptions of a two-day medieval festival, the Abbey Museum's Medieval Festival and Tournament, held in South East Queensland on an annual basis. This event, held on the museum's grounds, attracts approximately 18,000 visitors and includes workshops, demonstrations, re-enactments, a masque ball, and a Medieval banquet. Although attached to a museum, the site itself has no Medieval significance and was never populated by Medieval societies. Self-administered questionnaires asked respondents to the daytime events to evaluate various aspects of the experience with particular attention focused on the authenticity of the food and beverages served. Analysis indicated that overall, visitors thought the festival created an authentic Medieval atmosphere with the mean score on a seven-point scale of 5.94 (1 = dissatisfied to 7 = very satisfied). Questions relating to food and beverages revealed that authenticity was also an important factor in determining respondents' choices of food.

According to Breathnach (2006:107), "simulated" authenticity is successful because although it is obviously staged, it nevertheless gives visitors an intimate and immediate experience of the past that "involves a combination of social interaction and other mental, emotional and physical experiences." Often these experiences require multi-sensory responses from visitors (visual, tactile, vocal, and aural), and are augmented by multimedia exhibits and interactive activities designed to both entertain and educate. As mentioned, provided these are relevant to the topics being presented and are based on sound educational goals, they should enhance rather than detract from the educational value of the experience. The key is to ensure there are obvious links between entertainment or "fun" activities and the educational messages of the site.

Using Interpretive Techniques to Educate and Entertain According to Tourism Scholars

Archaeological sites and artifacts do not readily explain themselves; therefore, it is important that these are described or "interpreted" in a way that enables visitors to make meaning of the experience (Light 1995). To archaeologists, fragments of flint, bone, and pottery signify particular historical eras, cultures, and events. Visitors, however, are rarely experts and often have limited knowledge of historical periods and previous civilizations. Consequently, it is likely that in many cases they will fail to appreciate the significance of site features and artifacts unless they are effectively interpreted (Moscardo et al. 2007). Interpretation is particularly valuable at archaeological sites because it helps to create "links" between what is visible (archaeological digs/remains) and what it represents. Simply put, effective interpretation provides context and thereby helps visitors make sense of what they experience. It also helps to make the experience more interesting and entertaining (McIntosh and Prentice 1999).

Research consistently shows that people assimilate new information by relating it to something they already know (Ballantyne et al. 2000; Moscardo 1999). From a tourism perspective, it is critical to provide information and experiences that have meaning and personal value for visitors. While dazzling graphics, signs, and activities may initially attract visitors' attention, unless these enable visitors to make meaningful connections with their previous knowledge and experiences, much of the information will not be processed (Screven 1999). A range of interpretive techniques are commonly used to help people "connect with" the visitor site or experience. These include: telling stories, particularly those with realistic characters; explaining concepts, objects, and events through analogies and metaphors; asking questions; presenting examples, diagrams, simulations, and illustrations; and offering suggestions about how to use new information to "make sense of" other sites, situations, and experiences. These techniques help visitors understand new information about a particular site, culture, or civilization within the context of their existing knowledge (Ballantyne et al. 2000; Ham 1992; Moscardo et al. 2007; Tilden 1977).

Another common technique used to connect visitors with archaeological settings is to describe the everyday lives of the people who once inhabited the site. Through comparative examples and stories, visitors are encouraged to reflect upon their current lives and use this knowledge and insight to understand the past and its remains (Holtorf 2005:15). As an example, at Catalhoyuk in Turkey, there are the remains of a farming community where thousands of people once lived. Visitors are encouraged to compare the life stories of its Neolithic residents with their own life stories through prompts such as those presented in the attraction's teachers' notes in Figure 3.1.

This approach places the artifacts and remains into context and assists visitors make meaning of the topics and events being viewed. To do this effectively, however, it is important to have a current, reliable indication of the site's main visitor groups, and their knowledge, motives, experiences, and interests *prior* to designing interpretive signs, exhibits, and experiences.

Current approaches to interpretive practice also emphasize the importance of using themes to guide the development of interpretive materials and experiences. Themes in a tourism context are the "big picture" ideas that help visitors to connect the different elements of their visit. Again, the best themes generally build personal connections between the topic being interpreted and visitors' everyday lives, their previous experiences, and/or what is experienced at the site. From a learning perspective, a clear theme is an important aid to visitor understanding as it allows visitors to see the connection between what they already know and the facts, figures, and stories presented.

Imagine that you're living at Catalhoyuk 9000 years ago. There are no other towns around. In the winter, it's cold and snowy. In summer, it's hot. There's a river nearby, but there's no running water inside the house. There's no electricity – no heating or air conditioning. There are no matches to make fires – no computers or televisions. Nobody takes the trash away each week or delivers newspapers, so you can't really tell what's going on anywhere else. If you lived in Catalhoyuk 9000 years ago:

- What would you eat? Drink?
- What skills would you need to survive?
- What would your job be?
- What could you do to make sure you always had food?
- Would people in the Neolithic throw away the same kinds of things we do today? What do you think might be left for us to find?
- People lived with all their relatives – what sounds would you hear? What odors would you smell? How would you feel about living in a small house with lots of other people? How would it affect your day-to-day life?

Figure 3.1 Example of linking archaeological remains to visitors' experiences. (Source: *Remixing Catalhoyuk Teacher's Guide*, http://okapi.berkeley.edu.remixing.)

This is important, as visitors often lack the specialist knowledge and experience to "see" links and relationships between pieces of information or topics. Themes assist in this process by supporting the site's main messages. As highlighted earlier, this requires that interpreters have a comprehensive understanding of their target audience, particularly in relation to their areas of expertise, their previous experiences, and their common interests. The importance of developing archaeological interpretation based on themes is highlighted by Holtorf (2005:205):

A simulated participation in scientific practice and the magic of encountering enigmatic objects can provide visitors with very powerful experiences. They are even stronger when they are a part of themed environments that tell exciting stories, involving the visitor in metaphorical scenarios. These experiences are entertaining, but as visitors relate their impressions immediately to themselves, they can also be highly educational.

Another way of engaging visitors and providing interest and entertainment is to design interactive experiences. As with all interpretive techniques, the introduction of interactive elements needs to be based on sound educational purposes and goals. Simply providing interactive experiences to keep visitors occupied and entertained is inappropriate and may even cause confusion and visitor dissatisfaction (Moscardo et al. 2007). For some archaeological sites, basic interactive elements, such as lifting flaps to reveal answers to questions, may be sufficient. For others, multimedia virtual reality experiences could be appropriate. The choice will often depend upon the sophistication and location of the site; highly technical exhibits at remote archaeological sites are likely to detract rather than enhance the visitor experience.

While it will be impossible to appeal to every visitor, offering a range of interpretive techniques and activities allows visitors to choose ones that are personally relevant and interesting (Beeho and Prentice 1997). For archaeological sites, variety can also be introduced by designing activities that help visitors become involved in the site and its activities. Keen (1999) recommends using a range of approaches to educate visitors about archaeology. These include:

1. Simulation – making copies of the artifact or building with modern tools/materials. While these are fun and interesting to touch, they also have significant educational value.
2. Process and production – asking visitors to work out how things were made. Examples would include setting up experiments for firing pots or making coins.
3. Function – asking visitors to reflect upon what artifacts were used for. This process can include comparisons, experiments, and opportunities to use artifacts.

As stressed throughout this section, priority should be given to activities that support the learning process by "connecting" visitors to the site in some way. While these activities can be designed to engage and entertain, they must also have an underlying educational purpose or goal.

An Entertainment-Education Continuum According to the Archaeologist

To some extent, the view that entertainment and education are opposites finds echoes in the time-worn distinction between the "traveler," presumably looking to expand his/her education and worldview with an open mind, and the "tourist," presumably keeping his/her mind shut while on a trinket-collecting trip. "Experiential travel," as an important tourism trend, is relevant to the distinction, not least because it exemplifies how the divide can be narrowed (Wylie and Bauer 2008). Experiential travel is exemplified in archaeological tourism by programs where tourists either pay or volunteer to work alongside professional archaeologists. J. Kersting (n.d.), a volunteer with a Passport in Time (PIT) archaeological project at Chinese-mining sites in Boise National Forest in the western United States, shares her feeling about the experience:

> Adult life lessons included an appreciation for the Chinese culture that coexisted with the Anglos in a common goal to mine precious metals from the earth, while at times teaching the dominant culture a thing or two about mining. It was such a joy to spend time with people with no hidden agendas – a respite from our busy lives, a counterpoint to life out of balance. We understood our connectedness as human beings – a life lesson worth learning.

Experiential travel provides tourists with experiences that involve both education and enjoyment. Wylie and Bauer (2008:33) explain the potential outcome of educational and entertaining experiences that fully engage the tourist: "through a carefully staged set of memo-rable experiences, and perhaps multiple encounters, the final result is 'transformation' or permanent beneficial change to the participant." Adopting this assessment of a current tourism trend on a continuum between education and entertainment, transformational learning is the educational end. On the other end is pure diversion of the "we're in Greece so let's take our pictures with those obligatory ruins" variety. Archaeological tourism runs the full continuum, which might also be thought of anchored at either end by meaning (education) and fun (entertainment); each is an essential ingredient for happy balance, and each is subjective and variable. It may be possible for interpretation at archaeological sites and museums to provide tourists opportunities to move from entertaining diversion to educational transformation.

Although experiential travel might be transformational, there are other possible sources of transformation within archaeological tourism that do not involve immersion in an archaeological project. Archaeological tourism sites from the ancient and recent past raise important issues. Education at these sites can help challenge stereotypes and provide the kind of "disorienting dilemmas" seminal for transformational learning (e.g., Mezirow 1991). The human capacity for learning with both our rationality and intuition is served by interpretive goals that seek to provide visitors to historic sites the opportunities to form their own intellectual and emotional connections. Freeman Tilden was quoted at the beginning because he identified the "disturbing idea" – similar to a disorienting dilemma – as an important element of interpretation at historic sites. Tilden was a writer whose observations and principles of interpretation have been influential in interpretive practice for over a half century (Little 2004).

Transformational learning is not necessarily a matter of teaching per se, but rather of fostering opportunities, such as a learning environment where it is safe to take risks and where there is a community of learners. The interpretive profession's emphasis on creating opportunities for the "Ah ha – now I get it!" experience and opening up both the possibilities for emotional and intellectual connections is another. Archaeology can offer opportunities for disorienting dilemmas, perhaps by tracing the sources and origins of some persistent biases based on race, class, sex, ethnicity, and other factors. Innumerable forms of bigotry exist; most are based on perceptions of entitlement, including those often taken for granted in a nation founded through colonization. It can be quite disorienting to realize that one's sense of entitlement or superiority is based on false assumptions, but it is one entry into transformation. Through provocative displays, questions, and examples, archaeology can raise questions about such assumptions (Little 2007:164–165).

Intersections: Entertainment, Authenticity, and Education According to an Archaeologist

As Walker and Carr mention in the introduction to this book, the popularity of archaeological and heritage tourism has increased markedly. Organizations and governments are demonstrating increasing interest in archaeological tourism. Sustainability is the impetus for the effort by the Archaeological Institute of America, *Archaeology* magazine, and the Adventure Travel Trade Association to collaborate on a forthcoming guide to best practices for archaeological tourism (AIA n.d.). The General Assembly of ICOMOS adopted The ICOMOS Charter for the Interpretation and Presentation of Cultural Heritage Sites in September 2008 (ICOMOS n.d.). The United States Advisory Council on Historic Preservation released its Policy Statement on Archaeology, Heritage Tourism, and Education in August 2008 (ACHP n.d.). Authenticity is a key element in these documents. Sustainability of the archaeological heritage pertains to in situ sites and collections. Clearly, sustainability is related to the authenticity of the historical fabric of archaeological structures and, to some extent, to the surrounding landscape.

K. Slick (2002) of the US National Trust for Historic Preservation admonishes archaeologists to "get on the tourism train." She describes a regional approach based on resource protection, authenticity and quality, and marketing assuring archaeologists that, while entertainment is the primary motivation for people visiting historic sites, there is no need to fictionalize the stories being told. It is important to note too that one could learn a lot about "authentic" archaeology even at a contrived site. The process of working and discovery can be duplicated; the exploration of questions and demonstration of analysis can be simulated virtually.

What is archaeologically and historically "authentic" resides along a continuum within a defined context. We cannot substitute "believable" or "non-fiction" for authentic or "unbelievable" or "fiction" for inauthentic; otherwise literature – and all the humanities, arts, and spiritual concepts seeking to express truths of the human condition might be labeled "inauthentic." The concept of simulated authenticity is related to an acknowledgment of humanistic empathy as an essential part of connecting to the past. Does a staged event give people a sense of the past? Is visitor satisfaction an appropriate measure of authenticity? Research suggesting that people believe they have experienced an authentic sense of the past, as described for the medieval banquet described above, suggests that such experiences can be successful at opening the door for further learning. Perceived authenticity does not equal authenticity; I cannot, in fact, "feel *your* pain," but I can empathize given comparable human experiences. Whether the visitor is blissfully unaware of his/her ignorance or rates an experience as highly satisfying may not be relevant in judging the accuracy of an interpretation. Content of the available interpretation needs to be professionally defensible as the closest approximation of "reality" that can be offered. However, the tourist context affects the parameters of what can reasonably be offered, just as any medium of communication affects the choice and content of a message.

Nothing can force a visitor to be curious about the past. However, interpretive techniques that provide opportunities for a person to notice and appreciate that there is something different about the past may well stimulate that person to think differently or want to learn more. It is important for venues to make resources available for further learning. Such materials often reside on a website and can range from suggested readings to in-depth educational programs.

Although we cannot achieve "authenticity" in any absolute sense, we can be conscious and intentional about the messages that we seek to impart to tourists. We can create opportunities for tourists to engage actively with the ideas and interpretations that are offered. Raising questions about deeply taken-for-granted ideas may be one of the most provocative, disturbing, and ultimately most important contributions archaeological education at tourism sites can achieve. Part of the challenge for education at archaeological tourism sites is to design experiences that provide real opportunities to question inherited and implicit messages. Working with stakeholders, including descendant communities, is the key to meeting this challenge. The definition of descendents can be broad. In his study of narratives at the Royal Palace in Stockholm, N. Glover (2008), for example, draws on the idea that locals and tourists coproduce interpretations of history. The tourists include Swedes, other Europeans, and inter-continental visitors.

The challenge facing archaeologists and interpreters is to design relevant messages and experiences that are interesting and engaging and support opportunities for tourists to find a balance between meaning and fun along the entertainment-education continuum. Some degree of authenticity – of historic fabric, of scholarship, of Indigenous meaning, and of message – ensures that such communication can be placed in context. Presentations of sites should dare to leave people with questions about archaeology, archaeologists, the past, the peoples whose lives created the record, their descendants, and the relationships among these entities (Little and McManamon 2005:14).

Closing Thoughts from the Archaeological Perspective

Interpretation at archaeological tourism spots, whether sites, museums, or regional landscapes, can provide tourists opportunities to learn, to become open to new ways of thinking, to do both, or to do neither. All of those involved in the creation of opportunities – archaeologists, interpreters, tour operators, host communities, descendant communities, and the tourists themselves – have opportunities to make tourism potentially transformative. The preamble to the United Nations World Tourism Organization's *Global Code of Ethics for Tourism* (WTO n.d.) describes the purpose of the organization:

> In promoting and developing tourism with a view to contributing to economic development, international understanding, peace, prosperity and universal respect for, and observance of, human rights and fundamental freedoms for all without distinction as to race, sex, language or religion.

This high-minded principle is worth keeping in mind in the daily work. Our efforts must be intentional and explicit because it is not likely that most of the public would bring enough prior knowledge to question the interpretations offered to them. As Duke (2007) demonstrates, a tourist visiting Knossos in Crete can "learn" a whole array of things, including some simple facts and some deep ideological and potentially misleading assumptions. Perhaps the real contest then is not between entertainment and education but between mis-education and education, either of which can be entertaining.

Closing Thoughts from the Tourism Perspective

Having argued that learning and entertainment are not mutually exclusive concepts, Hughes and Ballantyne wish to caution that "too much of a good thing" can be detrimental to the learning experience. While seeking to appeal to a wide range of audiences and interest, there is the danger that educational objectives can get smothered by management's desire to provide experiences that are exciting, interesting, and entertaining. Indeed, critics argue that heritage sites are so often concerned with maintaining commercial viability and competing with other leisure activities that their educational role becomes secondary to their entertainment one (Light 1995). Throughout this chapter, it has been argued that visitor experiences (activities, displays, simulations, costume dramas, etc.) must be based on clear educational goals and objectives. Providing entertainment merely to attract or engage visitors is not sound educational practice and should be avoided at all costs. Thus, when designing interpretive experiences, care needs to be taken to ensure that visitor experiences develop skills, knowledge, and/or understanding in some way. In other words, as interpreters and educators we are tasked with the responsibility of encouraging visitors to search for meaning and to come to decisions based on their activities (Veverka n.d.).

Merriman (1991) claims that archaeology could (and should) be made more widely available and enjoyable by providing opportunities for individuals from outside the discipline to become involved in fieldwork. He also states that public participation should be an integral aspect of the archaeological process. Tourism offers unprecedented opportunities to both educate and excite people about their heritage and past civilizations. Education and entertainment are complimentary if not symbiotic concepts, and to continue to appeal to modern audiences, archaeological experiences need to offer experiences that are both entertaining *and* educational. As Lowenthal (1981:65) states: "the more we save, the more aware we become that such remains are continually altered and reinterpreted." We require a heritage with which we continually interact, one which fuses past with present. Thus, if archaeological sites have to incorporate entertainment, multimedia displays, simulations, and role plays to attract visitors and remain relevant, then so be it! Provided these are based on sound educational goals and that they clearly link to visitors' knowledge, experiences, and needs, entertainment should enhance rather than detract from visitors' on-site experiences.

Chapter 4
Cultural Sensitivity and Embeddedness

Tim Wallace and Kevin Hannam

The past is almost always about the present, and the "history" of the past depends on who does the interpreting. Archaeologists are the interpreters-in-chief of a site, and their narratives and "reconstructions" are part of a broader disciplinary narrative. In addition, archaeologists must work within the sociopolitical environment of the cultures-societies-communities where the site is located. The effect of these "constraints" suggests that understanding the issues of cultural embeddedness and sensitivity is necessary not only for those who observe-interact-participate in the site but also for those who serve as the professional experts in making the site ready for consumption as a product (Castañeda 2008; Duke 2007; Matthews 2008). Archaeological sites "tell" multiple, potentially conflicting "stories" that relate to past historical periods, as well as to everyday contemporary subcultures (Leone 2008; Smith 2006). Thus, the mutability of archaeological enterprise and the multicultural nature of

Tourism and Archaeology: Sustainable Meeting Grounds, edited by Cameron Walker and Neil Carr, 91–109. ©2013 Left Coast Press, Inc. All rights reserved.

visitors and members of communities adjacent to archaeological sites necessitate debate about how to present information and interpretation for multiple historical cultures at any one archaeological site to the potentially multiple, diverse, and even conflicting visitor cultures and subcultures. This is also the case with conflicting perspectives of professional archaeologists who provide the interpretation of the site (Handler 2008; McDavid 2004). We could also add here that often tour guides at the site add another level of interpretation that reflects both local perspectives (stories) and professional training (Diekmann and Hannam 2012; Handler and Gable 1997).

Conceptually, then, work in the intersection between heritage, tourism, and archaeology requires both an awareness of cultural sensitivity and an understanding of the ways in which cultures are "embedded" regionally, as well as the ability of the archaeologist to have developed sufficient collaboration with them to address their multiple, if not often, conflicting demands.

This chapter seeks to develop and discuss these ideas in the context of tourism and archaeology. We begin this chapter by discussing notions of cultural sensitivity before going on to examine the concept of "embeddedness." We draw upon examples from the authors' research to illustrate the broader conceptual points made. We also discuss the complexities of ethnographic archaeologies and how those regional cultures-societies come to be represented in the archaeologists' interpretations.

Cultural Sensitivity and Insensitivity

Notions of heritage and *inter alia* heritage tourism, of which tourism and archaeology form a part, are fundamentally contested from various social, cultural, economic, and political points of view. As Graham et al. (2000:2) note:

> Heritage is a view from the present, either backward or forward to a future. In both cases, the viewpoint cannot be other than now, the perspective is blurred and indistinct and shaped by current concerns and predispositions, while the field of vision is restricted to a highly selective view of a small fraction of possible pasts or envisaged futures.

Furthermore, heritage, as with history, reflects power, class, ethnicity, and gender. Jim Crisp, a historian who has spent many years uncovering the narratives surrounding San Antonio's Alamo battle between Mexican forces and Texan rebels, writes of his experience:

> In other words, though every narrator must make choices in selecting which facts are to be included and the significance attributed to them, sometimes, what is *not* said – not included in the narrative – is actually the most important part of the story as experienced by many of those who lived it. Not everyone's story gets told, not everyone's story is heard. The production and distribution of historical narratives is bound up with relationships of power – relationships that make some narratives possible (or even dominant), but silence others. (Crisp 2005:180)

Erve Chambers (2006:2–3) suggests that we ought to conceptualize heritage as belonging to two separate types: public heritage and private heritage. The distinction he makes is well worth considering. The former refers to "an expression of the past that attempts to preserve important though often fading social practices." Private heritage is a "focus on the ways in which the past is dynamically linked to the present, with heritage values identified and interpreted by community members rather than by outsiders" (Chambers 2006: 2–3). Public heritage is often associated with state-level attempts at manipulating local heritage locales for creating or sustaining support for the dominant group or maintaining the status quo. Nevertheless, local communities or a segment of a local community may claim a site or an interpretation of a site as "belonging" to their past, separate from the dominant group or the "national" or state-level community(s). Witness the situation of the well-known case of the African Burial Ground (ABG) (Hansen and McGowan 1998; King 2008). Discovered by chance during excavations for a federal office building in New York City, workers uncovered the remains of over 400 individuals buried in a Manhattan cemetery during the 17th and 18th centuries. The debate over how to treat the remains, study the remains, and commemorate the site was boisterous and contentious. Contemporary African-American New Yorkers claimed the site as their (private) heritage, and their interpretation of the meaning of the site was very different from that of the first archaeologists at the site for the majority of New York City politicians. Eventually, the ABG became a national monument under the mantle of the National Park Service. This is a case where the local community (private heritage) worked to control the definition and interpretation of the site and control its conversion into public heritage.

The historical narratives transmitted through heritage, public or private, are selective, partial, and frequently biased and distorted (Johnson 1999), because, to a significant degree, the narratives reflect political and social-structural themes of contemporary people (Crisp 2005:188). The study of tourism and archaeology thus involves acknowledging the contextual power relations that underpin various representations and interpretations. By conceptualizing this as a series of contested meanings rather than as a series of artifacts allows us to analyze the underlying conflicts and tensions and, therefore, remain culturally sensitive (Bruner 2005; Graham et al. 2000).

In this context, Graham et al. (2000:93) put forward the idea of the dissonance of heritage representations defined as:

The mis-match between heritage and people, in space and time. It is caused by movements or other changes in heritage and by migration or other changes in people, transformations which characteristically involve how heritage is perceived and what value systems are filtering these perceptions. The most pervasive source of heritage dissonance lies in the fundamental diversity of societies. The complexities of dissonance are further exacerbated by the contemporary expansion in the meanings and scope of heritage, and the concomitant multiplication of conflicts between its uses.

Heritage dissonance at archaeological sites can lead to very real conflicts when cultural sensitivities are not adhered to or recognized by visitors. Moreover, interpretative displays at archaeological sites can also provoke further conflicts. This is illustrated conceptually by examining the contested interpretation and representation of two archaeological sites: one in India and one in Israel.

India and the Reinterpretation of a Colonial Era Site

India's heritage tourism is largely maintained by the semi-autonomous Archaeological Survey of India (ASI), which was originally established in 1861. Today, it functions as a large and complex organization "attached" to the Department of Culture, in the Ministry of Tourism and Culture. Under the *Ancient Monuments and Archaeological Sites and Remains Act of 1958*, the ASI has declared over 3000 monuments to be of National importance in India. The ASI's major activities have expanded to include: the maintenance; conservation; and preservation of protected monuments and sites; archaeological exploration and excavations; chemical preservation of monuments and antiquarian remains; architectural survey of monuments, the setting up and reorganization of site museums; and the creation of greater awareness of the heritage of the India (ASI 2004). The ASI attempts to portray an all-India viewpoint independent of political bias. However, its independence has been questioned by the recent right-wing government in India associated with the BJP party. The BJP has actively sought the Hinduization of many archaeological sites and the renaming of many towns and cities.

Moreover, at archaeological sites associated with India's colonial past, the representations have also taken on a nationalistic pedigree (Hannam 2006). For example, The "British" Residency in Lucknow, the site of one of the most (in)famous conflicts between the British colonists and the Indian population, remains to this day almost exactly as it was over one hundred years ago as a monument to a colonial conflict. It was not erased, rebuilt, or restored but conserved by the ASI, the Indian National Trust for Archaeological and Cultural Heritage, and the Uttar Pradesh State Tourism Department. The Residency site was declared a monument of British "national" importance in 1920, but not opened to the general public until 1957, exactly 100 years after the conflict (Menon 2003). However, recent interpretations of the conflict by the ASI have begun to reinscribe the site as a memorial to the Indian resistance rather than as a memorial to British domination.

In a recent ASI publication, Menon (2003:5, emphasis added by authors), the Director General of the ASI, has argued that the ruins of The Residency, "stand as a mute witness to the *intense resistance* to domination by a foreign power." Another recent ASI publication contains a message from the former Prime Minister of India, Vajpayee:

> The revolt of 1857 forms an important turning point in Indian history. It marked the beginning of India's First War of Independence, demonstrating the national feeling and action against alien rule in India. . . . The Residency at Lucknow which was built by Nawab Saadat Ali Khan for the use of the British Resident in 1800 is a mute witness to the dramatic events leading to its siege during the First War of Independence in 1857. Every brick of the Residency echoes with the sense of patriotism, sacrifice and heroic deeds of countless freedom fighters who lost their lives when it was besieged. (Fonia 2002:1)

The museum exhibits, meanwhile, "comprise an extensive range of material from old photographs, lithographs, paintings, and documents to artifacts and memorabilia, *which invoke the high points of a revolt that has remained embedded in the collective memory of the people*" (Menon 2003:5, emphasis added by authors). The archaeologist in charge of The Residency, Fonia (2002:4) has similarly argued that "it is our hope that each individual who walks into the galleries of this Museum will be able to re-live the spirit of [the] First War of Independence fought in and around Lucknow." This reinterpretation of the archaeological site as one of Indian rather than British heritage was further demonstrated in 2007 when a group of British historians and ex-soldiers whose ancestors were involved in the conflict were forced to abandon a three-week tour of sites commemorating 150 years since the conflict after mobs pelted them with mud and bottles. The trouble began within days of the group arriving after sections of the Indian media described their visit as a "celebration of a British victory." Muslim clerics and Hindu nationalists joined to denounce the trip as an "insult to Indian freedom fighters" (Ramesh 2007).

The Zealots of Masada and the Israeli State

Despite the Biblical connections of Jews to the Middle East, the State of Israel is a recent nation-state. Founded in 1948, the Jewish state has perforce needed to acquire traditions that reinforce state nationalism. The archaeological site of Masada provides a dramatic narrative structure that fits well with the invention of modern Israeli nationalistic traditions. Edward Bruner's commentary on Masada argues that:

> Masada is simultaneously a tourist attraction (MacCannell 1976), a pilgrimage site (Turner and Turner 1978), an archaeological excavation (Yadin 1966), the idiom of political debate (Alter 1973), the topic of a novel (Gann 1981), a scholarly dissertation (Zerubavel 1980), a television spectacular (Cultural Information Service 1981), and, for some, a national symbol of the state of Israel. (Bruner and Gorfain 2005:174)

Masada, built by King Herod between 37 and 31 BCE, was the scene of a mass suicide by a besieged group of Jewish Zealots in 73 CE who, according to the one original, written document accounting for the story, preferred death over surrender to a stronger force of a Roman legion under the leadership of Governor Flavius Silva after the fall of Jerusalem and the Temple in 70 CE. The site today has enormous symbolic significance for the citizens of the modern Israeli state. Groups as diverse as tourists, school children, army draftees, and bar/bat mitzvah attendees meet there. The modern dialogic narratives of the site are supported by the archaeological research of Israeli politician-scholar Yigael Yadin (1966) who interprets the site as that of a heroic sacrifice made by the Masada rebels. For example, on *Amazon.com* a reviewer in 2008 – ostensibly a Rabbi – of a children's book version of Yadin's published works (Yadin and Gottlieb 1969) in 2008 wrote a glowing report of the value of this book for Jews and gentiles alike about the Masada siege. He writes that the archaeology of Masada is "totally amazing."

However, some scholars have called this interpretation of the site into question (Ben-Yehuda 1995, 2002; Bruner and Gorfain 1984). Nachman Ben-Yehuda, Dean of the Faculty of Social Sciences at Hebrew University, Jerusalem, has suggested that Yadin (1917–1984), who was not only an archaeologist, but a military figure in the War for Independence and a political leader and politician in the postwar period, preferred writing an analysis that supported the heroic storyline of Masada's Zealot Jewish defenders. Since Yadin's book is an essential component of the Masada "warriors as heroes" theme, called the "Masada mythical narrative" by Ben-Yehuda (1995:67), the underlying archaeological research for this narrative takes on a sense of historical accuracy that in fact may be open to different interpretations, but which remain undiscovered or viewed with disfavor. Indeed, both Shapira (1992) and Ben-Yehuda (1995, 2002) conclude that Yadin used his research to legitimize the use of force by Zionists in their independence. Prior to the work of Yadin and others, "Jewish rabbinical tradition ignored or suppressed the story [of Masada] for twenty centuries because the commentators disapproved of suicide and the secularity of the story's values (Bruner and Gorfain 2005:127, citing Zerubavel 1980:95–116)." The story of ancient the Zealots' suicides has taken hold as public heritage, and the primary narrative is clear, not only from tourist guidebooks and television specials, but also from a recent National Geographic story that concludes:

Herodium and Masada remain prominent landmarks for modern Israelis. Their defiant warriors symbolize a religious idealism and high-minded courage in the face of foreign invaders that, too many Israelis, resonates strongly with their country's position in the Middle East . . . On Masada . . . officers are inducted into the Israeli army, repeating the fateful phrase, 'Masada shall never fall again!' (Mueller 2008:59)

For both domestic and international tourists, Masada carries an important constructed narrative. Those who would, today, dare to contradict this interpretation could become the object of fierce and perhaps violent criticism. Ben-Yehuda has been heavily criticized in Israel for questioning the accuracy of Yadin's work. The narrative force for this UN World Heritage site cannot, at this time, be easily challenged without a backlash.

Notions of cultural sensitivity and insensitivity at archaeological sites demonstrate the underlying power relations involved in the contemporary (re)interpretation of the past. The notion of cultural embeddedness, to which we now turn, allows us to understand the power relations that underpin how individuals and groups experience these sites and develop their cultural networks.

Embeddedness

The notion of embeddedness can be traced back to the early work of Karl Polanyi (1944) in his book, *The Great Transformation*, which explicitly rejected the then-dominant view of the economy as somehow natural, self-regulating, and inevitable in form, arguing instead that markets are socially constructed and governed. Polanyi's work was then reintroduced into social science research in the mid-1980s by Mark Granovetter (1985), who used the expression "structural embeddedness" to indicate that not only do personal relations matter in understanding a regional culture, but also "the structure of the overall network of relations" (Granovetter 1990:98–99). Sharon Zukin and Paul DiMaggio (1990) later identified four different kinds of embeddedness: cognitive, cultural, structural, and political; with cultural embeddedness referring to the role of shared collective understandings in shaping strategies and goals. Indeed, the notion of cultural embeddedness has quickly become established in the social science literature, particularly in understanding processes of regional development and change by focusing attention on how people's everyday practices and experiences can shape a regional culture.

Another way of defining embeddedness is by placing actions, material culture, and ideology within behavioral and symbolic norms of particular groups, which may be social groups such as communities, political entities, such as municipalities and states, or cross-sectional groups, such as ethnically identified minorities and majorities. A third, more focused definition is as a set of sociocultural relationships between individuals and organizations that create distinctive patterns of constraints and incentives for human action and behavior. Of course, we also understand that collectivities of understandings do not exist except in the minds of scientific analysts, and that instead it is more fruitful to see human understandings as quite variable, dynamic, and affected by historical, social, and experiential events.

More recently, Hess (2004) has identified three broad aspects of cultural embeddedness. Firstly, societal embeddedness refers to the ways in which the actions and strategies of actors are influenced and shaped by their social, cultural, and political backgrounds, both at the individual and the aggregate level. Secondly, network embeddedness describes the structure and composition of the formal and informal relationships among different sets of individuals and organizations and how in turn that shapes their activities. Thirdly, territorial embeddedness refers to the extent to which actors are "anchored" in local territorial networks of institutions and place-bound, social dynamics. Ultimately, embeddedness must affect the work of archaeologists or they fail to understand the importance of their work for contemporary communities. Here we need to question the extent to which "communities" include tourists or does their voice need to be added as a distinct entity connected to the sites that archaeologists excavate, restore, and/or (re)interpret. The history and heritage of a site must reflect not only the perspective of the archaeologist, but also the voice(s) of the community as they interpret the site for the visitors. Likewise, tourists must be part of the equation, for the interpretative value can have little meaning without the audience (the tourists). While the tourist culture and the cultures of the tourists may be well understood (embedded) within the tourist industry, often neither the archaeologist nor the local communities involved understand nor anticipate the visitor's needs or culture. Just as the archaeologist works to lay the groundwork for the archaeological work within the community, so also must he or she work to ensure that the site itself can withstand the varied demands (both cultural and physical) of the tourist.

One example of these aspects of embeddedness as it relates to the work of archaeologists is the work undertaken by post processual archaeologist Carol McDavid (2004). Working with processual archaeologists on a historic plantation site in Brazoria, Texas (60 miles south of Houston) McDavid constructed an interactive website (http://www.saa.org/public/news/societyawardsforPublicArchaeology_McDavid.html) that weaves together the stories and histories of the descendants of masters and slaves on the Levi Jordan Plantation. It also serves the members of the contemporary community and anyone else interested in the issue of slavery and its effects on the modern era. Her work illustrates the need for archaeologists to carefully consider the effects of their research and how it connects to the life and times of contemporary communities, organizations, and individuals whose self-identities are intimately connected with the site's interpretation, yet not be so esoteric to alienate the curious, but perhaps less emotionally involved, tourist. Other complex examples of cultural embeddedness are Colonial Williamsburg, Virginia, and the Alamo in San Antonio, Texas, whose historical significances and meanings are being rewritten by each generation, changing according to the demands of the local community, as well as to the expectations of a more knowing, culturally aware tourist. In cases like these, the archaeologist who diminishes the importance of cultural embeddedness will soon find his/her work unwelcome.

To further illustrate the notion of cultural embeddedness, we now focus upon three extended examples from archaeology and tourism, one concerning Viking festivals and rituals, a second concerning Minoan archaeology on Crete, and a third from the Mayan regions of Yucatán, Mexico (Chichén Itzá) and the Western Highlands of Guatemala (Iximche').

Viking Festivals and Rituals

Participants in reconstructing the Viking archaeological past have developed both a networked and territorially embedded cultural structure across Scandinavia through the development of re-enactment organizations and festivals. On average, over 50 Viking festivals each year of varying sizes and duration take place. Most last three or four days and consist of approximately 200 transnational participants and around 3000 visitors per day. Most are in rural locations; however, a few take place in fairly large cities, such as Stockholm or Uppsala and have a very different atmosphere. Most Viking festivals are built upon or around an existing tourist attraction such as an archaeological site, a museum, or a heritage center. Indeed, many Viking festivals use their location to confer added authenticity and thus symbolic value (Halewood and Hannam 2001).

For example, in Sweden since 1994, Årsunda has been the home to a Viking festival that takes place each March. Årsunda's Viking project was created by a number of unemployed people who hoped to develop tourism and jobs in the region. The project is divided into three parts: a reconstructed Viking farm at Brudberget, archaeological finds from excavations, and a museum and exhibition center. During the festival, shopkeepers display their wares, like leather, glassware, textiles, ceramics, jewelry, and much more. Skillful artisans display their accomplishments in metal forging and other crafts. Viking competitions requiring strength, quickness, and technique go on throughout the day. Viking warriors challenge one another in archery, tug-of-war, tossing the caber, and other sports (Sandvikens 2003).

Like many other festivals, this festival is openly trying to emphasize the "quality" and "authenticity" of both its festival and its participants by drawing upon archaeological evidence to impress its visitors. Through this, they are firstly embedded *territorially*.

Secondly, the Viking re-enactment groups are fundamentally *networked* across space by using new technologies, such as the internet to put forward their interpretations of the archaeological past. Local organizers mobilize the support of a local council, tourism, or leisure organization or private sponsor – who underwrites the festival and provides a venue and services such as water, waste disposal, security, and parking. However, Viking festivals are advertised by the key organizers both locally, nationally, and internationally through the use of the internet, national advertising, and local word of mouth re-enactment networks. More recently, a Viking tourism network called Destination Viking Living with an internet forum and partners in Norway, Denmark, Sweden, Germany, Latvia, and Russia has been funded by the European Union.

Tourists may watch Viking history come alive or take part in activities presented by "real" Vikings. Visit one of the high-quality campuses in the Destination Viking network and live next door to a Viking village offering reenactments, Viking markets, and fun while planning to visit adjacent archaeological sites. Destination Viking Living history is a high-quality tourist concept provided by Nordic Viking villages, museums, and professional archaeologists and re-enactors from Denmark, Norway, Sweden, and Germany. The Destination Viking logo signifies a partner dedicated to present the Vikings' cultural heritage to the public in a way that gives a fresh experience of the Viking world (Destination Viking 2005). Through the internet, collective identity and group solidarity is recognized, defined, and maintained outside the festival arena itself, largely separate from the tourists.

Thirdly, the Viking festivals are embedded *socially*. It is through the actual social experience of the festivals themselves that collective affinity, consciousness, and identity are actualized and maintained. The key participants at Viking festivals are drawn from a wide variety of economic and social backgrounds with a range of academic and practical expertise. Most people participate on a part-time basis, although a few do pursue the organization of the various societies and events almost full-time. Many festivals have become established as annual features with their own histories, attracting the same traders and tourists from several countries each year (Hannam and Halewood 2006).

Viking festivals are ultimately a unique combination of two meaningful and competing cultural themes: *heritage* and *festival*. Heritage is used in terms of foregrounding a stratified *past* with historical and archaeological significance; festival refers to foregrounding a *present* embodied site of popular culture (Hannam and Halewood 2006). Both the archaeological past and the modern present are intimately entwined in the experience of Viking heritage, and both seek their own continuities with the past: heritage through notions of order and authority, and festival through notions of ambivalence and mobility (the peripatetic movement of festival participants from festival to festival, the itinerant movement from a fixed home to a home on the road).

Arthur Evans, Knossos, and Cretan Tourism

The dynamic development of embeddedness stemming from archaeological excavations and affecting heritage tourism can also be seen by a visit to the island of Crete. The foundations for our modern understandings of Minoan archaeology go back to the late 19th and early 20th centuries when the island was divided up among "scholarly fiefdoms" (Duke 2007:29).

Eventually, the archaeological work of Arthur Evans (1921) (and other contemporaries) through his excavation at Knossos, Crete, and restoration of the palace of Minos – though now widely recognized as problematic (Duke 2007:78) – continues to provide the main narrative of Minoan civilization. Evan's restoration serves as the basis for the government's training of official tour guides. They are required to provide a slavish repetition of his now-out-dated interpretations (Duke 2007:108). The tour guides must instruct the tourist to see a direct linear connection between Minoan and Western civilization, a view archaeologist Philip Duke (2007:105–6) believes is far from accurate. He believes Minoan society did not follow a linear civilizational pattern. In the 2nd millennium, more recent archaeological work seems to show that Minoan social structure and culture was actually less complex, and there is little evidence, he says, for greater heterogeneity. This finding weakens the case considerably for making an acute link between Minoan and Western civilization. Duke concludes that archaeological paradigms have obscured what really happened facilitated an uncritical development of a myth of Minoan greatness. He writes, "an unholy alliance has been unwittingly created between cultural ideology and intellectual paradigms."

Thus, the lower class of Minoan life has been studied less because that has been the historical tone of Minoan archaeology (an ideological sin of omission). It is also because neo-evolutionary archaeology tells us the inexorable development of human society is to greater complexity, even though on both empirical and epistemological grounds, the argument has no validity when applied to Minoan culture in the first place (an intellectual sin of commission [Duke 2007:105–6]).

Evans, a member of British society, had a profound effect on the narrative of Minoan culture and society. Once Minoan society was linked to ancient Greek political culture, it has been very hard to redirect the narrative and embark on a broader, postmodern search for other interpretations that may more accurately reflect the data. In turn, this interpretation has a profound effect on the way Cretans view their own heritage. There is no room for interpretations that detract from the narrative of Minoan culture as the foundational culture for Western civilization. Archaeology and tourism are thus embedded within the past and the present interpretation and understanding of the structural relations between resident and tourist. In this circumstance, alternative views of the past that distance the actors from this interpretation might be received with incredulity or even with hostility.

Chichén Itzá and Pist'e

In other cases, such as one in Yucatán, embeddedness continues to play a complex role, but here the residents have been left out of key roles in interpreting the importance of the site to tourists and to government officials. Cultural anthropologist Quetzil Castañeda (1996, 1997) has worked for many years in the community of Pist'e, located on the doorstep to the famous Late Classic Mayan site of Chichén Itzá. The interpretation of these ruins as a UN World Heritage site by its excavators and even today by the *Instituto Nacional de Antropología e Historia* (INAH) excludes the people living in nearby communities. Rather than being regarded as integral to understanding the long and dynamic history of the Maya people who still exist in large numbers through the Yucatán, Chiapas, Guatemala, Honduras, and Belize, they are seen as nuisances when they try to sell their art objects to tourists visiting a city of their ancestors (Castañeda 1997). Chichén Itzá has become an exclusion zone for the Maya descendants of the people who built Chichén Itzá. Not only are the Pist'e inhabitants/residents ethnically Maya, they often also claim a Maya identity, as do a majority of the indigenous people of Yucatán (see Castillo and Castañeda 2004; Gabbert 2004; Restall 2004). Ironically, Pist'eños were the majority of workers originally hired by the archaeologists of the Mexican government and the Carnegie Institution of Washington DC during Chichén Itzá's period of excavation and restoration (1923–1970s). Castañeda documents in numerous publications (1996, 1997, 2004) the ways in which the inhabitants of Pist'e have been denied economic opportunities and political and social recognition for their role as representatives of modern Mayan life. The Pist'eños are embedded within the structural relationship between tourist and archaeological site. The officials of INAH attempts to constrain their role by denying them opportunities to interact with the tourists to sell their art and souvenirs, and the archaeological community denies them recognition as part of the dynamic present of the great Maya past. Most tourists visit the site completely unaware that the Maya have not died out, oblivious to the fact that the Maya, in fact, are all around them. The inhabitants of Pist'e, as well as the majority of the people of Yucatán, are "not simply Mayans and descendents of Maya, but they are the Maya! They themselves typically have always claimed that they are cultural, linguistic, and ethnic descendents of the pre-Columbian Maya" (Castañeda, personal communication 2008). The narrative of Chichén Itzá excludes the contemporary Maya. One might say that the Maya are so much a part of Chichén Itzá, so embedded are they in the tourist and historical scene that they are invisible to both archaeologists and tourists alike.

Iximche', Guatemala

Embeddedness at another Maya pre-Columbian setting, however, does not result in invisibility, but rather a sense of connectedness and belonging. Iximche', in Guatemala's Western Highlands, stands in stark contrast to Chichén Itzá and even to Tikal, a Classic period site famous for its very tall pyramids and extensive grounds. Unlike Chichén Itzá, which is a Mayan exclusion zone meant only for tourists and guides, Iximche' is the home to the only pre-Columbian Mayan site that is still used by contemporary Kaqchikel-speaking Maya. Iximche' was burned to the ground in 1526, two years after the Spanish, under Pedro de Alvarado, broke their truce with the Kaqchikel leaders. This site in the middle of pine trees and set atop a high mesa near the colonial town of Tecpán was excavated and restored by the Swiss-Guatemalan George Guillemin (1965). What makes this site special is the active and constant use of the site by contemporary Kaqchikel in traditional dress who frequently picnic, play soccer, stroll over the ruins, and/or visit a sacred Maya altar (Schele and Mathews 1998:316). For example, after visiting Iximche' in 1990 during the feast of the Epiphany, Peter Mathews, a Mayan epigrapher, was awestruck by the fact that the place is often packed with Maya. He writes:

> We had been to other Maya sites and had usually had them to ourselves. Now we were in a place where there were thousands of other people. What's more they weren't tourists, as at Copan. Virtually everyone else at Iximche' on that day was Kaqchikel. . . . What [we] saw at Iximche' is something new. We have both been to Maya sites that were full of people, but in every case, the people were as much strangers as we were – whether Ladinos, Gringos, Europeans, or Asians. They [the Kaqchikels] had gone to their sacred ancestral place with the same respect and emotion people have when they go to such places around the world. . . . They have taken back its sovereignty after almost 500 hundred years. (Schele and Mathews 1998:316–317)

Visits to Chichén Itzá and Iximch'e by one of the authors of this chapter (Wallace) confirm the contrasting experiences of these sites. Although there are other ancient sites still sacred to the modern

Maya, the use and enjoyment of Iximche' remains unmatched (Evans 2008; McKillop 2004). The former is a tourist site where local residents are excluded from the site and alienated from their heritage by a government that exalts its Mestizo (racial mixing of European and Native Americans) present and Maya past but denigrates its indigenous peoples. Guatemala, by contrast, has been unable to develop a strong Mestizo identity, while a strong Mayan identity has been maintained in much of the country, especially in the region that surrounds Iximche'. This partially restored site is a focal point of Mayan, especially Kaqchikel, pride with multiple functions. The local staff treats Mayan and foreign tourists alike – no special favors for anyone. It is clear the site is for everyone. For each group there is a different meaning, a different narrative. At many archaeological sites, the stories of the workers and the women are often missing altogether, although much of the scholarship has more recently been refocusing on these topics.

Tourists view the site as a "Late Classic Maya" site, while Mayans see it as a sacred site, but one where they can also relax and recreate. The urban Guatemalan has been estranged from the majority of its Mayan compatriots due to hundreds of years of colonialism and, more recently, a thirty-year civil war. When President George W. Bush visited Iximche' in September, 2006, local Maya shamans retraced his footsteps throughout the site to perform ceremonies for decon-tamination after he left! The site has become embedded in local narratives and ideology, one that differs significantly from either tourists or archaeologists.

Conclusions

Edward Bruner (2005:169), following Mikhail Bakhtin (1981), suggests that the understanding of a locality such as an archaeological site is based on the embedded nature of an interactive process whereby on one level scholars and researchers are affected by their own narratives and paradigms at a particular point in time and on another by the narratives of non-scholars, including members of the local community, the nation-state, and the tourists and visitors. These levels are rather like a three-dimensional chess game with many multiples of stories that change and shift according to current events, the demands of local communities, and nation-states for symbols that reinforce their identities, the tour guides, and docents that contour the "official" stories, and finally, the tourists whose stories often start with the experience of the site itself. The meanings, narratives, and interpretations of a site are embedded within a dynamic, socio-spatial history and heritage that is intimately connected to a present that is differentially understood by different actors (locals, tourists, government officials, scholars, archaeologists, etc.). As at Iximche', the meaning of the site varies much according to the visitor, whereas at another, ethnically related site such as Chichén Itzá, which is only for tourists, the meaning is heavily contested among locals and officials. In contrast, at Cretan Minoan sites, Lucknow, India, and at Israeli Masada, the government officials and archaeologists have set the narrative discourse for which here is much agreement among local residents as it supports nationalist (public heritage) needs, at least currently, though this can change over time, as we have seen.

Archaeological sites are networked across space so that multiple sites and multiple actors play roles in the narratives and the dialogic interpretation of the site. They exist within a territorial context that is simultaneously a space within which multiple dialogues take place, refining, changing, and affecting those interpretations. Finally archaelogical sites embedded within a sociopolitical context whose narratives are also dynamic, where often the dominant stories are those of the powerful (including that of the archaeologist and the tourist industry), and where the stories of the less powerful are sub-merged or even missing.

In this chapter we have tried to outline the complexity of the issues surrounding the excavation, restoration, and interpretation of archaeological sites and tourism. Our knowledge and understanding of the past is embedded in the cultures, communities, and societies of the present. Additionally, each individual, group, society, or community may have their own "investment" in the interpretation of the site.

As the archaeologist and the tourist industry approach the site, it is imperative that they be aware of the potential for multiple dialogues and narratives among the residents and within the socio-political and economic structures present. They need also be mindful of the narrative expectations that the tourists bring to the site. The meaning of the archaeological site is part of a dynamic and ongoing process simultaneously uniting and separating residents, the broader community affected by the existence of the site, as well as the tourists. Though the archaeologist and the industry members, and even the local and national governments involved, may believe they "know" the meaning of the site, they may be mistaken how this meaning actually may be used and interpreted in different ways by locals and tourists alike. This is cultural sensitivity, that is, the need to understand that any heritage site exists within an embedded and contested context that is as much connected to the present as it is to the past.

Part TWO

Case Studies

Chapter 5

The Management and Marketing of Archaeological Sites: The Case of Hadrian's Wall

Gary Warnaby, David Bennison, and Dominic Medway

Introduction: The Topography of Hadrian's Wall

Hadrian's Wall dates from AD 122 and stretches over 70 miles between the mouths of the rivers Tyne and Solway and from coast to coast across the north of England, although nowhere now at its full height. It is the most spectacular and best known Roman *limes* or frontier system (Dudley 1970), and it has been described as "the greatest monument to Roman achievement in Britain" (Hunter Blair 1963:74). The Wall was not a closed frontier and, at regular intervals of one Roman mile, there were fortified gateways called milecastles, which were an adaptation of the normal fortlets constructed throughout Britain by the Roman army (Breeze and Dobson 2000). These milecastles provided a way through the Wall with double gates

Tourism and Archaeology: Sustainable Meeting Grounds, edited by Cameron Walker and Neil Carr, 111–126. ©2013 Left Coast Press, Inc. All rights reserved.

at front and rear, and the gap between milecastles was evenly divided by two observation towers, usually called turrets. Also, relatively evenly spaced along the Wall were a series of forts, positioned astride the Wall wherever local topography allowed (Breeze and Dobson 2000).

The topography of the Wall can be divided into three main sections. The Eastern section (between South Shields and Chollerford) is dominated by the Tyneside conurbation, within which today Hadrian's Wall exists mostly below ground or as excavated/conserved ruins. There are two popular visitor sites – the forts of Segedunum (which has a large interactive museum and a viewing tower that is 3.5m high) and Arbeia (which has a museum and reconstructions of buildings and a section of the Wall, as shown in Figure 5.1). The Central section (between Heddon and Birdoswald) is the most developed and well-recognized section, passing through environmentally sensitive rural landscapes (as shown in Figure 5.2). The Cumbria section runs between Brampton and the Solway Firth (west of the River Irthing, the Wall was always a turf rather than a stone structure). Although

Figure 5.1 Arbeia Fort in South Shields on the south bank of the River Tyne. The picture shows the reconstructed gatehouse and the urban setting of the site.

Figure 5.2   View of Wall from Housesteads.

the Wall itself ends at Bowness-on-Solway, remnants of a defensive network (in the form of free-standing fortlets and towers) are found for 26 miles to the southwest along the Cumbrian coast as far as Maryport (Mason et al. 2003). In tourism terms, the Cumbria section is less well developed, with knowledge of the links between Cumbrian sites and Hadrian's Wall largely limited to those with an interest in Roman archaeology, although the city of Carlisle emphasizes its links with Hadrian's Wall in its tourism promotion literature.

Post-Roman History of the Wall

Roman rule in Britain ended in AD 411, although Breeze and Dobson (2000) state that there is evidence for continuing occupation at several sites into the fifth century and beyond. According to Hingley and Nesbitt (n.d.:2):

> The wall has been extensively written about and documented; it has been captured by maps, paintings, poetry and photographs.

and its appeal has been wide-reaching. The wall's monumentality provided a flexible concept that depended on the socio-political climate of the day, with different authors emphasising its ruination or grandeur appropriate to the image they were trying to promote.

Indeed, Young (2006:204) describes Hadrian's Wall as, "possibly the British monument with the longest history of antiquarian interest," and also one of the longest traditions of conservation effort. In Medieval times, the Wall is one of the few features marked on maps of Britain, and land records show the Wall as an important boundary (Mason et al. 2003; see also Whitworth 2000). In the 16th century, the Wall was seen as an icon of national and imperial identity in the troubled relations between England and Scotland (Hingley and Nestbitt n.d.). More prosaically, the Wall also provided great utilitarian value as a source of building material (Mason et al. 2003; Whitworth 2000).

Hingley and Nesbitt (n.d.) suggest that interest in the Wall waned in the 17th century, but there was a revival in the 18th and 19th centuries. The first excavations and conservation date from the early 19th century, and were catalyzed by the efforts of learned societies in the region and men such as John Clayton, who bought and excavated stretches of the Wall, and John Collingwood Bruce, who published the results of Clayton's excavations and wrote important historical guides to the Wall (for further details see Mason et al. 2003; Young 2006). The latter part of the century also saw the first public acquisition of part of the Wall with the creation of the Roman Remains Park in 1875 by the South Shields Urban District Council (Austen and Young 2002). In the early/mid-20th century, acquisition of parts of the Wall by public bodies continued, consolidated by state protection of archaeological sites through the application of successive ancient monument acts (Young 2006). The state (through the Office of Works) acquired its first parts of the Wall in 1932. North Tyneside Council, the Northumberland County Council, and Cumbria County Council all acquired forts on the Wall for conservation (Austen and Young 2002). In the 1970s, the creation of the Vindolanda Trust (to implement excavation, research, conservation, and education programs at the eponymous fort) expanded the range of public and charitable ownership still further.[1] More recent acquisitions by local authorities include the forts at Birdoswald, Rudchester, and Wallsend. In the last case, the site of the Wallsend fort was bought by North Tyneside Council initially to clear and replace Victorian housing, but they subsequently decided to maintain the site as an ancient monument after rescue excavations revealed the survival of the fort (Young 2006).

Managing a World Heritage Site

Until the 1970s, it could be argued that these conservation and preservation efforts were somewhat piecemeal, and Young argues that with some relatively minor exceptions, "there was little attempt to visualize the Wall as an entity, and to manage it as such" (2006:207). However, in recent years, this has changed, because the site acquired status as an UNESCO World Heritage Site (WHS) – termed "Frontiers of the Roman Empire" – in 1987. Initially this was thought to be a largely honorific distinction (Young 2006), but it has led to Hadrian's Wall being viewed "more as a conceptual entity than as a particular place" (Mason et al. 2003:13). Indeed, the need for a management plan as part of its WHS inscription has led to various initiatives to coordinate management of the Wall. The initiation of the management plan process (led by English Heritage) began in 1993, coinciding with the creation of the Hadrian's Wall Tourism Partnership (formed to coordinate the development of sustainable tourism for the WHS area) and the creation of the Hadrian's Wall National Trail. According to Mason et al. (2003:18) "these initiatives created institutions and partnerships to manage the Wall and setting resources in ways that were coherent geographically and across sectors." In 1996, the first comprehensive management plan for the WHS was adopted and a management plan committee representing 39 stakeholder groups was created. Some key responsibilities of the Hadrian's Wall Management Plan Committee (HWMPC) included:

- oversight of the implementation of general and specific recommendations made within the management plan (and to monitor success in meeting targets set);
- establishment of a forum for management issues and to continue to coordinate efforts toward concerted management within the World Heritage Site;

- monitoring of the condition of the WHS and develop and agree on appropriate actions to deal with threats to its well-being;
- development of further policies and codes of practice for protection, recoding and research, access, interpretation, and preservation (as well as safeguarding the livelihoods and interests of those living and working within the WHS zone); and,
- promotion of the economy of the region, within the overriding need to conserve the WHS (Mason et al. 2003).

Recognizing the fragmented ownership of the Wall and its environs and the plurality of interests involved in the management of the WHS, the HWMPC stakeholders included 12 boroughs, city and county councils, two national parks, two universities, two central government departments, two organizations representing local/regional museums, the Council for British Archaeology, the National Trust, the National Farmers Union, the Countryside Agency, and the Country Land & Business Association among others. A key role was played by English Heritage, and its associated organization, the Hadrian's Wall Coordination Unit, created to oversee implementation of the plan on a day-to-day basis. English Heritage has a dual role – it serves as a partner and coordinator for activities, but is also the national authority that advises and approves or prevents certain interventions or activities of other partners (Mason et al. 2003). Young argues that the management plan has "created a more holistic approach to the management of the WHS as a whole. It has stimulated considerable investment, primarily related to access and sustainable tourism" (2006:209). The second version of the *World Heritage Site Management Plan 2002–2007* has been published.

Mason et al. (2003) argue that the 2002 management plan was influenced by its completion in the aftermath of the outbreak of Foot and Mouth disease (FMD) that devastated livestock in many rural areas of the UK and had significant impact on rural economies, particularly with regard to tourism. For example, Housesteads, one of the iconic forts on the Wall and a very popular destination for visitors was only open to the public for 10 days in 2001. The 2002 management plan had an explicit emphasis on economic recovery and implications for the archaeological heritage of the WHS:

The balance of values has changed in response to the FMD tragedy and the resulting stresses on the Hadrian's Wall landscape and stakeholders. The Management Plan goals remained focused on sustainable management – which is to say, development within a conservation framework – but this sustainability has been redefined by FMD. By bolstering the economic use of the landscape for diversified agriculture as well as for heritage tourism, the heritage values of the site and setting were protected.

Management has accommodated a shift toward emphasizing the economic values of the Wall in the context of conserving the core heritage values. In the new climate, the focus is now on tourism rather than on the crippled agricultural sector (Mason et al. 2003:12–13).

Following this in April, 2003, two regional development agencies (RDAs) in the north of England commissioned a year-long "major study" into Hadrian's Wall to "assess the potential of Hadrian's Wall to support the regeneration of the North of England through the growth of tourism revenues and to deliver a new Vision for Hadrian's Wall" (NWDA/ONE 2004:1). This study entailed a number of stages (NWDA/ONE 2004):

1. Fact-finding – Stakeholders were interviewed to ascertain their perceptions regarding issues identified in a SWOT analysis and their visions for the Wall. Consumer research was undertaken among current and potential visitors to the Wall to understand current perceptions and to identify any barriers to visitation.
2. Visioning – A workshop attended by study clients and representatives from key stakeholder organizations was held to develop a draft vision, which was then tested with a wider stakeholder audience through subsequent workshops. These workshops also included discussions about the implications of carrying out the vision for the visitor offer, its organization, and its supporting infrastructure. This was also tested among consumers at selected locations via group discussions, focusing on what best differentiated the Hadrian's Wall experience from other leisure attractions, and what aspects of the Wall experience were most likely to motivate incremental visits to the North. As

a consequence of this process, the following goal/vision was articulated: "To move Hadrian's Wall from a Northern "ought to see" to a Global "must see, stay, and return for more." This was to be achieved by positioning the Wall as the "Greatest Roman Frontier" (NWDA/ONE 2004:4). The committees identified a number of implications that bore weight if a cohesive visitor experience able to deliver this positioning was ever to be achieved. The fragmented nature of the Wall "product" and its ownership may make consistent communication problematic, and also the different styles and levels of interpretation of the different sites (and the perceived competition between them) may hinder the integrated approach required to successfully implement the "Greatest Roman Frontier" positioning.

3. Development of the strategy and recognizing the specific requirements of the different sections of the Wall – the strategic objective articulated for the Central Section was to grow visitor revenues in ways that recognize and address existing, as well as potential future, visitor management issues. The strategic objective for the less developed Cumbria Section was to establish a more overt connection with Hadrian's Wall and the role of the coast as part of "The Greatest Roman Frontier," and to ensure that there was a critical mass of related visitor experiences there to justify this link. The urban Eastern Section of the Wall in Newcastle upon Tyne includes Segedunum and Arbeia, along with the less well-known Museum of Antiquities, which is located on the University of Newcastle campus. There are existing plans to relocate the museum to incorporate it into a proposed larger museum in Newcastle. The objective here was to establish the existing and planned sites as part of the "Greatest Roman Frontier" with the aim of broadening the visitor market.

Hadrian's Wall Major Study Report, published in September, 2004, went on to articulate a number of actions regarding organizational strategy, resources and funding, interpretation and product development, and marketing and communications in order to deliver the required economic impact. Moreover, the report made recommendations as to the nature of the next steps to be taken in terms of: (1) improving organizational support structures; (2) creating the capability required to deliver the agreed vision in consultation and discussion with organizational support structures; and (3) gaining stakeholder buy-in to these improvements and also to wider study recommendations. Other key priorities included: (1) the creation of a detailed development and funding plan and concept design for "The Greatest Roman Frontier" and detailed development plans for each site; (2) the creation of a panel responsible for content details for each site within the context of the Wall-wide interpretation, content, and differentiation strategy; (3) the progression of development plans affected by other grant giving bodies' deadlines; and (4) the development of the "Greatest Roman Frontier" brand. This branding proposition was regarded as the unifying theme that would facilitate the coordination of activity across different stakeholders in order to create a cohesive visitor experience. The *Hadrian's Wall Major Study Report* recognized the symbiotic nature of products and brands emphasized in the marketing literature (see for example, de Chernatony and MacDonald 1993) in terms of "product development." Thus, it proposed the creation of "preview centers" and "story centers" to communicate the Wall as the "Greatest Roman Frontier" in order to increase public awareness and present a more effective overview of the Hadrian's Wall "story."

The need for greater cohesion with regard to more formalized organization/management was also acknowledged in the *Major Study Report*. In April, 2005, new structure proposals were published (NWDA/ONE 2005) in which it was suggested that the establishment of a single body with responsibility for the entire Wall was needed rather than the currently existing three entities involved in the governance and operational framework. It was proposed that this new organization should be a non-charitable, non-profit company limited by guarantee. Its "core priorities" were articulated as the WHS Management Plan, capital development and investment, heritage, education, and conservation, which would be captured in the "core activities" of strategic leadership, relationship management, brand and product development, conservation, and funding development.

Hadrian's Wall Heritage Limited

This effort culminated in May, 2006, in the creation of Hadrian's Wall Heritage Ltd (HWHL):

To realize the economic, social and cultural regeneration potential of the Hadrian's Wall World Heritage Site and the communities and environment through which it passes by sustainable tourism development, management and conservation activities which benefit local communities and the wider region. And all that done in a way that reflects the values embodied in the WHS Management Plan. (HWHL 2007a:1)

These values are articulated in the 2002 Management Plan in terms of the following "vision" that Hadrian's Wall should be:

- A World Heritage Site universally recognized as the best surviving example of a Roman frontier system in concept, design and achievement, with all aspects of the Wall and its setting protected, conserved and appropriately enhanced;
- A World Heritage Site and its Setting made accessible for all to learn about and enjoy in ways which are sustainable;
- A World Heritage Site which is a source of local identity and inspiration and an exemplar of sustainable development; and
- An increased understanding and knowledge of how the World Heritage Site was created, has developed, and is now used, as a basic tool for all current management and development decisions (Austen and Young 2002:77).

The aims underpinning this vision were arranged under the principal headings of: (1) protecting; (2) conserving; (3) using (focusing on the user experience and the creation of sustainable economic benefits for the region); and (4) managing (relating to structures, partnerships and resources) the World Heritage Site.

Its strategic plan (HWHL 2007a) envisages that HWHL would lead or contribute materially and measurably to Hadrian's Wall as an exemplar of World Heritage Site management would maximize the economic, social, and cultural regeneration of the Wall corridor through sustainable tourism. It would do so via: (1) improvement of the WHS offer to visitors and local communities; (2) optimizing accessibility to the WHS for all users; and (3) the establishment of an internationally successful brand. The strategic plan (HWHL 2007a:4) states that a series of key strategic documents would be developed to guide the work of HWHL and its partners. The new documents would relate to such aspects as communications and branding, interpretation, integrated access, development (i.e., initiating and implementing major projects), sustainability, community (i.e., facilitating engagement and support of the local population), education, and research (including "visitor information, the archaeological research strategy, geological, ecological and landscape research").

In its first two years of operation, HWHL has been involved in a range of initiatives in line with these aspects (see HWHL 2007b, 2008). These include capital improvements to sites, which are designed to enhance the visitor experience and work toward economic regeneration of the area. This applies not just to the famous sites, but also lesser-known attractions in order to encourage Wall-wide visits. Recent activities in the Cumbrian section of the Wall include capital development projects at Roman sites at Ravenglass and Maryport to draw these previously neglected elements closer to the rest of the Wall (HWHL 2008). In the Eastern Section, there are plans to enhance the visitor experience at the sites at Segedunum and Arbeia in terms of, for example, landscaping and on-site interpretation, and also further excavation, and these and other initiatives are closely linked to wider local development and regeneration.

The 2008 *Annual Review* of HWHL activities outlines a number of development initiatives at various stages that it and its partners are involved in. These range from concept development (e.g., "The Sill" World Heritage and Protected Landscapes Center in conjunction with Northumberland National Park Authority) and site assembly (e.g., proposals for the £11.5m development of the unexcavated Roman fort and civilian settlement at Maryport are completed, and land acquisition is at an advanced stage) and the development of bids for future expansion. One of the key challenges of this activity is "to ensure that current and future proposals are sufficiently differentiated to encourage visitors to explore more than one site" (HWHL 2008:10).

As mentioned above, interpretation is a crucially important factor and improving this aspect is an important part of HWHL's activities to enhance the visitor experience. HWHL has developed an interpretative framework:

Through which to work with partners to develop more strategic planning and coordination of interpretation and development.

The Interpretation Framework is described as 'a flexible and evolving document that puts forward some key ideas and principles. The challenge is to bring the story of the frontier to life through dynamic interpretation that engages with modern visitors. Visitors need to be able to grasp the overall story and to feel that each site tells a different part of the story or presents the story in a different way appropriate for a different audience. (HWHL 2008:23)

Indeed, HWHL has been keen to develop the Hadrian's Wall product as more than simply as a physical place or a collection of linked places but as an opportunity for *experience* and *adventure*. This also fits with HWHL's notion of moving the Hadrian's Wall place "product" from merely being a Wall to a *frontier*, and to facilitate understanding "so that visitors can absorb as much as they wish of about 2000 years of history" (HWHL 2008:23) in ways that are appropriate to their needs. Various key stakeholders have also bought into the experiential marketing stance. For example, the Vindolanda Trust, in addition to its invaluable scholarly archaeological activities, has been keen to invite voluntary battle re-enactment societies in full Roman dress to undertake special events at their sites. Similar activities have been implemented at sites in the Newcastle conurbation operated by Tyne & Wear Museums and also at sites operated by English Heritage.

The HWHL also has a sustainable access program, linking the planning, coordination, and direction of all modes of physical access. This is manifested in the AD 122 bus service along the Wall, which is the development and promotion of a network of circular walking routes based around the Hadrian's Wall National Trail.[2] It aims to diversify and grow the walking "product" by encouraging visitors to explore Roman sites as part of a walking holiday, to use local facilities, and to bike on the Hadrian's Wall coast-to-coast cycleway.

Marketing – and particularly marketing communications – is important in order "to build brand awareness, encourage more and prolonged visits, and grow the longer term visitor economy" (HWHL 2007b:24). A website – www.hadrians-wall.org – has been developed in order to provide "a multi-dimensional way of presenting the offer: [it] can present content in a more inspirational way, across different formats so that the HWC [Hadrian's Wall Country] offer can be brought to life" (HWHL 2007c:6). Linked to this, in 2007, the summer marketing campaign was built around the theme "Plan Your Invasion." The main focus of this was a stand-alone, web-based journey planner, with an interface that actively promoted the various destinations, facilities, and attractions of "Hadrian's Wall Country." This concept seeks to include a wide range of local businesses and communities through the fostering of a strong sense of place and identity. Indeed, the full-color press advertisements that ran in July and August, 2007, emphasized the range of activities, facilities, and attractions that were located in the area – not only those explicitly linked to the Roman heritage. They also include those with a more tangential relationship (e.g., art galleries, cafes, restaurants) but that nevertheless contribute to the overall visitor experience of the area. Recent initiatives include partnering with local businesses in the development of the "Hadrian's Wall Country Locally Produced" scheme that encompasses food, drink, arts, and crafts produced within a ten-mile corridor on either side of the Wall (HWHL 2008).

All of this activity is supported by promotional literature designed for use by visitors before and during their visit. The HWHL has also been actively engaged in public relations activities designed to stimulate and maintain media interest in the area at local, regional, and national levels through national and local print and broadcast media, as well as relevant websites. Recently, HWHL "has worked intensively to maximize the potential of the Hadrian: Empire and Conflict exhibition," which is a major exhibition on Hadrian at the British Museum that ran between July and October, 2008 (HWHL 2008:31). As part of this, a touring exhibition showcasing the British Museum's iconic bronze bust of Hadrian, titled "The Face of an Emperor: Hadrian Inspects the Wall" was exhibited at the Tullie House Museum in Carlisle and at Segedunum. Moreover, HWHL's summer marketing campaign for that year (in conjunction with the English tourism promotion agency, Enjoy England, and a range of other public and private sector partnerships) focused on advertising on the London Underground network and brand advertising in the national press and *BBC History Magazine* in order to capitalize on these connections with "Brand Hadrian" (HWHL 2008:31). In addition, the HWHL website was redesigned to tie in more explicitly with the British Museum exhibition.

Hadrian's Wall: Tourism, Archaeology, and the Future

In the 20th century, the growth of the tourism industry has had an obvious impact on Hadrian's Wall. Austen and Young state that since the Second World War,

> increasing car ownership and leisure have accelerated the growth of tourism within the WHS on the back of an increase in the number of sites managed for public access. These have brought their own impact on the landscape with car parks and visitor centers, but they also contribute to the conservation of the WHS and its setting and to the local economy through entry to paid sites and using local services and businesses. (2002:15)

Arguably, tourism – and the need to manage visitation – was regarded as an important issue, which in part catalyzed the management initiatives described above. As early as the 1970s, concerns existed that tourism was leading to damage through over-visiting and consequent erosion (Young 2006), and the relevance of such issues of sustainability remains as strong today as evidenced by the emphasis placed on them by Hadrian's Wall Heritage Limited. Such pressures have increased as the tourism infrastructure of the Wall has expanded with walking and cycle trails along the Wall. Indeed, concerns regarding the impact of these trails – and the need for enhanced resources for monitoring and for protecting the Wall – have been articulated in the media (see Alberge 2005; British Archaeology 2005). The impact of FMD on the area resulted to some extent in an increased emphasis on tourism as a means of economic regeneration – which arguably led in part to the creation of HWHL – meaning that balancing these competing pressures to enable sustainable development of the WHS will be an ongoing issue.

Notes

1. A detailed representation of Vindolanda is provided in the second case study of this book.
2. Walking the length of Hadrian's Wall has long been popular with walkers, and a long distance walk from Wallsend in Newcastle to Bowness-on-Solway was designated an official National Trail in May, 2003 with many new sections of path following the Wall itself. More details can be found at http://www.ramblers.org.uk/info/paths/hadrianswall.html.

Chapter 6
Vindolanda
Andrew Birley

Introduction

This case study examines how Vindolanda Trust has achieved a sustainable model for archaeological research financed by tourism on Hadrian's Wall at the Roman site of Vindolanda. The Vindolanda Trust is an archaeological charitable trust, founded in 1970, and is exclusively financed by visitors who come to see its two sites and museums along the line of Hadrian's Wall in northern England. It is a unique organization in the British archaeological landscape that successfully combines archaeological research with the needs and requirements of its primary stakeholders, the tourists who visit the site. Throughout its operations, the Vindolanda Trust has had to rely upon revenue generated by the visits of the public to fund its excavation/ research program. Without this direct funding, and an enthusiastic core of hard-working volunteers, progress would have been minimal. Conflicts with authorities (quasi non-governmental organizations/ university academics, and county council archaeologists), more accustomed to the minimalistic administration of the state's ancient

Tourism and Archaeology: Sustainable Meeting Grounds, edited by Cameron Walker and Neil Carr, 127–141. ©2013 Left Coast Press, Inc. All rights reserved.

monuments, was inevitable. For example, the construction of full-scale replicas of sections of Hadrian's Wall in the early 1970s seemed to be highly informative and educational to the Vindolanda Trusts staff. However, the county planners disapproved of Hadrian's design because there were no damp proofing or permeable membranes, and the windows were too small for modern housing. The Ancient Monuments Board for England and Wales wrote to inform the Trust that by building such things it was "bringing the integrity of Britain's ancient monuments into disrepute." Fortunately, the visiting general public did not agree.

By 1970, Vindolanda was well known to members of the archaeological community, but by very few outside of this. Although a series of notable antiquarians and archaeologists sporadically commented on and studied artifacts from the site, in real terms little had been done at the site in comparison to the large-scale excavations undertaken elsewhere along the line of Hadrian's Wall (Corbridge, Chesters, and Housesteads being perhaps the most famous of these). As a result, visitors to the site before 1970 were numbered only in their hundreds. Those that did come to visit found no car park or toilets and had to cross a farmer's field, often with a bull in it, and were obliged to navigate through a maze of cowpats and thistles to look at the very few consolidated remains. In this period most archaeologists were regarded with suspicion by local landowners, and visitors were viewed as potential pests by the local farming community.

As a result of these attitudes, most of the pre-1970 archaeological study on the site of Vindolanda was financed through personal investment by individuals or through university grants and bursaries. No government finance was made available to work on the site; and indeed, landowners would not have welcomed such work as the site was designated as agricultural land, and archaeological work or visitors disturbed the cattle grazing on the site. Early excavations were, therefore, conducted on a small scale and often only a few weeks at a time before trenches were backfilled and grass replaced. The findings of these excavations were then duly published in learned journals that had readerships almost exclusively restricted to either an academic or archaeological audience. It was thought in 1970 that Vindolanda consisted of three successive forts and a civilian settlement outside the walls. It is now known that there were at least nine forts spread out over nearly 40 acres rather than the previously assumed 12 acres (Birley and Blake 2007:3) – and that the anaerobic pockets in parts of the site have created some of the best preserved remains to be found anywhere in the former Roman Empire. In 1987, Vindolanda was designated as part of the Hadrian's Wall World Heritage Site.

Archaeology and Archaeological Tourism: The Savior or Destroyer of Hadrian's Wall? A Historical Perspective

Since its construction, Vindolanda and Hadrian's Wall have been visited by antiquarians and archaeologists in the capacity of curious tourists, many of whom made important contributions to the local economy and ultimately to our understanding of a World Heritage Site. Until the 18th century, most of the visitors could be regarded as adventurers, as the region of Hadrian's Wall has had more than its fair share of conflict and uncertainty (Moffat 2008:163). In Roman times, the area was a military frontier, and in the post Roman eras a large part of it became a new barrier between what would become England and Scotland, depopulated and rarely under lawful control by either kingdom (Moffat 2008:180). After the 18th century, Hadrian's Wall became more accessible, and for the next two hundred years the need to regulate tourism and monitor the preservation of the monument was neglected, often with dire consequences for the remains. Between the retreat of Rome at the beginning of the 5th century and the 18th century desires for preservation, tourists would be offered few facilities and little warmth in their visit to Hadrian's Wall, although their money was always welcome (Birley R. 1998:56).

As soon as the Romans completed Hadrian's Wall, it became a tourist attraction, and Roman memorabilia commemorating visits to Hadrian's Wall have been found many hundreds of miles away from the monument itself. These souvenirs include the Rudge cup (found in Wiltshire in 1725), the Amiens skillet (Amiens in France in 1949), and more recently the Staffordshire Moorlands Patera (found in 2003, including a quotation along its side of "*On the line of Hadrian's Wall*"). All of the souvenirs have place names/depictions of Roman forts we now know to have existed along the line of Hadrian's Wall, and one, the Staffordshire Patera, has the name of the manufacturer, Draconis. The fact that these finds have an international dimension, –

showing that in Roman times, just like today, people traveled from great distances to the monument – is telling. This speaks to modern audiences about the power of the monument as a tourist destination in a time when leisure time was at a premium, paid holidays did not exist, and traveling was a great deal more dangerous and laborious than today. To get to Hadrian's Wall, Roman tourists would have had to cross into a military zone populated with frontier forts and surrounded at times by restless and non-compliant natives. It is little wonder that after spending a night or two in an inn on a frontier town that many would have found their experience memorable enough to wish to remember it through the purchase of a souvenir. Modern archaeologists have had to comprehend that tourism is and always has been an important part of the fabric of the archaeology of Hadrian's Wall. A proportion of the collection of material culture studied by archaeologists is linked to the tourism of Hadrian's Wall in the Roman period.

Sadly, from the withdrawal of Rome to the rise of antiquarianism in the 16th century, we have little evidence of tourists going to the Wall. Those that did visit the monument had only limited access due to a high level of banditry and general lawlessness. The Elizabethan historian William Camden was one of the first to record a visit to Hadrian's Wall in 1599 before the 4th edition of his *Britannia* was published (Camden 1722). He mentions the remains at Vindolanda, although he was personally unable to inspect them due to the presence of "rank robbers" or moss troopers. As tensions eased in the 17th and 18th centuries after the Union of the Crowns, effectively removing the lawless border between England and Scotland, more visitors came to the Wall, and they have left us with some of the most important archaeological records of the monument. In 1702, Dr. Christopher Hunter wrote one such account and commented on what we now know are the remains of Vindolanda's third-century bathhouse:

Some years ago (probably well before 1702) on the west side of this place, about fifty yards from the walls thereof, there was discovered under a heap of rubbish a square room, strongly vaulted above, and paved with large squared stones set in lime, and under this a lower room, whose roof was supported by rows of square pillars of about half a yard high: the upper room had two niches, like (and perhaps in the nature of) chimneys on each side of the every corner or square, which made in all the number 16: the pavement of this room, also its roof, were tinged black with smoak. The stones used in vaulting the upper room have been marked as our joiners do the deals for chambers; those I saw were numbered thus – x, xi, xiii. (Hunter C. 1702, reproduced in Birley E. 1961:185)

This clearly shows that some buildings in the settlement at Vindolanda, as well as the fort walls, were standing to a great height until relatively recent times. It is reports like this, from tourists to the Wall that galvanized the archaeological community into action and a series of small-scale excavations were soon to follow both at Vindolanda and along the line of the Hadrian's Wall.

But this work was to come too late for the protection of some of the better-preserved parts of the monument. By the time of the publication of Warburton's *Vallum Romanum* in 1753, farming had been re-established in the area during more peaceful conditions created by the Union of the Crowns in 1603 and the later the *Act of Union in 1707*. There is evidence of a great deal of disturbance from stone robbing, plowing, and drainage work being undertaken as a consequence. Perversely, it was an Act of Parliament in the 1750s that saw the construction of a new road (much of it along the line of the Wall itself) between Newcastle and Carlisle in response to the 1745 Jacobite rebellion that was to be both the initial doom and savior of Hadrian's Wall. The new road allowed easy access to Hadrian's Wall sites for tourists and opened up the Wall to stone robbing and destruction on an unprecedented scale. Farmers had better access to markets, and as a result started to demolish the remains of the World Heritage Site to bring their fields into a more profitable state of bearing (Birley R. 1998:56). During this work, some incredible finds came to light, many of which were sold to passing tourists. It is difficult to accurately determine the scale of impact of tourism on the preservation of the monument at this time. Tourism money was certainly a motivating factor for some farmers to speed up the destruction of sites to collect more Roman artifacts to sell to tourists and to allow the fields to be ploughed once the Roman remains had been destroyed. Yet, while farmers and landowners were more than happy to sell what they found, often they were less happy to preserve remains on their land, preferring to destroy fine Roman buildings in case people tramped over fields in an attempt to visit them (Birley R. 1998:64). Tourism was a new and ill-defined phenomenon, and the farmers along the line of Hadrian's Wall had no concept of how they might use tourists as a resource, beyond selling what they found on their land to passers-by (an extension of farming in every sense).

By 1849, the mood started to change. The shambolic destruction of Hadrian's Wall and the selling of the remains to tourists by landowners met a new challenge from academic tourists who were motivated because they were horrified by the destruction, and they had a deep desire to explore what was left more fully through scientific means. In 1849, John Collingwood Bruce led the first academic pilgrimages along Hadrian's Wall with members of two northern antiquarian societies (Bidwell 1999:1). He described it as a larger version of a family holiday he had undertaken the previous year and was joined by 20 colleagues. The purpose of the pilgrimage was to examine excavation work that had been undertaken in the previous 10 years, and it is a tradition that remains to this day with a subsequent pilgrimage in 2009. This pilgrimage focused the minds of academia and was followed by the first guide to Hadrian's Wall, *The Roman Wall* (Collingwood Bruce 1867).

In 1863, John Clayton of Chesters acquired Vindolanda in a land grab that would ultimately hand him a great deal of Hadrian's Wall. Clayton was a lawyer and town clerk for the city of Newcastle and a champion of the railways with a passion for Romans and their remains. His ownership of much of the central part of Hadrian's Wall put a stop to much of the previous destruction, and importantly, he carefully collected material culture from and restored mile after mile of the central section of Hadrian's Wall. This section of Hadrian's Wall is now known by many as Clayton's Wall, because the stones are Roman but the Wall is not. This created some controversy and raised questions about what constitutes archaeological conservation or restoration. Many World Heritage Sites have similar problems; the Great Wall of China, Masada in Israel, and Leptis Magna on the Libyan coast have been treated in a similar way, and each have been "rebuilt" to a much greater extent.

Clayton would have regarded his work as restoration, not rebuilding. At the time of his death in 1890, and thanks to his charitable work, a new era in archaeological research had been ushered in, watched over, and admired by both tourists and academics. In the end, it can be argued that it was the partnership of academics and tourists that helped to save Hadrian's Wall from landowners and developers, government road building programs, and stone robbers, and it is through their continued shared interest and participation that the future of the World Heritage Site remains most secure.

Archaeology Financed through Sustainable Tourism

Upon its foundation in 1970, the Vindolanda Trust had very few assets. They consisted of a thirteen-acre "camp field" (in which the principle remains were thought to lie), a small garden shed, a few wheelbarrows, picks, shovels and spades, and £21 in the Bank (left over from the previous year's excavation grant from the Durham University Excavation Committee). The Director of the Vindolanda Trust, Robin Birley, was still in post as Senior Lecturer in History at Alnwick College of Education, and the planned work for 1970 was confined to the school and college holiday weeks in July and August, which was assisted by a variety of volunteers. At this early stage, and on a superficial level, there was little to distinguish between the early plan of work to be undertaken by the Vindolanda Trust, what had gone on before at the site, or indeed on other sites along the line of Hadrian's Wall. Although the Vindolanda Trust planned to consolidate any outstanding remains for permanent display, it was not initially thought by many that this would massively raise the profile of the site. In 1970, there was no museum, no electricity, no telephone, no water supply, no toilets, and nowhere for any visitors to park. The Vindolanda Trust's own trustees were divided on the issue, with half wanting things to remain as they always had done, and the other half, along with Robin Birley, keen to expand the operation to a full-time project. A full-time research project, with staff and facilities was not possible with the meager resources that the Vindolanda Trust had at its disposal in 1970, yet there were signs that this could change, with the support of visitors who came to watch the excavations taking place.

During the Vindolanda excavations in the summer of 1969, a year before the Vindolanda Trust was founded, the excavators appointed one of their number to act as a site custodian/guide to the few visitors who came to see what was going on. On one Sunday, a sum of £20 was raised by charging adults one shilling and children six pence for this experience. At the time, the nearby Roman fort site of Housesteads attracted over 100,000 visitors annually, and the excavators felt that with suitable publicity, it ought to be possible to attract sufficient people to make the short journey down to Vindolanda, thereby making a serious contribution to excavation funds.

The Director put the proposition for full-time working to his Trustees along with a movement from a short-term summer excavation to a research center that could operate on a full-time basis. After a long debate, he eventually managed to persuade the Trustees to agree, and he became the first full-time member of staff; although he was self-employed because the Trustees did not want to pay any National Insurance contributions. He was shortly to be followed by a second member of staff, Patricia Burnham, who gave up her own teaching post, and received £19 per week to take on the Custodian duties (as well as being responsible for the care of the finds and a good deal else). With volunteer excavators only available on weekends and school holidays, it was vital to attract some form of labor to keep the work going at other times. The solution was to run archaeology courses each week for senior pupils from regionally based, north of England, secondary schools for a small fee and to run other courses for adults on weekends for slightly larger fees. This arrangement had the additional advantage of creating a supply of excellent additional volunteers during the holiday periods, drawn from the keenest members of the schools' courses, several of whom went on to become archaeology graduates.

The initial drawback to this system was the imposition of seven days a week working for the first two members of staff. For the Vindolanda Trust to survive, all manner of things needed to be attended to, and not just during the time-honored 9 a.m. to 5 p.m. The Director of the Vindolanda Trust could be regularly seen cutting the grass on the site, emptying the elsan toilet, doing the accounts, dealing with correspondence, and writing excavation research reports. The strain placed on the organization, and in particular the two founding members of staff during the years of 1970–1973 was enormous. It is during this time that the Vindolanda Trust came closest to being a failed concept rather than a successful organization. To build up the necessary resources to enable investment into the site, to secure a museum for the archaeological collection, car parks, toilets, and other visitor facilities, the staffing costs were kept to an absolute minimum. In 1973, the profile of the site, which had slowly been rising through continued excavation, bringing in more visitors every year, and giving the Vindolanda Trust the financial muscle to operate successfully, was to change dramatically.

The discovery in the spring of 1973 of the superbly preserved remains of early timber forts at the site, with their extraordinary writing tablets, completely changed the archaeological landscape of Roman Britain. The writing tablets, thin postcards made from wood, covered in ink, with handwritten Latin text, are the largest archive of Roman written material from Roman Britain and include such gems as the earliest example of female handwriting from the Roman Empire and Western Europe. Their finding and subsequent excavation was heavily publicized by the *Observer* and the BBC's children's TV show *Blue Peter*. The visitor numbers moved up from 35,000 in 1972 to 88,000 in 1973. This should have been a great boost to the fledgling Trust, but at the time there were still very few facilities on the site. Fortunately, Northumberland County Council came to the rescue by providing, in 1974, a car park and toilet block, and the increased visitor flow gave the Trust the courage to acquire, with the support of the English Tourist Board, the house of Chesterholm (a small cottage nearby the site) as a Museum. It also became possible, gradually, to engage the essential support staff of custodians, cleaners, a grounds staff, and a full-time finance officer.

While the boost in visitor numbers was extremely welcome, the publicity generated by finding the writing tablets provided new challenges for the Trust in its dealings with the wider archaeological community. There were some who thought that a small charitable Trust should not be allowed to excavate such an important site in light of the recent discoveries, and who actively sought either the closure of the excavations or advocated that the Vindolanda Trust be taken over by the state, a *quango* (a quasi non-governmental organization), or another larger body. The publicity generated by excavations put the Trust in the harshest of spotlights, and some vocal critics who had watched the success of the Trust's work, were quick to seize upon anything that they did not like while the topic was hot.

In 1973, three of the founding Trustees of the Vindolanda Trust left the organization, disappointed by the direction that the Trust was taking. They had lost the argument that work on the site should be limited to summer months and that provision for tourists should be minimal. Shortly after their resignation, a newspaper article appeared stating; "three of the leading figures involved in the Vindolanda Trust – now one of the country's leading archaeological tourist attractions – have resigned after 'internal disagreements' on how the site should be managed" (*Hexham Courant* August 3rd, 1973). It was to prove to be the start of a number of negative newspaper articles. A local landowner summed up the mood of this struggle by complaining about "the plight of unfortunate farmers" who, upset at tourists visiting the site in droves, demand that "the fort should be either temporarily closed or the public warned of the position by the same national wide media that has brought them" (Portnell H.B. – August 3rd, 1973, writing in the *Hexham Courant*). But there was no going back, and shortly after the writing tablets were discovered in 1973, the Vindolanda Trust acquired the adjacent cottage of Chesterholm in which it was to base its museum. The new museum had an old coaching house in its driveway, and this building was converted into a cafe. The cafe, along with the replica's of Hadrian's Wall that were built on the site, proved to be very popular with tourists but controversial with academics at the time. Articles in various newspapers accusing the Vindolanda Trust of bringing the monument into disrepute and creating a Disneyland. In 1974, Dr. Grace Simpson wrote a letter to *The Times* stating that "last autumn J.C.B. earth moving machines was used to tear two huge holes in the stratified Roman deposits," which was followed by a piece accusing the Vindolanda Trust of destroying a once-beautiful place and creating "an opencast quarry" (Grace Simpson – April 23rd, 1974, *The Times*). *The Journal* (a regional paper) led with the headline Roman site "Like an Opencast Quarry" (*The Journal* – April 24th, 1974) and its sister paper the *Evening Chronicle* stated "Vindolanda 'Treasure Hunt' Rapped" (*The Evening Chronicle* – April 24th, 1974). The wooden and stone replicas of Hadrian's Wall came in for particular criticism, being described as "full of archaeological errors" (*The Times* – April 23rd, 1974). The timber replicas of Hadrian's Wall at Vindolanda used cut-timber planking instead of logs with their bark on, as had been used elsewhere (the Lunt, Coventry), and this was a particular source of

Figure 6.1 The stone and timber replicas of Hadrian's Wall at Vindolanda with a part of the archaeological site in the foreground.

criticism. However, this ignored the archaeological facts from the site of Vindolanda where excavations on the timber layers of the site had shown that timber planking was widely used. Figure 6.1 shows the timber and stone reconstructions at the site of Vindolanda.

In line with this criticism, other aspects of the Trust's work were seized on. The running of educational courses, so important to the early finance and pace of the archaeological work, were regarded by some as sinister. False accusations about the use of paid-child labor, which inferred that the excavations were not only morally wrong, but amateur, were made (*The Times* – April 24th, 1974). At the time, the Vindolanda Trust was taking 16–18 year old students and their teachers onto the excavations for week long courses during school time and as part of their education, providing (as the Trust saw it) a unique experience in front-line learning in archaeology and history. The structured school courses survived this criticism and continued from 1970–1981 until changes in the UK educational system made direct participation by schools in the history of the Roman period more difficult (by removing the study of Roman Britain from key parts of the new national curriculum). However, the principles of these courses survive to this day, and anyone over the age of 16 is entitled to volunteer to join the Vindolanda excavations.

It is perhaps important to stress that the school courses that were offered by the Vindolanda Trust in the 1970s and early 1980s were educationally driven and well structured by qualified and published archaeologists who had worked on a range of sites and were themselves former school teachers. What perhaps grated with some then-prominent members of the academic community was the fact that they themselves had nothing directly to do with it. This is partly due to the fact that most universities were not set up to be able to directly offer such opportunities to 16–18 year olds themselves and that the much-heralded but relatively new concept of "archaeology in the community" was not widely practiced, aside from at Vindolanda where it has always remained core to the Vindolanda Trusts' philosophy. While such a strategy was perhaps "cutting edge" at the time and, therefore, for some people seen as divisive, there was also support for the initiative from sections of the archaeological community which included six of the Vindolanda Trustees who were academics and archaeologists, working in universities and who were fully behind the program at the site.

The nature of the debate in the early 1970s can be viewed as a watershed. On one side, there was the end of an era in "antiquarian" thinking where archaeology was a gentleman's activity rather than a modern profession. On the other side was the recognition of a need to provide facilities for tourists along the Wall and to allow for a new level of engagement between academics and the wider general public, to make archaeology accessible to modern audiences. Popularization of archaeology through long-running television shows in the UK, such as *Animal, Vegetable, Mineral* which aired throughout the 1950s had raised the profile of archaeology to a very wide audience, and many of the new students coming through the university system during the following decades had been introduced to archaeology in this new way. But it took time for this higher profile to filter through into the ways in which archaeologists were to engage with a more knowledgeable general public who wished to continue to be informed.

It is difficult to comprehend visiting a major site along the lines of Hadrian's Wall today and having no refreshments available, no museum shop, or bathrooms, but this was the reality for visitors to Hadrian's Wall in the early 1970s. To meet modern demands, the Vindolanda Trust needed to prove that it was up to the task of excavating such an important site, and more than this, it needed to prove that its model of research and associated development through sustainable tourism was possible. The only way it could do this was to make the needs of visitors a priority.

The Vindolanda Trust survived the turbulent 1970s period thanks to a core belief that the way forward was to engage the general public in the work of the organization, to enfranchise as many people as possible, and to offer them a stake in the project being undertaken. Many of the 550 volunteer excavators who now annually work on the excavations started their association with Vindolanda as visitors to the site. Over the past 38 years, more than 6000 people have actively participated in the archaeology of Vindolanda. The excavations have always provided direct access to the archaeology of the site, and through this, ordinary people are offered a personal role in shaping our understanding of the history of Roman Britain.

If the Vindolanda Trust's relationship with the wider academic and state-funded archaeological community became fragile in the mid 1970s, its relationship with its stakeholders was never in doubt. By 1978, more than 115,000 visited the site annually. In the 1980s and 1990s, work continued on the excavations and improvement of the facilities at Vindolanda. Although external economic pressures started to tell on the visitor figures for Vindolanda and Hadrian's Wall (averaging out to around 85,000 Vindolanda visitors per year), the Trust maintained a healthy balance between the needs of visitors and research on the site. Some of the most remarkable discoveries made at Vindolanda came during this time with the recovery of hundreds more writing tablets and many thousands of other special objects from the excavations. Continuing to consolidate the stone remains on the site offered a constantly refreshing and changing archaeological experience. During this time, good relationships with the wider academic community were rebuilt. Today, the Vindolanda Trust is regarded as an exemplar in the fields of research/excavation/consolidation and education in Britain and beyond. Other sites along Hadrian's Wall have followed the Vindolanda model in investing in visitor facilities, and the replica's of Hadrian's Wall at Vindolanda have been complemented by reconstructions at other forts along the line of Hadrian's Wall, such as South Shields and Segedunum in Tyneside, which are both run by local authorities. The revenue generated by visitors coming to the site allowed the Trust to make modest but continual investments into the infrastructure at both Vindolanda and The Roman Army Museum. Redevelopment of the cafe's, shops, museum display, and galleries continued consolidation/excavations/research of the remains, and a new admissions building to the site of Vindolanda have all taken place over the past 10 years.

The "Vindolanda model" of continuing yearly investment into the archaeology/infrastructure of the site through sustainable tourism has enabled the organization to maintain its market share of tourists to Hadrian's Wall from the mid-1970s to today. The pie chart in Figure 6.2 shows the present market share of the Vindolanda Trust in relation to its main competitors along the line of Hadrian's Wall. Vindolanda's market share remains second behind Housesteads, which has the advantage of free admission to groups, members of English Heritage, Historic Scotland, and The National Trust. This market share is maintained partly thanks to the ongoing excavations at the site, which constantly renews and enhances the visitor experience. The Vindolanda model can offer a successful blueprint for research and development but only if energy, commitment, and expertise are combined with good business principles. In September, 2008, against a background of economic recession and stiff competition, the Vindolanda Trust was awarded a £4 million Heritage Lottery Fund

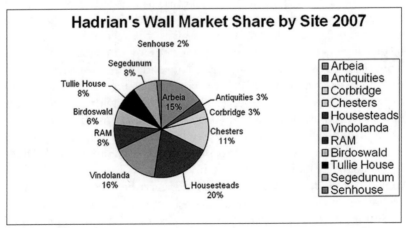

Figure 6.2 A chart showing the market share in visitors to Hadrian's Wall sites in 2007. RAM represents the Roman Army Museum.

grant to further develop its facilities and continue to deliver the aims and objectives of the Trust. This grant enabled important work to take place at both Vindolanda and the Roman Army Museum but does not change the fact that nothing could be achieved for the Vindolanda Trust or for furthering the understanding of archaeology of the sites without the partnership of its key stakeholders, the tourists, who visit its sites.

Chapter 7

Casa Malpais: Development of an Archaeological Park in Rural Arizona

Teresa L. Pinter

In 1990, the Town of Springerville, a small rural Arizona community, embarked on a mission to develop nearby Casa Malpais National Historic Landmark as an archaeological park. This ambitious pursuit would present many challenges but would also open up significant opportunities along the way. Nineteen years later, there is a lot to learn from this case study, which highlights some of the critical issues involved in archaeological park development, particularly with respect to rural communities. These include the important processes of identifying and evaluating sites as heritage tourism resources and their preservation and protection, interpretation and education, community involvement, and sustainability through broad-based partnerships (Pinter 2005).

Tourism and Archaeology: Sustainable Meeting Grounds, edited by Cameron Walker and Neil Carr, 143–154. ©2013 Left Coast Press, Inc. All rights reserved.

Casa Malpais National Historic Landmark

With a population of 2000 individuals, the Town of Springerville is located in northeastern Arizona at an elevation of 7000 ft. As the "Gateway to Arizona's White Mountains," the Town provides access to many popular recreation areas and is an approximate four-hour drive from major metropolitan areas such as Phoenix, Tucson, and Flagstaff (Town of Springerville n.d.). The Town was founded in 1879 and still retains its rural setting and character. Tourism revolves around the relatively mild climate and proximity to a wealth of year-round outdoor recreation opportunities, including camping, hiking, mountain biking, fishing, hunting, winter skiing, and snowmobiling.

The area also has a rich archaeological heritage, with several large ruins representing the prehistoric Mogollon culture. Casa Malpais is one of the most significant of those sites. Located just north of Springerville, this site is situated on terraces below a basalt cliff along the upper Little Colorado River (Figure 7.1). The site's name, Spanish for "House of the Badlands," apparently reflects the early Spanish settlers' characterization of the lands to the north of town (Hohmann 1990:22).

Figure 7.1 Overview of Casa Malpais with the Little Colorado River Valley in the background.

Figure 7.2   The Great Kiva at Casa Malpais.

Casa Malpais is a prehistoric pueblo ruin that contains a large masonry pueblo, a Great Kiva (Figure 7.2), masonry compounds, an enclosing wall, two masonry stairways that lead to the top of the basalt cliff, prehistoric trails, numerous isolated rooms, bedrock grinding areas, rock art panels, and trash middens. The site dates from late Pueblo III to early Pueblo IV times (AD 1240–1350). The entire complex was built upon an extensive basalt lava flow, and the builders took advantage of deep fissures created by the lava to construct some of their architecture underground.

The ruin was visited by anthropologist Frank Cushing in 1883, but the first formal recording of the site was accomplished as part of the Peabody Museum's, 1947–1949, Upper Gila Expedition that extended across west-central New Mexico and east-central Arizona (Danson 1957:63). It was again recorded in 1956 as part of the Chicago Natural History Museum's Southwest Expedition (Martin et al. 1961). A 1962 National Survey of Historic Sites and Buildings further recognized the site's potential significance, and the National Park Service designated Casa Malpais as a national historic landmark on July 19, 1964. On October 15, 1966, it was automatically listed on the National Register of Historic Places following the passage of the *National Historic Preservation Act of 1966*. The original national historic landmark contained more than 350 acres, which included a large buffer zone. In the 1980s, the National Park Service Western Archaeological and Conservation Center contracted with the Arizona State Museum (ASM) to update the documentation for the site and revise the landmark boundaries to more accurately reflect the site's extent. The ASM's work reduced the boundary to 14.5 acres (Neily 1987).

Situated on Arizona State Trust Land on the outskirts of town where it was not subject to developmental pressures, the ruin was never tested or excavated by archaeologists, although locals had explored and collected resources from the site since the late 1800s. In 1986, two local men were arrested and convicted of illegal pothunting at the site (Hohmann 1990:24).

Evaluating Casa Malpais for Heritage Tourism

With the heightened visibility of the site at a number of levels, and with the local economy struggling due to the faltering timber industry, the Springerville Economic Development Commission recognized the recreation potential of Casa Malpais. To the Commission, development of the site represented a means of diversifying the local economy, as well as protecting and preserving the ruin. In 1989, the Springerville town manager approached the Arizona State Historic Preservation Office (SHPO) with a proposal to develop Casa Malpais as an archaeological park and turn it into a viable visitor destination. The process of creating the park was complicated by a number of factors, not the least of which was transfer of ownership from the State to the Town. The eventual development of the archaeological park would require a broad range of partnerships and collaborations.

"Respect for the Past" was the theme selected by the Town for its project, and a 1990 Survey and Planning Grant from the Arizona SHPO helped to finance *A Master Stabilization and Development Plan for the Casa Malpais National Historic Landmark Site* for the Town (Hohmann 1990). The plan outlined the potential opportunities for development of Casa Malpais as an interpretive park and recreational area. The plan also proposed a park complex that would consist of a series of self-guided interpretive loop trails; this visitation program would be integrated with ongoing archaeological research activities that would represent a key aspect of the overall interpretive and educational program. A prerequisite for full implementation of the development plan was acquisition of Casa Malpais from the State. The tourism potential of the site as an archaeological recreation area, rather than simply an archaeological park, was explored. This broader concept allowed the Town to capitalize on additional recreational opportunities afforded by the site's location along the Little Colorado River floodplain, surrounding nature and hiking trails, and additional cultural sites available for viewing and exploration. This comprehensive plan contained three components, including: (1) a conceptual design; (2) a stabilization, development, and interpretive plan; and (3) a cost benefit analysis.

The conceptual design addressed a broad range of issues, including the natural, cultural, and archaeological settings, site development and interpretive potential, resource management issues, park interpretation goals, and interpretive trails and themes. The Stabilization, Development, and Interpretive Plan laid the priorities and groundwork for interpretive park development, including site-specific planning for the park boundaries, park and site entries, site trails and facilities, park circulation, a visitor's center, picnic facilities, and utilities. A trail plan was laid out with general interpretive themes. Specific recommendations for Casa Malpais included two interpretive trail systems, one within the park, and a second trail beginning at either a visitor's center or Arizona Department of Transportation rest area facility along nearby US Highway 60. The latter trail would extend along the Little Colorado River and incorporate adjacent natural and cultural attractions. The issue of excavation at the site was also discussed. The plan recommended that minimal excavations be undertaken and that most excavation work should be directed toward archaeological features damaged by pothunters or exposed to damage from the elements. The need to balance interpretation and research was given particular consideration as was the importance of ruins stabilization and maintenance.

The cost benefit analysis addressed a number of issues, including park visitation in Arizona, economic benefits, the phasing required for park development, park management, and staffing needs. Park visitation potential was evaluated primarily on the basis of national and state parks operating in Arizona. Approximately 30,000 visitors were projected for Casa Malpais within the first two years of operation, with the potential for upward of 85,000 visitors within four years of operation. With respect to potential economic benefits, this level of visitation was projected to generate between $2.9 and $3.8 million for the local and regional economy. However, the plan also indicated that predicted park revenues would not equal the initial capital outlay and operating costs during the first eight years of operation. Only after that time would park revenue meet operating costs and begin to pay back the initial capital investment (Hohmann 1990:90). Visitor expectations were not given extensive consideration beyond noting that the top outdoor recreation activities for Arizonans were hiking and walking, with visiting archaeological and historical sites ranking seventh out of 25. The plan anticipated that "an interpretive program at Casa Malpais, which highlights the visitation and walking opportunities in outdoor recreation, coupled with archaeological and historical attractions, could anticipate substantial park visitation from both in-state and outside visitors" (Hohmann 1990:88).

With the advantage of hindsight, it is worth pausing at this stage to recognize that Casa Malpais illustrates a common misperception that especially small rural communities may have. This is the assumption that their particular resource is a destination resource, when the reality is that it may be more feasible for that resource to play a supporting role in a larger tourism effort. This is also a strategy that requires multiple levels of collaboration and funding. As noted above, the initial cost benefit analysis for Casa Malpais in 1990 projected that upward of 85,000 people would visit the park annually. So far, the highest visitation levels were around 5000 in 2008 (Eastern White Mountains Heritage Program n.d.). Perhaps one reason these initial numbers were so out of phase with the eventual reality is that they were based on established state and national park visitation rates in Arizona, which do not accurately reflect expectations for smaller community-based parks.

The situation at Casa Malpais was not unique, but it was one of the earliest community-based parks of its type developed for tourism in Arizona. Issues arising out of the creation of this park in particular, and similar efforts (and outcomes) at other archaeological sites across Arizona, led to the creation of guidelines for archaeological park development by the Governor's Arizona Archaeology Advisory Commission in 1997 (Arizona Archaeological Society 1997).

Development and Operation of the Park

With momentum from the feasibility study, the Town was successful in obtaining an acquisition and development grant from the SHPO in 1991. This provided funds for a protective barrier installation around the park perimeter, stabilization of eroding and vandalized features, and initial trail development and signage. With significant progress being made, and the Foundation laid for operation of the interpretive park, the Town signed a contract with an archaeological consultant who had prepared the master stabilization and development plan, and the Casa Malpais Advisory Committee was created to provide input into the site development. The Committee was composed of professional archaeologists, as well as Town officials and local business interests, but it did not include anyone with direct ties to the tourism industry. In March of that same year, the Casa Malpais Museum opened in a storefront in downtown Springerville. The Museum showcased materials from the site and surrounding area, and served as the starting point for guided tours of the site. The Museum also featured a laboratory that allowed visitors to view the reconstruction of ceramic vessels and other artifacts. The Museum and laboratory were staffed by local volunteers. Community support was evident in the establishment of a local chapter of the Arizona Archaeological Society (AAS) in Springerville. Founded in 1964, the AAS is a well-known and respected avocational organization with numerous chapters statewide and a comprehensive certification program (Arizona Archaeological Society n.d.). Many of the chapter members volunteered at the Museum, laboratory, and site.

Casa Malpais Archaeological Park officially opened in 1993, and that same year the Malpais Foundation replaced the Advisory Committee to oversee park development and to raise funds. The Foundation included professional archaeologists, local business owners, an accountant, the town manager, the town attorney, and representatives of the Hopi and Zuni tribes, but no tourism professionals. The Foundation held its initial meeting in September 1993, and one of its first acts was to hire a fulltime project director to oversee the Visitor Center and Museum, train volunteers, and conduct tours at the site. The Town appropriated $22,950 that first year to hire the director, to operate the visitor center, and to maintain and stabilize the site (Malpais Foundation 1993). The Foundation achieved non-profit status in 1995, so donations could be deducted by donors as charitable contributions.

Over the next few years, the park continued to operate out of the visitor center and museum in downtown Springerville with most funding coming from the Town and supplemental funding from the County for the park's operation. Visitation gradually increased from a low of 82 in 1993 to 3002 in 1997, but it remained relatively low. Park revenue from the tours and sales at the Museum varied, and 1994 was a particularly tough year.

In 1995, Casa Malpais was purchased from the State of Arizona by the Town. The sale followed extensive negotiations among the Arizona State Land Department, SHPO, ASM, and the Town to ensure that the site would continue to be protected under the *Arizona Antiquities Act of 1960* (Arizona State Land Department 1995; Figure 7.3).

Following the Town's purchase of the site, there was an initial increase in visitation and revenue in 1995, but the Park's financial situation began deteriorating in late 1996. By mid-1998, the full-time director had resigned, and in 2000, the Malpais Foundation was dissolved, leaving management and operation to the Town. In the meantime, the

---

- The successful bidder agrees not to excavate in any prehistoric or historical archaeological deposit on the subject property without obtaining a project-specific *Arizona Antiquities Act* permit from the Arizona State Museum.
- The successful bidder agrees not to collect or remove any prehistoric or historic archaeological specimens from the subject parcel without first obtaining a project-specific *Arizona Antiquities Act* permit from the Arizona State Museum.
- All artifacts and records recovered or produced as a result of activities on the subject parcel that are permitted by the Arizona State Museum shall remain the property of the State of Arizona, regardless of the repository institution.
- The successful bidder agrees to comply with all other provisions of the *Arizona Antiquities Act* (A.R.S. § 41-841, et seq.) and its implementing rules.
- Before causing any ground disturbance on the subject property, the successful bidder shall consult with the SHPO and agree to preserve the subject property according to recommendations of the State Historic Preservation Officer.

Figure 7.3 Conditions for continued protection of Casa Malpais National Historic Landmark.

visitor center and museum had been combined with the local Chamber of Commerce to allow sufficient staffing of both establishments. Over the next few years, the Town persisted in its efforts to keep the Park open. With limited resources, most of the Town's appropriations were needed to keep the Park and Museum operating at a basic level, with little money left over for marketing and promotion (Malpais Foundation 1995). Volunteers were invaluable in assisting with tours, stabilization, and other efforts. To enhance marketing and promotion efforts, the Town took advantage of opportunities to publicize the park as part of a regional suite of attractions; this maximized opportunities for publicity and made more efficient use of funds.

Regional Partnerships

One such regional effort for promoting heritage-based tourism was the Trail of Many Tracks (2008). This historical driving tour high-lighted the prehistoric and historic heritage of the region. Beginning in 1999, Casa Malpais was listed on the Trail of Many Tracks map for Navajo/Apache County (Malpais Foundation 1999). The Trail of Many Tracks provides an educational tour of Arizona's White Mountain region and the Little Colorado Plateau. A CD series provides a narrated, self-guided driving tour that allows visitors to "get to know the real people of the west, past and present, whose tracks have crisscrossed [the region]." The CDs are available at participating Chambers of Commerce, and the files are also available online for downloading to a portable audio device or burning to a CD. The Trail of Many Tracks was an initiative of the Four Corners Heritage Council, a multi-state regional heritage tourism partnership and coordinating body consisting of the states of Utah, Colorado, New Mexico, and Arizona. The governors of these four states established the Four Corners Heritage Council in 1991.

In 2001, the non-profit Center for Desert Archaeology began working on archaeological and heritage tourism projects in communities along the Little Colorado River (Center for Desert Archaeology 2008b:6), including the Town of Springerville and Casa Malpais. The Center's focus was on promoting "the stewardship of archaeological and historical resources in the American Southwest and Mexican Northwest through active research, preservation, and public educa-tion" (Center for Desert Archaeology n.d.). The deterioration of some of the stabilized rooms at Casa Malpais was part of the impetus for the Center's initial involvement. Although it has no direct links to the tourism industry, one of the Center's strengths is its ability to bring diverse groups together for a common goal. As part of the Center's regional efforts and meetings with a variety of stakeholders, it became clear that there were shared concerns about "the challenges of protecting important sites, interpreting them for a variety of audiences, and linking the stories of one community to those of neighboring communities throughout the region" (Center for Desert Archaeology 2008b:6). In 2003, building on their previous success with the Santa Cruz River Valley National Heritage Area in southern Arizona, the Center began exploring the idea of a Little Colorado River Valley National Heritage Area (Center for Desert Archaeology 2005). As a non-regulatory federal designation, a National Heritage Area is a framework that helps to preserve defining landscapes and important regional cultural traditions and resources through a network of federal, state, and local partnerships (Center for Desert Archaeology 2008b:1; National Park Service 2008). The concept of local recognition and control of important resources is at the heart of this community-based conservation strategy. The Town of Springerville with Casa Malpais as its main attraction was one of the first entities to join this regional effort, and in 2008, the draft *Feasibility Study for the Little Colorado River Valley National Heritage Area* was completed (Center for Desert Archaeology 2008b). As part of a broad spectrum of local stakeholders seeking this designation, the Town thus expanded its potential opportunities to reap the benefits of this regional effort as it moved forward (see Figure 7.4).

Partnerships have been a significant catalyst for more recent improvements at Casa Malpais (Gann 2007:11). In 2004 and again in 2006, the Center for Desert Archaeology, the Town, and the Casa Malpais Museum and Visitors Center were successful in obtaining grants from the Arizona Humanities Council that allowed development of an updated interpretive plan, stabilization treatments, development of new interactive exhibits, and remodeling the Museum's gift shop and storefront.

An additional benefit of the grants was the ability to bring in Hopi and Zuni scholars and elders as part of the interpretive planning process.

1. Development and increase in heritage tourism.	4. More efficient pooling of resources for tourism, education, and conservation projects.
2. Additional sources of funding.	
3. Increased ability to network with multiple entities on a regional scale.	5. Expanded opportunities and resources for volunteer stewardship of resources and components of regional heritage.
	6. Balanced preservation and promotion.

Figure 7.4 Some of the anticipated benefits of National Heritage Areas (from Center for Desert Archaeology 2008b:2).

In 2006, the Town hired Linda Matthews as the full-time manager of the Park, and that same year the Town received a Preserve America Grant (Preserve America 2008). This funding supported the development of a three-dimensional computer model of the site and other interpretive improvements that were designed to provide visitors with a clearer understanding of prehistoric life at Casa Malpais. As a result of a National Park Service Challenge Cost Share Grant, all of the site architecture previously listed as threatened has now been documented, stabilized, or backfilled (National Historic Landmarks Program 2008).

Casa Malpais Today

According to the National Historic Landmarks Program (2008), "Casa Malpais is now in excellent condition, thanks to efforts by the National Park Service, Intermountain Region, the Town of Springerville, Little Colorado Chapter of the Arizona [Archaeological] Society, and the Center for Desert Archaeology." Threatened architecture has been stabilized and interpretive programs have been improved. Nine excavated or looter-damaged rooms have been stabilized and backfilled. Using limited reconstruction techniques, room outlines have been re-established over backfill. These room outlines can be easily distinguished from native architecture by a layer of non-native orange soil on which the walls were reconstructed.

In early 2008, the Casa Malpais Museum and Visitor Center moved to its new home in the Springerville Town Hall with assistance from Douglas Gann of the Center for Desert Archaeology and volunteers from the Little Colorado Chapter of the AAS (Center for Desert

Archaeology 2008a). The Museum is open every day except Thanksgiving, Christmas, and New Years. The site is accessible only via guided tours that depart from the visitor center. A modest fee is charged for these services.

Conclusion

As illustrated by this case example, expectations and reality can diverge even with careful attention to critical issues. In collaboration with the archaeological community, state officials, Hopi and Zuni scholars and elders, and regional economic interests, the Town attempted to address many of those critical issues early on with its *Master Stabilization and Development Plan for the Casa Malpais National Historic Landmark Site* (Hohmann 1990). Over the long-term, Casa Malpais has built an integrated interpretive and education program through its museum and visitor center, and recent improvements in exhibits and interpretive programs reflect a proactive approach to keeping them current. At the time of writing, low visitor numbers were a concern, and it was too early to tell what the impact would be of the recent visitor center move to a less visible location in the Town Hall (Linda Matthews, personal communication 2008).

As noted earlier, the Town recognized that Casa Malpais was not a destination resource, but one of many important regional attractions. The quest for National Heritage Area (NHA) status is ongoing, and it is anticipated that NHA designation "will create opportunities for new tourism development" (Center for Desert Archaeology 2008b:188). Studies of other NHAs indicate that, in the 10 years following such designation, annual economic impact from tourism activity doubled (Center for Desert Archaeology 2008b:196). Only time will tell if the same results will hold true for the proposed Little Colorado River NHA. However, by building upon a series of regional partnerships for heritage tourism, the Town has adopted a diverse strategy that has the potential for growing tourism demand and a sustainable heritage tourism program for Casa Malpais that has a positive impact on the local and regional communities.

Chapter 8

Visitors at the Trench Edge: Outreach and Archaeology at Historic Dilston, Northumberland, UK

Emilie Sibbesson

Introduction

The site of Historic Dilston is situated on an escarpment overlooking the Tyne Valley in Northumberland, UK. Today, the site comprises a Medieval tower house, a post-Medieval chapel, and a Victorian mansion. A number of cottages are found scattered around, and substantial archaeological remains lie buried in the surrounding fields. The best known chapter of its history relates to the dramatic demise of the Radcliffe family in the early 18th century, although the site has been occupied almost continually for at least 800 years. After

Tourism and Archaeology: Sustainable Meeting Grounds, edited by Cameron Walker and Neil Carr, 155–163. ©2013 Left Coast Press, Inc. All rights reserved.

decades of neglect, an extensive program of recording, consolidation, and archaeological fieldwork was initiated in 2001. For the majority of its duration, this program has been undertaken with an explicit emphasis on community involvement and public awareness of the site and its history. This case study describes how outreach became integral to the ongoing program of research and restoration and how this posed a number of new challenges during the 2008 season of large-scale excavation.

History

Much research into the history of Dilston has been driven by interest in the Jacobean period and the Radcliffe family. During their heyday in the 17th century, the Radcliffes, Earls of Derwentwater, were amongst the most influential Catholics in northern England (Dickinson 2001; Forster 2002; Gooch 1995). It was during this period that the Dilston Chapel was built, although it is likely to stand on the foundations of a Medieval structure. Early in the 17th century, a village was still thriving in what is today a pasture field a little to the East. The extensive building work initiated by the first Earl, Francis Radcliffe, probably began to encroach on the village outskirts, and this might partly explain its eventual desertion. The seventeenth-century hall was built to incorporate the Medieval tower house, which still stands today as the "Castle." By the early 18th century, James Radcliffe, third Earl of Derwentwater, again took up expanding and modernizing the Hall. As conflicts between the Protestant government and Catholic aristocracy intensified, however, his vision of Dilston Hall was never fully realized. The Radcliffe era at Dilston came to an end when the Jacobite Rising of 1715 failed to reinstate the exiled Prince James Stuart on the English throne. In 1716, James Radcliffe, cousin of the exiled prince, was executed for his involvement in the Rising, and the family fell into disrepute. Some decades later, Dilston Hall was demolished, and the Castle eventually left in disrepair.

James Radcliffe soon became a legend in local folklore, and to this day, these events dominate public and historical understanding of the site. Yet the Radcliffe family were not the first inhabitants of Dilston. A Medieval manor house is likely to have stood on the site of today's Castle. It is probable that the name Dilston is a derivative of Dyvelston, which was the name of the Medieval village. We know that the lords of Tynedale governed the area in the 13th century, and that today's version of the Castle was built by the Claxton family in or around 1417. Some traces of pre-Radcliffe phases of construction and occupation were encountered during the 2008 season of excavation.

Dilston was not deserted when the Radcliffes left, and indeed, occupation continues to this day. John Grey, landowner and progressive agriculturalist, lived at Dilston with his family for the most part of the 19th century, and today's Dilston Hall was built for them in the 1830s. The social reformer and campaigner for women's rights, Josephine Butler, was one of his daughters. The Castle and parklands were maintained and used as pleasure grounds during the Victorian period. The modern day hall was occupied in various ways during the 20th century. It was used as a hospital for soldiers during the Second World War and became a maternity home in the late 1940s. Today, these episodes are best attested by the graffiti that can still be seen on some walls in the Chapel and Castle (Figure 8.1). In 1970, the

Figure 8.1 Graffiti from the 19th and 20th centuries is still visible on some walls in Dilston Chapel.

grounds were taken over by MENCAP, a UK charity for people with learning disabilities, and the 19th century Hall became a residential college for teenagers and young adults. Thus, apart from the recent archaeological work and visitors to the historic site, Dilston is still today very much alive.

The Historic Dilston Project

By the late 1990s, the ruins and remains at Dilston were recognized as historically and archaeologically significant. The Chapel and Castle are both designated Grade I Listed Buildings, and the latter is legally protected as a Scheduled Ancient Monument. The earthworks that can be seen at the site of the deserted Medieval village feature in the region's Sites and Monuments Record. However, the Chapel and Castle were in a dire state of disrepair, as evidenced by their inclusion on English Heritage's register of Buildings at Risk. Parts of the landscape setting and associated structures were also in need of conservation. In 2002, management of the historic buildings was taken on by the North Pennines Heritage Trust (NPHT), a registered charity that works toward conservation and appreciation of historic sites across the North Pennines area. The first program of conservation, restoration, and research at Dilston began in 2001, with the primary aim of removing the Chapel and Castle from the Buildings at Risk register. The initial phase of archaeological investigation on the site was designed to inform the consolidation work. The program was completed in 2003, and it was at this stage that the historic site was officially opened to the public for the first time (Giecco et al. 2003).

The buildings were taken off English Heritage's register in 2007. Shortly after, a second phase of archaeological investigation got underway, and this time the aim was to enhance understanding of Dilston's past.

The 2008 Season

At the time of writing, the most extensive fieldwork season to date ran from May to September, 2008. Work that had commenced in 2007 was continued, and structural remains from the 17th and 18th centuries were excavated and recorded. One of the main aims was to explore the episodes of expansion that were made to the Castle and hall during the Jacobean period, and the digging of a large trench in the field to the east did, indeed, reveal foundations and floors of the Radcliffe Hall that was demolished in the late 18th century. Investigation of the foundations of a range of service buildings to the northeast, initially uncovered in the previous season, was also continued. Enhanced knowledge of the service range and hall was required for two aspects of the development of Dilston as a heritage site open to the public, as improved understanding of these features fed into both the heritage management strategies and the information about the site offered to visitors archaeologically. The 2008 season was highly successful as the structural layout and sequences of construction were exposed and a range of artifactual material was recovered (see Figure 8.2).

For two years and with support from the Heritage Lottery Fund, the project hosted a field school enabling students of archaeology to gain experience and skill in excavation and recording techniques.

Figure 8.2 Dilston Castle towering over remains of the seventeenth-century Hall excavated in 2008.

Apart from archaeologists and students, some members of the support organization Friends of Historic Dilston joined the excavations as volunteers. At times, it was a large and diverse group of people who took part in unearthing the remains of the Medieval tower house, the partially intact paved floor of the Radcliffe Hall, and a wide range of artifacts from different centuries. Finds included Medieval and post Medieval ceramics, ranging from coarse, utilitarian cooking vessels to finer, decorated tableware. Metalwork, such as delicate cufflinks, pins, and a thimble, was also found in addition to animal bones, oyster shells, and clay pipes. The extensive and well-preserved structural remains along with the numerous artifacts testify to the wealth of some of the past inhabitants of Dilston, as well as to the continuity of occupation. They also provided an excellent opportunity for members of the public to catch a glimpse of an archaeological excavation (Binks et al. 1988).

The chapel and Castle are kept open during the summer months by members of the Friends of Historic Dilston, the NPHT, and visitors to the historic buildings were encouraged to have a look at the ongoing excavation. Fieldworkers got accustomed to sometimes having visitors looking over their shoulder. In June, the weather improved and visitor numbers increased. My responsibilities changed from excavation to outreach, as it became clear that the needs of student excavators and visitors could not all be met by the site director.

The following is an account of experiences made and lessons learnt.

Visitors at the Trench Edge

In retrospect, it is fair to say that people's eagerness to see the ongoing archaeological work had been underestimated. Moreover, the chapel and Castle were already staffed by the NPHT. The archaeological work was undertaken by North Pennines Archaeology Ltd, a contracting consultancy that was part of the NPHT. This arrangement was entirely practical until the 2008 season, when the combination of large-scale excavation and radically increased numbers of visitors who came to see the open trenches as well as the historic buildings necessitated a new strategy.

Despite its long and colorful history, Dilston is not widely known. One of the longer-term goals of the Historic Dilston Project was to raise public awareness of the site. This objective was never intended to be placed on hold until the completion of the research and restoration program, and it was this approach that made it possible to bring visitors into the excavation. It was a rare opportunity for people to see what we were uncovering, including, for example, the faint traces of an early timber hall, as well as the more tangible stone wall foundations. Newly recovered artifacts were visible next to the fieldworkers, and it was thrilling for many visitors to handle muddy pottery sherds. Apart from describing Dilston's past, the tour of the excavation became an opportunity to explain aspects of the fieldwork itself. It was, for example, entirely workable to mention standard procedures such as the designation of context numbers, recovery of environmental samples, and meticulous creation of the drawn and photographic records. Contrary to expectation, perhaps, these kinds of details about archaeological practice were for many visitors as interesting as the history of the site. I spent the time in-between tours working on the excavation and I soon realized that my muddy clothes made the archaeology more "real." I kept a trowel with me also on days when I had no time for digging as it seemed to make the visitor experience more entertaining and authentic. The trench edge was not an impassable boundary as visitors had to walk through a shallow trench at one corner of the excavation. Elsewhere, they remained outside the trenches for safety reasons, but the fact that I walked in and out of the open trenches as I explained the archaeology again appeared to enhance the experience of ongoing excavation.

Working on the excavation also enabled me to update interpretation of the site as more features were uncovered. At times I encouraged visitors to challenge tentative interpretations of newly uncovered features.

People visit a multi-period site like Dilston for a variety of reasons. Some came to see and hear about the Roman tombstone built into the chapel wall, Anglo-Scottish warfare and raiding during the Medieval period, the "Bonnie Lord" (James Radcliffe), or Josephine Butler and the Victorian period. Others were mainly interested in the ghosts that allegedly haunt Dilston. Still others came to visit because they had been born in today's Dilston Hall. Many visited primarily to see the excavation in progress. No predefined package of information was sufficient; instead, it was necessary to play it by ear and meet, as far as possible, the aspects that each visitor or group of visitors took an interest in. Time and again, it was the archaeological process of excavation, interpretation, and recording that captured people's curiosity and imagination. The fragments of past lives and activities that were being unearthed made the historic buildings "come alive" to the visitor.

The Future: Archaeology — Visitor Interaction

The patchwork of occupation that has lasted nearly a millennium makes Dilston remarkable, historically and archaeologically. The decision to encourage and cater for visitors to have a look at the on-going excavation provided a unique opportunity to engage the public in the everyday events and procedures of archaeological fieldwork and interpretation. However, the more "authentic" experience of archaeology-in-action could not be sustained beyond the fieldwork seasons of 2007 and 2008. Since the archaeologists left the site, newly recovered information is communicated to the public through formalized media such as leaflets, information boards, and artifact displays.

In addition, some of the trenches that were excavated were left open, and a complex set of features is on display. The ground level has been lowered in order to enable visitors to see more of the architectural blueprint of the Medieval tower house and former hall. The exposed foundations were capped with lime mortar.

The restoration work that was part of phase 2 of the Historic Dilston Project continued after the excavation season of 2008 ended. The second floor and staircase of the Castle were restored, and the walls that flank one of the original walkways up to the site was con-solidated using traditional dry-stone techniques. A longer-term plan that has yet to be realized is to recreate the garden and orchard that flanked the river during the Radcliffe period. More immediate tasks involved meeting the increased numbers of visitors through improved ticket and retail facilities.

Apart from tourists at the site, the Education Team of the NPHT continued to use the buildings at Dilston for a range of different activities tailored to school children and teenagers.

The Historic Dilston Project was initiated to halt deterioration of the buildings and grounds, and community involvement has increased with each season. The concept of community archaeology encompasses a variety of practices; although, certain criteria have recently been outlined (e.g., Marshall 2002; Simpson and Williams 2008; Tully 2007). Work at Dilston fulfils a few, if not all, of these criteria, and the NPHT ran a number of more explicitly community-based projects elsewhere. Members of the local community with an active interest have been directly involved through the Friends of Historic Dilston, which is chaired by one of the foremost experts on the site's past. The project generated enhanced awareness of the site in the wider region, and many visitors returned repeatedly during the 2008 season to find out how the work was progressing. Some had succinct ideas about how the remains at Dilston should be presented in the future, and at times I engaged in rather lengthy discussions about, for example, how some of the artifacts should be placed on display once they had been studied by specialists. Outreach work does not have to be postponed until fieldwork is completed but can be successfully integrated with archaeological investigation. At Historic Dilston, this approach proved stimulating and rewarding for archaeologists, heritage managers, and visitors alike.

Chapter 9

Archaeology, Tourism, and Other "Marriages of Convenience:" Examples from Western Canada

Scott Hamilton

Introduction

I begin with a confession. As a professional archaeologist with applied and academic experience, cultural or heritage tourism has never been more than a secondary research outcome for me. This is in spite of directing projects where heritage tourism was a proximate goal and sometimes the ultimate outcome. I do not think that I am alone in this assessment. The generally subordinate status of cultural tourism in archaeological research may indicate that few archaeologists have cultural tourism training despite its role in furthering public heritage education. It also reflects general discomfort about how archaeological and other cultural heritage information has been used for tourism. Given that archaeological deposits are finite and non-renewable, one

Tourism and Archaeology: Sustainable Meeting Grounds, edited by Cameron Walker and Neil Carr, 165–180. ©2013 Left Coast Press, Inc. All rights reserved.

must also ask whether excavation to support tourism is a sufficient rationale for consumption of archaeological deposits.

The examples offered in this case study draw upon archaeology in the northern Plains and Subarctic of western Canada, with a few others to provide a broader context. The past 40 years has been a time of significant growth in Canadian archaeology as a consequence of heritage legislation that underlies cultural resource management (CRM). As the environmental impact assessments became entrenched in the environmental planning process, of which CRM is a part, applied archaeology grew to the point that most Canadian archaeologists now work within this subfield. While private consultants conduct most CRM research, some public agencies employ archaeologists to monitor legislative compliance and conduct research. This usually involves cultural heritage inventory, construction, and management; but it also includes archaeological assessment and salvage. Public education, often in support of tourism, has also been part of the public mandate and usually involves: (1) heritage education outreach; (2) research in anticipation of development at heritage properties; and (3) public archaeology.

Public funding for cultural tourism and heritage education is not surprising given Canada's relative youth, and the general angst regarding a national or cultural identity. Such programming also provides a rationale for publically funded documentation of a largely unknown "heritage landscape." Ironically, since the late 1980s, there has been a steady decline in substantive archaeological research and dissemination by public heritage agencies due to staffing and budget cuts and a shift in emphasis to policy development and regulatory compliance monitoring (see Klimko 1998). Even during its heyday, public education and cultural heritage tourism involving archaeology was rather ad hoc and short-term in its impact. The archaeological research at Red Rock House provides a case in point.

Red Rock House

Red Rock House was a late 19th century fur trading post operated by the Hudson's Bay Company (HBC) (Arthurs n.d.; Hamilton and Richie 1985; Hamilton et al. 1986) (Figure 9.1). The Ontario Ministry of Northern Development and Mines provided project funding, with technical supervision by the Ontario Ministry of Citizenship

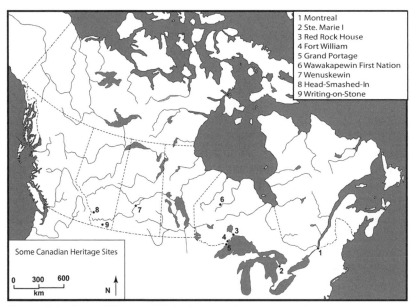

1 Montreal
2 Ste. Marie I
3 Red Rock House
4 Fort William
5 Grand Portage
6 Wawakapewin First Nation
7 Wenuskewin
8 Head-Smashed-In
9 Writing-on-Stone

Some Canadian Heritage Sites

0 300 600
km

N

Figure 9.1   Map of Canada with the heritage sites mentioned.

and Culture. Historical and archaeological information was sought to evaluate heritage tourism potential as part of waterfront redevelopment to support recreational boaters touring the north shore of Lake Superior.

The site is located along the Nipigon River, an important water route from Lake Superior north into the Canadian Shield (Figure 9.1). While the regional fur trade dates from the 1600s, investigation focused on the late phases (post 1850) when the HBC maintained a "guard post," and later a steamboat landing for inland cargo transshipment. After 1870, the post was expanded in anticipation of becoming an important railroad terminus and steamboat landing. This transportation boom failed to materialize, and Red Rock House slid into relative obscurity with key buildings being destroyed in an 1891 fire. The waterfront remained locally important for commercial fishing and logging until they too declined in the 1960s and left the waterfront virtually abandoned. The proposed waterfront redevelopment was to facilitate recreational yachting on Lake Superior, and heritage tourism was designed to encourage extended visits in Nipigon by water- and road-based tourists, thereby contributing to the economic diversification of northern Ontario.

The archaeological work at Red Rock House relocated several key buildings and assessed their depositional integrity. Historical interpretative themes were identified, and artifacts suitable for interpretative exhibition were recovered. In collaboration with the Nipigon Museum, a public archaeology program was offered to tourists and local residents through excavation tours, brochures, and exhibits. While water-based visitation was the ultimate goal for waterfront redevelopment, the public archaeology program focused on summer tourists traveling along the nearby Trans-Canada Highway. This involved distributing interpretative materials at regional tourism kiosks, establishing highway signage, and soliciting radio and television news coverage.

Such public archaeology programs also served auxiliary political goals in demonstrating provincial funding for projects in the under-developed north, a region generally alienated from urban southern Ontario. Similar mixed public education, tourism, and economic development motivations drove other public archaeology projects conducted by these government agencies at this time (Halverson 1992; Hamilton 1981; McLeod 1984; Rajnovich and Reid 1987; Taylor and Gliddon 1989). From my perspective, the primary motivation was to use public archaeology funding to enable collection of new knowledge about a largely unknown northern Ontario. While significant effort was devoted to public archaeology, tourism, and education, my primary professional instinct was to develop archaeological insight through conventional reports and publications.

Hindsight reveals that while the Red Rock House project efficiently addressed its CRM goals over two nine-month contracts, it was less effective in making long-term contributions to heritage tourism. The eventual waterfront redevelopment focused on wharf and marina infra-structure and no ongoing heritage interpretative programming. This is likely due to the sponsoring agencies not having expertise or a mandate to implement heritage tourism ventures. This was compounded by the destruction of the Nipigon Museum in a fire and the local heritage community's preoccupation with collections remediation and fund-raising for a new facility. This loss of a long-term focus remains a problem for many such projects, particularly local initiatives that are not well-financed and permanently staffed with heritage tourism professionals.

Archaeology and National Heritage

The use of archaeological sites to aid public education and cultural tourism reflects the foundation of historical archaeology in North America (Klimko 1998; Orser 2002:430–432, 456–458, 2004:30–38; McDavid and Babson 1997; Trigger 1994). While it has expanded far beyond these intellectual roots, most early research involved excavation and interpretation of sites deemed to have heritage significance. Such national monuments are carefully selected to represent what were thought to be pivotal moments in the nation's history, or embody elements of national cultural identity. Aboriginal culture and history has been less-frequently identified for public commemoration, but one possible exception is Ste. Marie I (Figure 9.1, Kidd 1949; Orser 2004:193)   (http://www.saintemarieamongthehurons.on.ca/english/index.htm). However, initial motivation for excavation, reconstruction, and commemoration of this Huron agricultural village was because the nearby Catholic mission is the earliest known European settlement in Ontario, and eight Jesuit missionaries were martyred there in 1649 during the Huron-Iroquois wars.

Some Canadian tourism facilities that feature precontact Aboriginal heritage include Alberta's Writing-on-Stone (http://gateway.cd.gov.ab.ca/siteinformation.aspx?id=177) and Head-Smashed-In sites (http://www.head-smashed-in.com/) (Brink 2008), and Saskatchewan's Wanuskewin Heritage Site (Figure 9.1; http://www.wanuskewin.com/). Head-Smashed-In is a bison jump where Native people drove the animals over a cliff in carefully planned and executed hunts. Writing-on-Stone Provincial Park contains cliffs carved with an array of images. Wanuskewin documents nearly 6000 years of occupation involving various modes of bison procurement and domestic encampment. These western Canadian sites, with predominately Aboriginal heritage themes, form a sharp contrast to most other Canadian sites that focus on European colonial settlements.

Development of public heritage tourist sites reflects considerations that include revisionist approaches to history and gradual transformation of power relationships within the state. We are often left with the disconcerting feeling that history is "relative" and vulnerable to manipulation, deliberate or otherwise. Interpretative narratives developed for public education (or info-tainment) are seldom subjected to critical reflection, with minimal attention paid to historic themes that might be unwelcome to a consuming tourist public. This issue is addressed with reference to Fort William Heritage Park.

Fort William Heritage Park

The Ontario Ministry of Tourism, Culture, and Sport operates the Fort William Heritage Park (Figure 9.1; http://fwhp.ca/index.php), which commemorates the North West Company's (NWC) primary inland fur trade depot. It was one of several British firms that facilitated British colonial expansion into the continental interior of North America. Established in 1804 along Lake Superior, Fort William was the largest fur trade post in North America, and it was the scene of important historic events. It persisted until the late 19th century when it was demolished to make way for a railway marshaling yard. Like the slightly earlier Grand Portage (Figure 9.1; http://www.nps.gov/grpo/index. htm), Fort William served administrative and warehousing functions to support the inland fur trade. Every spring, canoe brigades carried trade goods from Montreal through the Great Lakes to Fort William. Meanwhile, the "North men" transported furs to Fort William from widely dispersed winter stations. These crews converged and exchanged cargos, and the company shareholders planned for the upcoming year. The Montreal brigade then returned east with the furs, and the wintering crews returned inland with new trade goods.

Between 1968 and 1973, Fort William underwent archaeological exploration in anticipation of the 1973 construction of a heritage interpretative facility along the Kaministiquia River, some 18km upstream from the original site. The archaeological investigations were small-scale in light of the still-operating railway yards (Campbell 1976; Cloutier 1976), and much of the eventual reconstruction and heritage tourism relied upon written documents.

The fort reconstruction is a remarkably faithful reflection of what is thought to have existed in ca. 1815, a time of fierce competition among British traders (Figure 9.2). The tourism program focuses on trade post operations and the integration of Anglo-Scots mercantile organization with French Canadian voyager "country skills." Cost-umed heritage interpreters re-enact daily life, with its mix of European

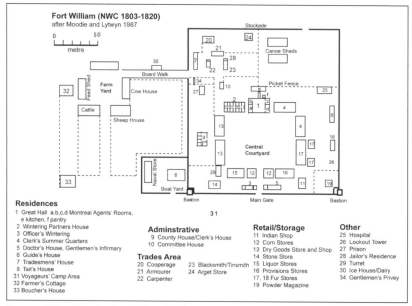

Figure 9.2 Sketch plan of Fort William.

and Aboriginal technologies and lifestyles. Also featured are the annual summer rendezvous of the canoe brigades and the 1816 capture of the post by Lord Selkirk and his hired troops. Early in its history of operation, the Fort William heritage program took great pains to remain authentic to the 1816 period. In more recent times, I detect a relaxation of the "reenactment" priority and a new emphasis on more generic heritage theme park entertainment experiences. This ensures continued fiscal viability by rendering the site more attractive to casually interested tourists.

Tourists are drawn into a visually rich interpretation of the early 19th century fur trade, but does this approach represent "reality" or "totality?" The site interprets the NWC corporate headquarters, but not interior wintering outposts where most of the trading occurred. European fur trade participants are emphasized, but Aboriginal heritage has become an increasingly important part of the interpretative program. This includes reconstruction of an Ojibwe camp located in the forest surrounding the main site. Costumed staff members demonstrate 19th century Aboriginal life and technology, but do not offer details of the diverse and changing roles of Aboriginal people in the fur trade.

Fort William Heritage Park does not represent the more troubling aspects of the British North American fur trade, with its violence and sectarian tension. It does not speak of the social chaos associated with the alcohol trade that rapidly escalated with European competition or the successive epidemics that devastated Aboriginal communities. It also does not address the ecological havoc caused by the fur trade that contributed to Aboriginal famine and hardship during the mid-19th century. I propose that these historical realities are not part of the interpretative program because of their complexity, and also because most tourists visit such sites primarily to be entertained. Politically incorrect or controversial elements of that history are unlikely to be welcomed. Similarly, visitors to the Head-Smashed-In Site are spared the gore of the actual operation of a mass bison kill. Imagine the public outcry if small bison herds were stampeded off the cliffs for the entertainment of casually interested tourist visitors.

Challenges exist when telling the history of Canadian Aboriginal people, particularly themes that address the consequences of European exploration and colonial appropriation. While initially holding relative power in their relationship with Europeans, recent Aboriginal history is one of disease pandemics, environmental devastation, treaties, and forced assimilation, all of which drove Aboriginal people into a subordinate relationship with Canadian authorities. While this narrative is "historic," it is also the basis of contemporary reality for most Canadian Aboriginal people. How do we talk about such realities through cultural tourism?

Northern Canadian Tourism and Heritage Interpretation

Northern Canada has a well-developed "wilderness tourism" industry involving sports fishermen and hunters who visit comparatively rustic resorts on remote northern lakes. Such tourism is marketed as an opportunity to experience what is imagined to be a pristine wilderness. It traditionally attracts middle-class, male sportsmen – a rather finite (and perhaps shrinking) market demographic. Many tourist outfitters seek to diversify their market appeal by improving the amenities at the "fly-in" resorts by offering a broader range of tourism experiences. This might include canoe or kayak camping, observation of wildlife or natural landscape features, and chances to learn about local history and culture. A major challenge for developing Subarctic cultural tourism is determining what to interpret. In general, there is little published information about northern culture and history, and it predominately consists of academically oriented archaeological and historical reports (see Rogers and Smith 1994 for a useful summary of Ontario Aboriginal history). Another rich information source is Aboriginal oral history.

Some Aboriginal communities are seeking to develop a broader economic base through cultural tourism. This involves more than new economic opportunities. Traditional modes of intergenerational cultural learning are breaking down, and many Elders fear that the young are becoming disconnected from their cultural and spiritual identity. Documenting local history and culture to support tourism is seen as one means of expanding local employment opportunities while simultaneously developing new means of cultural education for young Aboriginal people.

Some northern Ontario First Nations have commissioned cultural tourism feasibility studies (see, for example, Hamilton et al. 2000, 2003). As these reports were produced for specific First Nations, much of the information was and is proprietary, but Mr. Simon Frogg has permitted description of the developing ecotourism and cultural heritage program at Wawakapewin First Nation (Figure 9.1; http://www.wawakapewin.ca/). This community initiated several interrelated programs, one of which involves ecotourism business development to attract tourist visitors. Closely tied to this initiative are educational and healing programs for Aboriginal people (i.e., *Nadawehik Kakina Kedodumuk* Wilderness Healing Program) that, at the time of writing, sought to address the multigenerational consequences of forced assimilation, including the residential school system (see Miller 1996 or Milloy 1999).

Aboriginal cultural tourism projects often involve Elders recounting a time of traditional foraging coupled with commercial fishing and fur trapping. Direct memories generally date from the 1930s to 1960s; some datable information extends back into the 1890s, and undated indirect memories reflect much earlier times. Such recent history has clear utility for heritage tourism since many northern Ontario Aboriginal communities only recently signed treaties with Canada (Treaty #9 dates to 1905, with some signatories as late as 1929). In small isolated communities like Wawakapewin, many elements of the traditional lifestyle remain part of living memory. Elders' memories often feature winter trapping throughout extensive territories serviced from widely scattered cabin camps. Men made multiday treks on snowshoes and dog sleds to check and reset traps. Women with the children spent the winter operating the isolated base camps, running local trap lines, ice fishing, processing furs, cutting and hauling firewood, and other household chores. This traditional lifestyle has gradually disappeared over the past 50 years, and few people under 40 practice it for more than brief interludes.

Modern northern Canadian Aboriginal communities seldom exceed 1000 residents and are aggregations of extended families that formerly sustained themselves on widely dispersed trap lines. After World War II these groups coalesced into the modern reserve communities when the Canadian federal government established local day schools, nursing stations, and other administrative services. These communities have experienced rapid population growth and severe problems with housing, community infrastructure, chronic unemployment, limited local schooling, and social problems far in excess of the national average. Consequently, some communities seek new social and economic development opportunities, some of which include cultural heritage and ecotourism. Such local perspectives on cultural heritage emphasize oral history of life on the trap line.

Elders' reminiscences often include maps recording land use and travel patterns, burial and other sacred places, traditional harvest areas, old camps and cabins, place names, and so on. Documenting heritage, ostensibly for cultural tourism purposes, also provides baseline information for ongoing land claims and land-use planning, it documents traditional occupancy of lands subject to development, and it provides educational resources for future generations of Aboriginal people. It is my sense that these latter goals are the more urgent motivation for many Elders and other community leaders.

This information also reflects traditional Aboriginal land use that is more than a stereotypic image of Native people passively harvesting nature's bounty. Rather, it reflects people's operational knowledge of the ecological dynamics of their homeland, the timing and distribution of resources, and seasonal harvest strategies suited for long-term sustainability. For Aboriginal people, the Subarctic is not a pristine wilderness, but rather, a familiar cultural landscape of known resources defined by familiar place names assigned by their ancestors. Traditional Aboriginal perspectives about the land are fundamentally spiritual and can evoke a world animated with powerful "other-than-human" beings. Elements of this ancient spiritual perspective remain despite widespread Christianity. Indeed, Simon Frogg (2009, personal communication) speaks of his desire to "close the gap" between traditional spirituality and Christianity. I propose that elements of these spiritual relationships and responsibilities underlie what many traditional Elders seek to preserve for their descendents. It remains to be seen whether documentation of land use and lifestyle offers a faithful representation of this complex spirituality, and whether it is appropriate to integrate sacred knowledge into a cultural tourism program.

While cultural survival and revitalization reflect local Aboriginal priorities and motivations, the potential of cultural tourism is recognized. Elders' information represents a legacy from an ancient past; some of the last societies on earth to have practiced a band-organized foraging economy. Such information has significant academic value, and is of great interest to people living an urbanized and industrialized life. Hearkening back to the philosophical musings of Jean Jacques Rousseau, or more likely to the fiction of James Fenimore Cooper, Karl Friedrick May, or Archibald Belaney (Grey Owl), this interest is often quite simplistic and reflects a yearning for an imagined simpler time when people lived in harmony with nature. The challenge for those seeking to interpret Aboriginal history and culture is to reflect more than one-dimensional stereotypes of an imagined past. This is a significant problem that requires great care and sensitivity to do well.

Aboriginal cultural heritage has substantive value in revitalizing and expanding conventional northern tourism. This might involve colecting place names and the underlying stories to be integrated into the visitors' experience. For example, Wawakapewin place names reveal the depth of knowledge about the landscape and demonstrate how storytelling perpetuated such knowledge to successive generations.

Traditional lifestyles could become a featured part of tourism with visits to abandoned or reconstructed trapping cabins. These log cabins date from the early to mid-20th century. They were often only 2 × 4 meters in size with low, moss-covered pitched roofs, a single narrow low door, and sheet metal woodstoves or stoves made from oil drums for heating. They were the winter homes for families who remained isolated for months at a time. Even winter camps dating as late as the 1950s reveal that "country food" formed the basis of subsistence, with only a narrow stock of purchased goods being available (flour, lard, tea, ammunition, snare wire, blankets, textiles, and cookware).

The Wawakapewin Elders indicate that traditional moss-covered and conical winter houses (*akeqiganun*) were used into the early 20th century, with foundations and frames of such structures marking some of their birthplaces. This includes the birthplace of Mrs. Patti (Frogg) Nanokeesic who was born in 1933 (Figure 9.3).

This site contains shallow circular depressions, but test excavation revealed at least one with a central, stone-lined hearth yielding smashed food bone and sheet metal fragments from recycled containers. In the context of resource scarcity and fur trade retrenchment, E. S. Rogers (1994:310, citing Rogers 1963) suggests that such winter houses were introduced in the second half of the 1800s due to a scarcity of large mammal hides and the financial inability of Native people to purchase canvas. The limited archaeological visibility of Euro-Canadian consumer goods at sites dating to the first half of the 20th century is consistent with these generalizations and implies a persistence of nineteenth-century lifestyles into the recent past. At such places, a more ancient past is readily apparent in the archaeological debris of living memory.

The Elders also report summer gathering places where scores and sometimes hundreds of people briefly gathered. Such "in-gathering" places were strategically chosen where seasonal food supplies were rich and reliable. They were named places where spawning fish could be trapped in stone or wood weirs and preserved for future need. These seasonal gatherings were the means by which the larger community socially reconstituted itself through visiting, planning future harvests, ceremonies, courtship, and marriage. Thus, while Elders' memories represent direct experience supplemented with those of their grandparents, it often reflects continuities to the more distant past. Indeed, locations used in the early 20th century often reveal underlying precontact archaeological deposits (see Taylor-Hollings 2006a, 2006b; Taylor-Hollings and Hamilton n.d.).

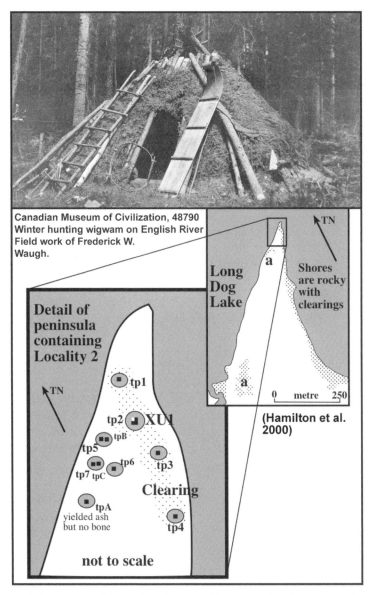

Figure 9.3 Sketch of Patti Nanokeesic's birthplace site, Wawakapewin First Nation, Ontario.

What can emerge is an understanding that Subarctic Aboriginal people lived and worked in a well known and carefully managed cultural landscape. While oral history reflects the comparatively recent past, it forms part of a cultural trajectory dating back for thousands of years. The tourist visitor begins to comprehend the north as a familiar homeland occupied by successive generations of Native people and not a "pristine and empty wilderness." The audience for such insight is not limited to tourists seeking authentic heritage experiences. An important underlying motivation for community Elders is the preservation of a fragile and beleaguered cultural legacy for their own descendents.

Conclusion

An uneasy symbiotic relationship exists between tourism and applied archaeology that involves multiple agendas. At its most developed, heritage tourism involves public agencies that undertake archaeology at sites deemed to have cultural heritage significance. What constitutes "significance" often reflects carefully selected "origin stories" that celebrate pivotal events, places, and people in Canada's colonial history. For example, Canadian political tensions during the 1960s and 1970s fostered heritage themes that celebrated French and British colonial history as the "two founding nations." It is only comparatively recently that sites explicitly commemorating Aboriginal culture and history have been identified and developed at major interpretative facilities. While reflecting gradual transformation of the power relationships within Canada, it also mirrors shifting priorities among archaeologists, historians, and tourism professionals toward examination of the non-elites and those who are not part of the dominant cultures.

Such shifts in orientation also reflect local initiatives for cultural and heritage tourism development. This can reflect stories with more local relevance and which also serve local agendas. Some projects, like Red Rock House, were overtly structured to collect planning information to address the feasibility of heritage tourism. In other circumstances, archaeology served the existing tourism market by offering public archaeology venues. In effect, the tourism opportunity focused on observing (and sometimes experiencing) archaeological investigations rather than consuming educational or cultural insight through museum exhibits or site reconstructions. I confess to viewing public archaeology programming as the "price" paid for receiving funding to conduct archaeology in an under-studied and under-serviced region. I suspect that this reflects the training and prejudices of most archaeologists, and I remember being admonished by my supervisors for my slightly dismissive attitude toward cultural tourism. This may have contributed to projects that effectively addressed short-term cultural tourism goals, but failed to deliver long-term benefits through permanent facilities, museum exhibits, or heritage interpretation literature. Such failures do not reflect upon the long-term public interest in such heritage resources, but rather the archaeological terms of reference and local capacity to sustain such programs over the long-term.

Mixed motivations are also evident with initial efforts at developing Aboriginal cultural tourism and ecotourism in northern Ontario. While archaeologists are often involved, such research usually empha-sizes Aboriginal oral history and ecological knowledge centered on traditional land use and occupancy. The rationale underlying such pilot studies is to identify heritage themes to be embedded into already existing "wilderness" tourism businesses and to attract new client groups interested in less consumptive cultural and "eco" tourism. As the northern Ontario economy shifts away from primary reliance on natural resource extraction, expanded tourism opportunities may become critically important, particularly for remote and under-serviced Aboriginal communities. However, such communities are also motiv-ated by local objectives that include preservation of traditional knowledge. This is calculated to enable cultural survival and revital-ization for future generations, to document past and contemporary Aboriginal land use and occupancy in the face of proposed development, to protect Aboriginal and treaty rights, and to facilitate development of locally based land-use planning capacity. In this sense cultural tourism is the proximate goal, while the long-term motivations remain firmly embedded in local priorities not involving tourism.

There is a steadily growing popular appetite for observing the process of archaeology and learning about diverse cultures. When coupled with authentic narratives, whether written or oral, cultural heritage is a powerful force for public education and tourism. It drives a significant part of the tourism economy and reflects a yearning to understand from whence we came. Yet, cultural heritage tourism can be readily subverted to perpetuate simplistic or stereotypic images and comforting messages about national or cultural origins. We must also recognize that tourism remains essentially a leisure pastime for the social and economic elite, and it remains a kind of entertainment. Developing cultural tourism venues and interpretations must be reflexive and self-critical exercises that do justice to the long-dead participants of that culture, as well as their living descendents.

Chapter 10

Saving Punalu'u: Ka'ū as a Cultural Kīpuka

Julie Tate-Libby

Introduction: Kapu Ka'ū

The district of Ka'ū covers the southernmost portion of Hawai'i Island,
locally known as the "Big Island." Its boundaries include the active
caldera Kilauea, most of Hawai'i Volcanoes National Park, rolling
upland mountains, and the sloping plains of Kama'oa. It is a windy,
isolated district considered by many local residents to be one of the last
kīpukas of Old Hawai'i. A kīpuka is an untouched oasis of vegetation
in the middle of a lava flow, which over time, develops its own unique
ecosystem. As a concept, it is used to describe places considered
pristine or "pockets" of Old Hawaiian culture (Fuchs 1961). To the
residents who live there, it is this quality which characterizes Ka'ū. As
one respondent said, "Ka'ū is the last bastion that still has the ways
of the 1800's in it [*sic*]."

Tourism and Archaeology: Sustainable Meeting Grounds, edited by Cameron
Walker and Neil Carr, 181–193. ©2013 Left Coast Press, Inc. All rights
reserved.

In the middle of Ka'ū's rocky, undeveloped coastline lies Punalu'u Black Sands Beach, a popular tourist stop and local hangout. It is the only accessible swimming beach in the district and has been a prime target for tourist development plans for over 30 years. It is also home to numerous Native Hawaiian archaeological sites, including several *heiaus* (religious temples), native fishponds, ancient trails, and burials. The physical and historical aspects of the landscape are integral to the existing Hawaiian lifestyle, and repeated attempts to further develop the beach as a tourist destination have served to highlight its importance within the local community. To date, no major development of Punalu'u has been carried out, but the beach remains unprotected by County, State, or Federal jurisdiction. The research on which this case study is based was undertaken over several extended trips to Ka'ū in 2008. During the course of fieldwork, controversy over the newest development proposal for Punalu'u sparked a series of community meetings, which in conjunction with interviews carried out for doctoral research, formed the basis of this study. While multiple perspectives on the usage and preservation of Punalu'u exist, this chapter focuses on local and Native Hawaiian perspectives. A thorough analysis of the multiple stakeholders surrounding Punalu'u remains outside the focus of this chapter but has been considered elsewhere.[1] This case study will provide a brief historical sketch of Punalu'u, its foremost archaeological and culturally significant sites, and the impacts of tourism and related development on such sites. In addition, it will analyze the significance of the most recent development proposal and the decision-making processes that reflect shifting political agendas. Finally, it will consider how such sites should be managed as archaeological and touristic endeavors.

History of Punalu'u

In ancient times, Punalu'u was the site of a busy fishing village and part of the Punalu'u *ahupua'a* (traditional Hawaiian land distribution system, which ran from *mauka* (mountains) to *makai* (the sea) (Handy and Pukui 1998). These pie-shaped wedges of land form the basis for Hawaiian social and economic systems as extended *'ohana* (families) traded agricultural goods from the mountains like sweet potato, banana, or taro for marine goods from the ocean, including *'opihi* (a type of limpet), *limu* (a seaweed), various species of fish, and salt. Punalu'u was particularly known for its 'opihi, which could be found scattered all over the low-lying rocks and tidal pools, as well as salt, which was collected from the dried pools and used to preserve meats and fish. The coast between Honu'apo and Punalu'u was also valuable for a series of fresh water springs that ran from the mountains of *Kumauna* (a rain god) to the ocean where they surfaced in a series of anchialine and freshwater ponds, Nīnole, Puhau, and Punalu'u. The Hawaiians diverted and built up these ponds to form holding reservoirs for surplus fish, as well as breeding pools for certain species like mullet; additionally, some of the ponds were culti-vated as *loi* or wetland taro patches. *Punalu'u*, which literally means, "the spring dived for," derives its name from the practice by ancient Hawaiians of diving under the water with empty gourds to procure fresh water. These elements contributed to a prosperous fishing village at Punalu'u in ancient times, and form the cornerstone of a Hawaiian lifestyle and identity that is still practiced at Punalu'u today.

Historical Sites of Punalu'u

In the late 1700s, Punalu'u served as the summer home of Keoua, the last native chief of Ka'ū and as the district's capital in an insurgent war with Kamehameha, who was an ambitious chief from the northern district of Kohala (Cordy 2000). After a series of bloody defeats, Keoua surrendered himself to Kamehameha's forces on Makanau, a broad, flat-topped mountain overlooking Punalu'u (see Figure 10.1).

Makanau was also the site of the Kohaikalani heiau, destroyed during sugar cane planting in the late 1800s. Some local residents say that Kohaikalani was built by the mythical *menehune*, or little people (Ka 'Ohana o Ka Lae 1987) who are popularly believed to have been the original inhabitants of the Islands before the Polynesian migrations from present day Marquesas and Tahiti. In a survey of Hawaiian heiaus by John F. Stokes from 1901 to 1919, the remains of Kohaikalani consisted of a rectangular enclosure with walls 4.5 to 5.5ft high on the inside and 6.5ft on the outside. The interior pavement of the temple was covered with sea-worn pebbles called *'ili 'ili* stones, which can still be found today scattered throughout the sugar cane fields.

In ancient times, priests annually went up to the mountain to pray for rain where a stone dedicated to Kumauna remained on the top of

Figure 10.1 From the beach at Punalu'u, Makanau on the left and Pu'u 'Enuhe or Caterpillar Hill on the right.

Makanau well-into the 20th century. When sugar oligarch C. Brewer acquired the top of the mountain for planting sugar cane, a *haole* (white) plantation manager destroyed the stone by shooting it to pieces with his rifle. That year an earthquake shook the mountainside and destroyed half the village of Hilea, including the manager's house. When men went to look for his body, they found it devoured by wild pigs. This story is recounted today to illustrate the importance of respecting the old gods and the significance of Makanau as a site imbued with meaning for Native Hawaiians. The neighboring hill to the right of Makanau is Pu'u 'Enuhe, or "Caterpillar Hill," named after the *kupua* (supernatural being) Kumuhea, who could assume both human and animal forms. Ka'ū people who trace their ancestry to Kumuhea refuse to eat or harm any caterpillar or its related forms (Handy and Pukui 1989).

In ancient times, the village of Punalu'u was composed of a dense cluster of house sites around the bay and fishponds with another group of farm lots located two miles inland at the foot of Pu'u 'Enuhe (Cordy 2000). Mahele records (land awards distributed during the Great Mahele of 1848) show that the main inland trail through Ka'ū passed by these inland parcels while the major coastal trail (*Ala Kahakai*) passed by the coastal sites before heading diagonally inland

Figure 10.2 Anchialine fishponds near Punalu'u.

east of Punalu'u and continuing to the Kilauea Crater (Kelly 1980). Archaeological surveys in the 1970s show scattered platforms, walled areas, and stone terraces on the bluff edge overlooking the shore (Barrera and Hommon 1972; Crozier and Barrera 1974).

The series of naturally occurring anchialine pools (see Figure 10.2) around Punalu'u and Nīnole Cove were utilized by Native Hawaiians for several purposes. In some cases, they were dug deeper and reinforced with rock walls to form reservoirs for holding surplus fish and breeding certain species. As well as being archaeologically significant, the fishponds have been used by Native Hawaiians for traditional gathering and fishing purposes since time immemorial and were protected under the Civil Code of the Hawaiian Kingdom from sale or private ownership even after the Great Mahele, when most of the land was privatized (Kelly 2006). Tax maps as late as 1935 identified the ponds as government property. During the 1980s, however, C. Brewer unveiled plans for a destination tourist resort that would have destroyed several of the ponds, which produced strong opposition from Native Hawaiians and community members who argued that C. Brewer had no legal right to the wetlands at all.

Arguably, the most significant archaeological sites at Punalu'u are the several heiau that lie within its immediate vicinity: Punalu'u Nui heiau, Ka'ie'ie, Lanipau, and the now-destroyed, Imakakoloa. The largest of these, Punalu'u Nui heiau (also called Kane'ele'ele, Halelau, or Maile'kini), can be seen from the beach at Punalu'u. Archaeological surveys from 1906 suggest that it was the district's *luakini*, or human sacrifice temple (Kelly 1980; Stokes 1919), and bone pits discovered during the construction of a sugar warehouse before 1906 concur. Luakini or human sacrifice temples were associated with war and politics and dedicated to the god Kū. The dates of Punalu'u Nui are difficult to determine; local tradition claims it dates back to AD 600–700, but Cordy (2000) maintains that heiau of this size did not appear until AD 1200–1300. Keoua used it during his reign, and scholars believe his residence would have been adjacent to the heiau (Cordy 2000). Later, Kamehameha's successor, Liholiho visited this heiau, leading historians to believe that each district had one "national" heiau that was utilized by the high chief (Ii 1959:137). Below the heiau, a large, flat-topped sacrificial stone overlooks the ocean. Here, bodies were sacrificed, literally *kahiholo* (cut and let go) into the ocean; their remains fed the shark, an *'aumakua* (guardian deity and ancestor) who lived in a cave below the heiau and protected the bay. As one local resident explained, "that's why nobody got bitten by the shark in Punalu'u. That's why, when I was young, I could swim all over the place and now I wasn't afraid of shark biting me. We never had. Because there was the akua that was watching the bay, see [sic]" (Ka 'Ohana o Ka Lae 1987:74).

In 1906, the site consisted of a large level area (700 × 500ft) that was partly paved with beach pebbles and the eastern wall, which stood 8.5ft high and 9ft thick. The shape of the heiau suggests that at one point there were two heiau, Halelau on the south and Punalu'u Nui on the north (Kelly 1980).

Two heiaus lie within the Sea Mountain Five Resort golf course and were heavily impacted by its construction. Lanipau heiau is a small, L-shaped enclosure with walls 6ft high and 6–7.5ft thick. The southern wall is composed of three terraces, each one rising about a foot. Lanipau is said to have been built by Laka of Kauai (Kelly 1980). The Imakakoloa heiau has not fared as well, having been completely obliterated by construction of the golf course.

Just to the west of what was once Nīnole fishpond, Ka'ie'ie heiau, named after a type of fishing trap or weir made from the fibrous *'ie'ie* vine, sits on top of an old *a'a* (rough, jagged lava) flow, overlooking the ocean. Ka'ie'ie is thought to have been a fishing shrine and may have been associated with the *koas*, or "fish houses" off-shore at Punalu'u. Traditionally, as well as today, Hawaiian fishermen used natural features of the landscape, when fishing off-shore, to locate underwater koa where certain species of fish lived. The fish are fed throughout the year with cooked pumpkin or taro, and in return, they supply a reliable source of protein; in this sense, they are considered "farmed" fish. Fishing heiaus were dedicated to *Kaneko'a*, a form of the god Kane, rather than that of Kū (Valeri 1985). Although recent scholarship considers Ka'ie'ie to have been a multipurpose heiau (Ka'ū Preservation n.d.), it is likely that at one point it was dedicated to fishing and the off-shore koas at Punalu'u. Today, the site includes several walls and a raised stone platform, but an adjacent jeep trail is often used by tourists "off-roading" from Nînole to Honu'apo.

Another significant site at Punalu'u is the Hokuloa chapel dedicated to Henry Opukahaia, a young man whose untimely death inspired New England missionaries to come to Hawai'i. It is said that he was born at Punalu'u. Perched high on a bluff overlooking the ocean, the original wooden structure was built in 1843 and boasted, on average, a congregation of around 350 people. This building was replaced in 1957 by a stone chapel and was dedicated as a memorial to Henry Opukahaia (Clark 1985). Many Hawaiian residents' ancestors are buried in the graveyard beside the church and are regularly visited today.

A final archaeological feature of Punalu'u is the *Ala Kahakai* (trail by the sea) that served as an important link between ritual centers and coastal communities (State of Hawai'i Department of Land and Natural Resources 2007). The trail is said to have divine origins and according to tradition is thought to be the original route taken by the god Lono from North Kohala to the southernmost tip of the island. Originally paved with the *'ili'ili hânau* (birthing stones), the trail was designated as a National Historic Trail by President Clinton in 2000. Remnants of the trail can be seen near both Punalu'u Nui and Ka'ie'ie heiaus.

Most of the archaeological sites at Punalu'u were scattered in 1868, when a major series of earthquakes and tidal waves shook the Ka'ū coast sending waves over 50ft tall onto the shore. The tsunamis wiped out the original Hawaiian village at Punalu'u along with several others along the coast. Although the residents of Punalu'u rebuilt their village, replanted their coconut groves, and resumed their off-shore fishing, other changes, including the introduction of sugar in the 1860s and the influx of foreign labor including Chinese, Japanese, and Filipino immigrants would soon alter the district (Lind 2004).

Punaluʻu as a Port Town

By the late 1800s, the village at Punaluʻu had become an established port town with interisland steamers arriving twice a month to unload cargo and transport sugar cane to the West coast of the United States (Clark 1985). A stagecoach line soon linked Punaluʻu with the neighboring villages of Honuʻapo and Pahala. During this time, Punaluʻu became a popular stop for tourists on their way to the volcano. Tourists arrived by steamer at Punaluʻu and rode the five-and-a-half-mile railroad to Pahala, after which they would then embark on a seven-hour stagecoach ride to the volcano. Traffic decreased considerably after 1893 when improvements on the road between Hilo and the volcano house made it the more desirous route.

Even Punaluʻu's commercial port would not last; by the 1940s with automobiles and established roads connecting the deep water ports at Hilo, the port at Punaluʻu was abandoned. A year later, after the attack on Pearl Harbor, US army personnel destroyed what was left of the warehouse and wharfs and stationed troops at the pier for the rest of World War II (Clark 1985). At the same time, the military constructed barracks next to Punaluʻu Nui heiau, destroying part of the original *Ala Kahakai* trail. During this period the US military occupied most of the shorelines and beaches and banned access for local residents who had to resort to fishing and gathering at night (Ka ʻOhana o Ka Lae 1987).

After the war, union strikes among the sugar workers and the incorporation of Hawaiʻi as part of the United States began to dismantle the sugar industry. Free trade agreements between the US and other countries like Puerto Rico and the Caribbean nations rendered Hawaiian sugar less competitive, and sugar oligarchs C. Brewer and Hutchinson began a series of consolidations. Previous ethnic-based camps scattered throughout the district were now lumped into the two towns of Naʻalehu and Pahala. Consolidations and the mechanization of much of the labor required for sugar could not save the industry; the mill in Naʻalehu closed in 1986, and the Pahala mill closed 10 years later.

Tourism at Punalu'u

Anticipating the demise of sugar, C. Brewer began plans for a large-scale tourist resort development at Punalu'u in 1970, but opposition and an ill-timed tsunami frustrated the process, leaving a modest seventy-six-unit condominium and golf course development. A cultural center and restaurant, built at the same time, were destroyed in the 1975 tsunami. Residents claimed that Pele (the volcano goddess and *'aumakua*) disapproved of development, as some of the sites (like the restaurant) were built directly over burial grounds or surrounded by golf courses. As local artist Herb Kane (1987) recounts, the miraculous preservation of his mural depicting Punalu'u in ancient times is proof to many residents that Pele's anger was invoked by attempts to develop Punalu'u. This time, Pele had prevailed. Since then, numerous developments have been proposed for Ka'ū, including a space port and theme park, a jail, and several resort developments at Punalu'u. All proposals have failed due to local opposition. Despite opposition, the beach receives over 30,000 visitors each month, most of them on their way to Hawai'i Volcanoes National Park (State of Hawai'i 2006). Recent attempts to renovate the existing development and add a luxury resort complex have divided community members between those who believe the beach should be preserved and those who want to see economic growth. Controversy over the development initiated a series of meetings where residents voiced concern over existing management practices at Punalu'u and moved to create a community-based management program for the beach.

Local Management for Punalu'u

During these meetings, several issues regarding the care of cultural and archaeological sites were discussed. Presently, the County of Hawai'i manages the seven-acre beach park while the rest of the Punalu'u area, which extends for some 433 acres from the coast to Pu'u Enuhe and Pu'u Makanau, is privately owned by a Japanese-based corporation. Adjacent lands, on which Punalu'u Nui heiau is located, are held by Bishop Estates. It became clear during the community-management meetings that with limited resources, the County was not doing enough to manage Punalu'u, and several key issues were identified.

Residents expressed that lack of regulation was a major problem, particularly with the number of tourists coming to the beach. They suggested that limits be placed on the number of tour buses allowed on the beach at one time. Those whose livelihoods depended on tourism, however, adamantly refuted these suggestions. A related issue was the removal of black sand for tourist souvenirs. Although taking black sand is illegal, there are no attempts to enforce the ban and some tour bus guides have been known to hand out baggies for tourists to collect sand. Having weathered direct tsunamis in 1868, 1946, 1960, and 1975, portions of the coastline have sunk over 10ft and buried much of the original beach. The sand is disappearing at an alarming rate, aided by tourists and tsunamis. Local residents cite "Pele's curse," the belief that removing lava rock or black sand will bring bad luck. Originally, a story made up by Hawai'i Volcanoes National Park officials in the 1940s to keep visitors from taking lava rock (Ching and Stephens 1994), "Pele's curse" endures in Ka'ū as a well-established tradition, which many take seriously.

Some residents addressed "cultural issues," like tourists stumbling through family birthday parties, walking on the walls of Punalu'u Nui heiau, or driving jeeps over archaeological sites (see Figure 10.3). Today, tourists disturb the walls of the heiaus by moving rocks and looking for the sacrificial stone, which is advertised in several guidebooks. Local residents voiced the need for educational signage on this heiau to encourage more respect and less impact on the site.

Figure 10.3 Tourist jeep near Ka'ie'ie heiau.

Additionally, some of the walls and the altar have been recently reconstructed, but Native Hawaiian practitioners feel that this is inappropriate due to its origins as a temple devoted to politics and war. Part of the problem with attempting management of this site is that it lies on land adjacent to the Bishop Estates, a private trust that manages the estate of Bernice Pauahi Bishop (King and Roth 2006), the last descendent of the Kamehamehas, so any changes would need to be cleared through this agency first. Currently, the two heiaus, Lanipau and Imakakoloa, lie within the rarely used golf course constructed by C. Brewer in the 1970s. While the sites were all but destroyed during construction, they are now relatively protected from tourist impact. Yet, there is no guarantee that they will stay that way under new development.

Part of the problem with archaeological sites in Hawai'i is that they are often discovered in conjunction with development. As one respondent described it to me:

> If they find bones the development stops. But if it's just a site, a place, an old house, a heiau . . . there's no law that they can't build. You have to have an appreciation of these sites and their cultural significance. When the Hawaiians get together to protest, the development gets all this publicity and that's the last thing they want, so this is the only thing that makes them stop or preserve that site.

At issue for Native Hawaiians is the ability to control culturally significant sites, particularly those of burials containing ancestors. One of the sites where developers have proposed locating a hotel overlooks the Hokolua chapel and graveyard as it lies on a bluff with prime views of the ocean. Hawaiian residents frequent the chapel to care for the graves, and the idea of doing so under the gaze of several hundred tourists is abhorrent.

Ultimately the series of meetings initiated by the new development proposal exposed the complexities of local management. While the group Ka'ū Preservation had long been advocating preservation of Punalu'u, a newer group called *O Ka'ū Kakou* (we are Ka'ū) had recently undertaken volunteer management activities, like putting up recycling bins and cleaning out Kauila pond. This group favored the resort development, and relations between the two groups grew more and more strained as both asserted their right to have a say in Punaluʻu's management. The meetings held at Punaluʻu from January to April of 2008 reflected these internal tensions and eventually produced a third management group called *Malama Ka ʻAina Kapu o Nīnole-Punaluʻu* (take care of the land, Nīnole-Punaluʻu) which advocated a new vision for Punaluʻu. Instead of a destination resort catering to wealthy tourists, many members expressed that they would like to see Punaluʻu once again as part of an *ahupuaʻa* (traditional Hawaiian land distribution). They envisioned the site as a living history center where the ahupuaʻa could be recreated with cultural practitioners engaged in subsistence activities like taro and sweet potato cultivation, net fishing, and gathering. Members suggested that it would be a place where children and visitors alike could learn about Hawaiian culture and sustainability. Most importantly, it represented a local vision for Punaluʻu. As one resident said during a planning meeting, "it's a bigger story about the community getting involved and saying no, this is what we want for Punaluʻu. This is what we want for development. It isn't any big developer's idea for Kaʻū. . . . It's about the real Kaʻū becoming again."

While this vision did not reflect the entire community of Kaʻū, it did represent the views of those who have been the most passionately involved in protecting, managing, and "saving" Punaluʻu for the past several decades, and who have articulated some of the underlying issues between archaeological sites as relics of a past era versus an ongoing, living Hawaiian culture.

The Hawaiian Lifestyle at Punaluʻu

The archaeologically significant sites at Punaluʻu are not simply ancient sites to be preserved for viewing by tourists, but are associated with the continuation of a traditional lifestyle still practiced at Punaluʻu. Several *kuleana* parcels located at Punaluʻu are private lands that were redistributed to individual families during the Great Mahele. These lands are directly impacted by tourists who inadvertently wander onto their premises or take pictures of private structures and homes. One family has erected a statue of a Hawaiian man in chains in his yard for public viewing, but most visitors have no idea that this monument represents the ongoing struggle for Hawaiian political sovereignty. One morning, for example, the author visited this home and saw several tourists lined up at the "No Trespassing" sign taking pictures. Those living at Punalu'u on their kuleana lands still practice a traditional hunting and gathering lifestyle, but must do so under the scrutiny of hundreds of tourists. Many of the sites like the chapel, the fishponds, and the heiaus are still used by Native Hawaiians and cannot be considered relics of a past era. Instead they must be viewed as culturally significant sites whose maintenance and ongoing use provokes controversy over who "owns" such sites and how they should be regarded.

Conclusion: Local versus Outside Agendas

The most recent development proposal for Punalu'u is part of an ongoing struggle for ownership and local control. What was once a thriving Hawaiian fishing village is now a run-down resort and local hangout whose future remains undecided. While not all residents of Ka'ū agree on what should be done with the site, the two groups currently involved in its local management, Ka'ū Preservation and Malama Ka 'Aina Kapu o Nīnole-Punalu'u, have their own vision for Punalu'u.

Ultimately at Punalu'u, the past is in constant negotiation with the present. Hawaiian culture is not dead or relegated to the historical sites of Punalu'u Nui heiau, the fishponds, or the *Ala Kahakai* trail. Rather, these sites become emblematic of living Hawaiian culture, which is also kids hanging out on the beach, fisherman motoring in on the waves, and families barbequing on Sundays. Preserving the historical sites of Punalu'u and managing tourism is about allowing local voices to tell their own stories and come up with their own visions. How to do this within the complex interrelations of local, state, and international agencies remains unsure, but at Punalu'u, local groups have found ways to protect their beach in the past, and will doubtless do so again.

Note

1. See unpublished doctorial thesis, "Place, Preservation, and Mobility: Amenity Migration and the Politics of Preservation in the Ka'ū District of Hawai'i Island" (2009).

Chapter 11

Framing the Mogao Caves in the Encounters between Tourists and Site Interpreters

Ming-chun Ku

Introduction

Public access to archaeological sites in the era of mass tourism presents challenges to the principles and practices of site management.[1] Tourists' increasing access may change what Erving Goffman calls the "interaction order"[2] (Goffman 1974, 1983) of face-to-face interaction on the sites, especially in locations where definitions and management of the sites have predominantly been maintained by archaeologists, heritage professionals, or other non-tourist actors with relevant expertise or legitimacy. To address the issues of management and interpretation of archaeological sites in the context of heritage tourism, this article analyzes how the interaction order of the sites is framed and reframed during encounters between tourists and site interpreters.

Tourism and Archaeology: Sustainable Meeting Grounds, edited by Cameron Walker and Neil Carr, 195–210. ©2013 Left Coast Press, Inc. All rights reserved.

Figure 11.1 Outlook of the Mogao Caves.

This study is based on my field research at the Mogao Caves. They are one of the more important archaeological sites of the ancient Silk Road, a national heritage site of China, and an UNESCO World Heritage Site (Figure 11.1). They were preserved as a result of limited public access; however, this changed in the late 1970s when tourism boomed as a consequence of China's Economic Reforms and Opening. One major change concerning public access to the Mogao Caves, which is addressed in this chapter, is the emergence of tourism interaction, namely the interactive dynamics between tourists and non-tourist actors on the sites.

My field research took place in 2001, 2009, and 2010 using research methods that included interviews and participant observation. I interviewed the director, resident researchers, guides, and other staff of the on-site institute, the Dunhuang Academy. I also interviewed several tourists, domestic as well as international, as a means of ascertaining their expectations and experiences during their visit to the site. For research purposes, I participated in, and observed, 18 tours of the Mogao Caves. Five of these tours were arranged by the staff of the Dunhuang Academy subsequent to my interviews. During the remaining 13 tours, I participated as an anonymous backpacker, where, along with other individual visitors, I was assigned randomly to the tour groups.

The Mogao Caves as a Tourist Site: Background and Context

The Mogao Caves are situated near the town of Dunhuang, located on the edge of the Gobi Desert in Northwest China. The grottos were built between the 4th and the 14th centuries, and today there are 735 caves in the protected area of the site where they are monitored and preserved under the supervision of the Dunhuang Academy.

The archaeological excavation of ruins along the ancient Silk Road was started in the early 20th century by international explorers and archaeologists who discovered the historical value of the Mogao Caves. One of the major archaeological sites was the Library Cave, also known in China as *Cangjing Dong*, which is Cave 17 in the Academy's records. This cave was sealed and hidden for centuries before it was rediscovered in 1900 along with tens of thousands of manuscripts. While some of the archaeological findings from the early 20th century have been dispersed to institutions across the world, the Mogao Caves still contain large amounts of preserved Buddhist artwork, manuscripts, and historic artifacts with artistic, academic, and historic value.[3]

The official cultural institute, the Dunhuang Art Institute, was established in 1947 for on-site protection, research, and daily management of the Mogao Caves. After the Chinese Communist Party (CCP) assumed power in 1949, ideological concerns constituted major principles with regard to heritage affairs, and these principles were institutionalized during the process of socialist state formation. Consequently, historic artifacts and heritage sites were taken over by the CCP, as they were considered to be under state ownership (Ku 2008). The CCP took over the management of the Mogao Caves in 1950. Since, the on-site institute, first known as the Dunhuang Relics Institute in 1950 and has changed to the Dunhuang Academy in 1984 (Ku 2011).

Compared with its counterparts in the United State or in western European countries, the authority of the state in socialist China has played a dominant role in the definition and management of heritage sites considered under state ownership. In Mao's China, the functions of on-site institutes were cultural protection and propaganda. Discursively, the framework was provided by nationalism and Marxism-Leninism-Moa-Zedong-thought for authorized discourse of heritage in Mao's China. State ownership guaranteed the dominance of the authorized discourses in the definition and interpretation of heritage and history (Ku 2008). In such regimes of cultural governance, the on-site institute in the Mogao Caves plays multiple roles that include an academic institute conducting research projects, a professional cultural institute focusing on grotto preservation, and a government agency in charge of the daily management and supervision of on-site activities. In Mao's China, the Mogao Caves were preserved by the limited public access to the site. In addition, the rigid restrictions imposed on ordinary people's ability to be mobile, limited the number of people who were able to visit to the Mogao Caves in person. Most Chinese people were aware of the dispersion of the Dunhuang relics to overseas institutions through state propaganda that was developed for specific political purposes.

At the dawn of China's economic reforms during the late 1970s, the government decided to develop inbound tourism in order to pursue tourism revenue. The Mogao Caves and several other world famous sites were officially assigned to be opened to foreign tourists. Since that time, the Mogao Caves have become one of the most famous tourist destinations in China. When the restrictions on geographical mobility were lifted in post Mao China, many Chinese people traveled to the Mogao Caves to visit the places widely spoken about in classrooms, the media, or at public exhibitions. Since 1980, when domestic tourism flourished due to China's economic growth, domestic visitors to the Mogao Caves have outnumbered that of foreign tourists. The inscription of the Mogao Caves as an UNESCO World Heritage Site in 1987 further augmented the site's fame, both nationally and internationally. Since opening to the public in the late 1970s, over six million visitors have traveled to the Mogao Caves (Ku 2011). In the year 2011 alone, the Mogao Caves received over 680,000 visitors (Figure 11.2).

Figure 11.2   Tourists outside the caves.

Guided Tours as Means of Control in Site Management

The large number of visitors presents many challenges to the management of the Mogao Caves, and issues regarding regulations and the control of tourists in order to reduce the impact of tourism on the site have become a concern for the Dunhuang Academy. In addition, the Dunhunag Academy aims to maintain its authority over the interpretation and definition of the Mogao Caves in the interactions with the tourists.

Since the late 1970s, the Dunhuang Academy has gradually improved the daily management of the site. One of the major improvements has been the introduction of guided tours, by which the institute can manage the speed of tourist flows as well as the number of visitors to the caves. According to information obtained through interviews with staff, in the mid-1980s when the number of visitors reached over 100,000, the Dunhuang Academy was concerned with the potential damage to the grotto relics caused by an increase in tourist numbers.

Today, the total number of caves that make up the Mogao Caves, comprising 243 caves in the northern area and 492 caves in the southern area. The Academy decided to open approximately 40 caves in the southern area to the public and make them accessible only through guided tours as a way to reduce the possible impact of mass tourism. The caves are selected every few years by the Dunhunag Academy based on the following criteria: the type of Buddhist art located in the caves, the historic period during its construction, the state of preservation, and whether adequate space exists for visitors. The Reception Office of the Dunhuang Academy arranges different groups of guided tours led by its staff for visiting eight to ten of the forty caves. Groupings of caves and the order of visits can be adjusted by the Reception Office, and are based on the circumstances on that day and the intention to minimize the impact of tourism to certain caves at peak times.

Visitors to the Mogao Caves do not wander alone during their stay in the protected area. Special guests such as political leaders are accompanied by the director or researchers of the Academy, while general visitors are required to join the guided tours. The guided tour, as an organized activity, constitutes the order of tourism interactions with specific schemata of interpretation, and it is where the face-to-face interactions take place between the visitors and their guide. Although the visitors may be quite diverse with different expectations and imaginations about the Mogao Caves, they are nevertheless treated as "tourists" and are organized into groups during their visit. The guide is a part of the staff at the Academy and takes the lead on the pacing and direction of the tour. Unless the guide unlocks the door, the visitors are unable to enter the cave, although the guide can be flexible enough to adjust the order in which the caves are visited, or to speed up or slow down the group's movement, as a way to control the number of tourists in a specific cave. If a visitor raises any doubts or challenges the guide during the tour, the guide will either encourage or curb the visitor's behavior.

A large proportion of the guide's narration also constitutes the major frame of interaction. During my participation in the tours, I observed that the guide begins the educational spiel subsequent to entering the cave, which takes up a majority of the time. If time allows, there may be a simple question-and-answer session, or the guide may allow more time for the group to look around. When time is up, the group leaves the cave, so tourists spend most of their time in the cave viewing, listening, and following the instructions of the guide. When a tourist speaks, unless the topic reflects the theme of the introductory remarks, he or she may not get a reply. A sustained dialogue among tourists is extremely rare.

Guided tours have a strong sense of regulation in three dimensions: flow controls, discursive controls, and control over tourists' behavior. In terms of flow controls, tourists are led by the guides along specific routes and at a certain pace to visit the caves that are open to them. These "open-for-visiting" caves are actually always locked, and only the guides have keys since they are responsible for controlling the length of time the tourists spend in each cave.

In terms of discursive controls, the guide gives information and commentary in each cave the tourists visit. Inside the caves, it is dark and only the guide has a flashlight, so when the guide mentions a specific point of interest, he/she points his/her flashlight to highlight it for the tourists. This means that the gaze of the tourists typically follows the weak light. When I joined tours in 2009 and 2010, wireless headsets were in use, and the guide's narration was received clearly in my headset throughout the visits. With headsets, even if I walked some distance away from the guide, or two or more groups entered the cave at the same time, I still received the narration from my assigned guide throughout the tour, which told me what to look at and why.

The guided tours at Mogao Caves are available in several languages, and in order to compare them, I joined tours in Mandarin and in English. I noted that in both the Mandarin and English tours, the remarks were standardized and some wording was identical. These remarks focused on specific subjects, such as the artistic attributes of particular grotto relics, the religious and scientific dimension of the wall paintings, and other historic findings in the caves. The guides constantly used jargon in their remarks to highlight the artistic or scientific value of the grotto relics, and all guides mentioned that the Mogao Caves are listed as an UNESCO World Heritage Site. During subsequent interviews with staff, I learned that during the off-season, the guides are required to attend training classes taught by the resident researchers at the Academy. They may memorize standardized remarks related to individual caves. At the end of the training, the guides are assessed, and they are required to give oral introductions about randomly selected caves to make sure that they have been able to memorize what they have been taught. The scores received are taken into consideration with regard to determining the guide's ranking, salary, and other benefits. Through staff training and evaluation, the Academy is able to maintain the discursive controls via well-trained professional guides capable of delivering officially approved remarks, using preferred referential frameworks of meaning or even identical scripts in the tours.

In terms of control over tourists' behaviors, the duties of the guide include enforcing bans on certain types of behavior during the course of the tour. These include bans on photography, touching the relics, and eating or drinking. In the tours I attended anonymously, I often heard guides admonish tourists in a very loud voice for touching relics or taking photographs. Sometimes, the guide would use a moralistic tone, such as, "this is destroying cultural relics." At other times, guides would invoke their authority by issuing warnings, such as when a guide noticed one of the visitors using a camera during the tour, "switch your camera off. If I see you using it one more time, I CAN have you removed immediately." During the tours, the guides kept a watch on visitors' behavior to prevent anything "improper" from taking place, such as touching the relics or spitting, even though such behavior is common elsewhere in China.

Framing and Reframing the Interaction Order on the Sites

In these tours, guides maintain the interaction order in a tourism frame defined by the Academy, and that is the frame of "public education." I observed that in most of the tours, tourists consented to this frame and behaved in the same way as a "flock of sheep." They followed the lead of the guide, listened to guides' narration, and refrained from doing anything "improper." When the guide completed the narration, tourists typically took another look at the wall paintings or statues, asked a question or two about what the guide had just told them, and then followed the guide out of the caves. When the guide announced the tour was over, they did not linger and left the protected area of the Mogao Caves.

However, I also observed that occasionally some tourists would break the rules. The most common form of rule breaking was leaving the group to walk around as they pleased or, either wittingly or unwittingly, entering forbidden areas. When a guide noticed such a situation, he/she might do something to maintain the interaction order. For example, I observed that when a tourist was clearly falling behind and looked like he might become separated from the group, the guide said to him, "you have bought the entrance ticket. You have paid for our introduction. The wall paintings and statues in each of the Mogao Caves are genuine art. You may not be able to understand them yourself. So stay close to the group and let me introduce them to you." Sometimes, while noticing "the potential trouble makers,"[4] the guides would redefine the situation and reframe it to something other than public education. The following field note, from one of the Mandarin tours I joined, provides an example of this. The guide introduced himself to the group, then started handing out headsets and explained the visiting rules to us, and in doing so, somehow reframed the professional-oriented public education tour into a theme of "supervision from Big Brother," a theme that most Chinese people are familiar with.

First, I would like to welcome you to the Mogao Caves. I am a professional guide of the Dunhaung Academy. If you have any questions during the trip, please ask me. I will do my very best to give you an answer. I want to talk a bit about the visiting rules. They are very simple. Only a few points. First, after you have entered the caves it is important that you do not touch any of the wall paintings or statues. This is because the paintings and statues are all made from clay. They are many hundreds of years old and very fragile. If you are not careful and cause a piece to break off, then you have damaged a cultural relic. The consequences will be serious. The second point is about photography. Regardless of whether you are inside or outside the caves, until you have exited through this ticket gate do not use either your mobile phone or camera to take pictures. Our entire tour will be photographed by digital cameras. If you take pictures or touch relics, even out of my notice, when you leave here someone will track you down and give you a hard time. The third point is that the electronic tour guide systems (the headset) you are carrying are the same as the machines used by museums across the country. If you want to use one of the machines elsewhere, there is a separate charge. But here at the Mogao Caves we let you use the machines for free. If for any sudden reason you need to leave during the tour, please return the machine to me first. Do not take the machine out with you, as it has a tracking system inside. I hope everyone pays attention to these points. Now, we will move onto the main topic.

In my field research, I also noted that not all tourists act as part of the "flock of sheep" during the guided tours. During a visit in 2001, I witnessed tourists expressing their disapproval and transforming the frame in a Mandarin tour. When the group came to Cave 17, well known across China as Cangjing Dong, our guide gave a brief introduction that focused mainly on the intellectual contributions contained in the historical scripts found in this cave. She did not touch on the topic of the dispersion of these relics overseas. Cave 17 is a very small cave, too small for visitors to enter, and it is situated along the passageway to Cave 16; a much larger cave with wall paintings of Buddhist stories. After her brief remarks, the guide intended to lead us directly to Cave 16; however, one of the Chinese tourists stopped and began an enthusiastic speech about Western imperialists' theft of China's national treasures from the Cangjing Dong. This topic immediately evoked responses from the rest of the group who started interjecting stories about how many "good things" were "stolen" by the "foreign devils on the Silk Road." Everyone seemed to have something to say on this topic, and the opinions espoused were identical to popular nationalist discourses concerning the Mogao Caves, particularly Cangjing Dong as a symbol of "national shame." At that moment, the tour was transformed into nothing less than a spontaneous mass forum for patriotism and nationalism. Our guide silently stood aside, unable or unwilling to intervene in the interactions among these domestic tourists until she finally said to the group that we were running behind schedule and needed to move on to the next cave. When we left Cave 17, I asked the tourist who had made the initial speech why he had done so. He responded:

Of course, we need to talk about it. How can someone talk about Dunhuang without referring to the history of imperialism in China? There is so much to say on this topic. You must be from Hong Kong or an overseas Chinese, otherwise you would no doubt know how important this topic is. The guide did not mention it at all. The guide's introduction totally misses the key point. I was doing her job for her.

When they visited Cangjing Dong in this tour, the Chinese tourists' interactions with the guide did not fall into the pattern of "you narrate, I listen. Then we have questions and answers." Instead, they spontaneously and enthusiastically narrated stories they knew and expressed their opinions surrounding Cangjing Dong. They took the lead in the process of tourism interaction and transformed the tour into a kind of public forum. In addition, these tourists did not bring up the artistic or scientific value of the relics. Instead, their narratives focused on whether those items were either damaged or dispersed overseas by foreign explorers. Their narratives followed a nationalist discourse that was widely spread through public exhibitions and mass education programs in Maoist China. In such discourse, the stories about the Mogao Caves revolve around Cangjing Dong, which symbolizes the "national humiliation" when "our national treasures were lost overseas by rapacious Western imperialists."[5]

Such discursive inscription of nationalism on this archaeological site has symbolically constructed the Mogao Caves as a national space, projecting collective feelings and images regarding the imagined community of "nation." For some domestic tourists, if not for all of them, Cangjing Dong was the must-see in the Mogao Caves, and their visit constituted a journey to express their sentiments toward "our nation." The tourists I met in front of Cangjing Dong that day showed me the possibility of transforming the frames by redefining the situation into a public forum of patriotism and nationalism.

I also observed that not all tourists are capable of expressing their disagreement and transforming the frames in the same way as I witnessed in Cangjing Dong. During my visits in 2001, a Chinese backpacker named Zhang started chatting with me on the tourist minibus when he learned that I was from Taiwan. He sat next to me and asked me how I "felt" about the flying angels (*feitian*) on the cave walls. I told him that I had read about them in art books in Taiwan, but I did not realize how splendid they were until I saw them firsthand in the caves. Suddenly, he told me that he had seen the flying angels in his practice of *Falun Gong*[6] and the purpose of this trip was "to feel

and to experience the power of flying angels and that of this place."
Unsure of how to respond, I then asked him, "what did you feel and
experience in the caves?" He then told me mysteriously how those
flying angels were flying off the walls and, as though alive, gesturing
to him. He said that he directly captured the profound meaning of
these gestures and the sacred power in the spaces of the Mogao Caves.
I admitted to him that I had not "felt" as he had, and he replied that,
"most people could not feel that either. See how those guides introduce the cave? They emphasize the color of the painting and the
gestures of the sculpture. Very superficial. Unless you learn and practice Falun Gong, you may neither feel nor experience either the holy
power or the law of the Universe."

I joined the same tour as Zhang that day because what he had said
to me on the bus made me pay particular attention to his behavior in
the caves. Zhang did nothing at the grotto site that would have singled
him out as a Falun Gong practitioner. He simply followed the guide,
moving from one cave to another and listening to the narration. I
would have had no idea that Zhang was a Falun Gong practitioner if
he had not told me. After the tour, I could not help asking Zhang why
he had not practiced Falun Gong in the caves. Zhang replied, "Well,
our tour was led by the guide and with a routine schedule. In each
cave we only stayed a few minutes and then immediately moved on
to the next cave. How can I practice with such a schedule?"

The Mogao Caves and grotto relics on the site are sacred for Zhang,
and he wanted to "feel" these spiritual powers. However, his behavior
appeared no different than that of other tourists. For me, Zhang was
a closet pilgrim hidden within the arranged tour, and two factors
may account for Zhang's status: the first is surely the illegal status of
Falun Gong in China; and the second is that the Academy requires
all tourists to join guided tours where the guides keeping a watch
on visitors' behavior. During the guided tours, no religious activities
including meditation, praying, chanting sutras, or burning incense are
allowed. In fact, the rules as drawn up by the Academy specifically
stipulate that burning incense is forbidden. Among all of the on-site
cultural units administering grotto sites in China, the Dunhuang
Academy clearly has the most administrative strength and prestige.
Therefore, religious activities such as praying or chanting sutras,
which I occasionally came across while visiting other grotto sites, are

unlikely to take place at the Mogao Caves. Even though the guided tours may introduce the Mogao Caves as the location of Buddhist art, the Academy does not frame this grotto site as a holy space with ritual practices for Buddhists or for believers of other religious of spiritual movements.

Nevertheless, during a number of tours, I noticed that after the guides had completed their introductory remarks, some visitors would neither return to look at the items introduced by the guides or ask specific questions concerning the introductory themes. Instead, they walked toward the main Buddhist statue and placed money in a collection box then put their hands together to pray. Only then did I realize that there was a collection box inside the cave, something that the guides never mentioned, and the box was full of both coins and paper money. According to a guide I interviewed later, visitors would throw coins toward the statue if a collection box was not supplied. Not only would this make it difficult to keep the place tidy, but it also might damage the artifacts. It was difficult to ascertain exactly how much money was in the collection boxes, but clearly there were a large number of coins that probably came from a significant number of visitors.

During guided tours that did not allow the burning of incense and with limited time scheduled to remain inside the caves, visitors still clasped their hands in prayer and donated money. Therefore, I infer that pilgrims were hidden among the mass of tourists, and the pilgrims are more than likely not limited only to the Falun Gong members, but also include believers of Buddhism, Daoism, and various other religious movements. Given that some visitors were praying, donating money, and even secretly touching the statues when the guides were not looking, I believe that for these pilgrims, the statues and wall paintings inside the Mogao Caves still possess a degree of sanctity.

Since all visitors to the caves are required to join the guided tours, and the Academy clearly forbids the burning of incense, it is easy for these pilgrims to remain hidden in the framework established by the institute. These hidden pilgrims may join the tours, but for them the meaning of this site is not framed as a World Heritage Site, and their visit is not for the purpose of learning the artistic or scientific merits of the relics. Rather, their impetus is a religious one, which if not illegal as is Falun Gong is permitted to appear occasionally, as long as it does not challenge the dominant framework of the guided tours. My research also finds that at certain times the religious framework emerges and replaces the framework of public education. For example, according to a local custom, a temple fair for pilgrims and the community is held in the caves on the Buddha's birthday, which is the eighth day of the fourth month of the lunar year. The Dunhuang Academy pays respect to this tradition by opening several of the caves for pilgrims on the Buddha's birthday so that visitors may pray and make circuits around the Buddha.

In my 2010 field research, which coincided with the Buddha's birthday, I witnessed many people from nearby towns and villages, both young and old, praying inside the caves (Figure 11.3). The Academy set up an incense burner outside the protected area and allowed believers to worship in several caves containing large Buddha statues (Ku 2011). Guides were assigned to each of these caves, but they did not carry out their usual narration since their main task was to keep the worshipers moving along in an orderly manner and to ensure that no activities damaged the relics. During this event, the

Figure 11.3 Believers praying outside the caves on the Buddha's birthday.

dominant framework of public education gave way to a framework centered on religion and pilgrimage.

Conclusion

In the context of cultural governance in socialist China, specific cultural institutions have been the legitimate actors who have occupied the dominant position regarding interpretation and site management. Yet, mass tourism amid China's economic reforms presents new challenges to their dominance because of the changing interaction order that has emerged with public access to archaeological sites in the era of mass tourism. In this case study, the interaction order in the encounters between tourists and professional guides of the Dunhuang Academy has been explored through an analysis of how the interaction order and the meanings of archaeological sites are maintained, negotiated, or changed in face-to-face interactions.

Tourism activities at the Mogao Caves are organized through guided tours, which are designed as a means of managing the flow of tourists to the protected area. Although the guided tours define the participants' roles and their activities in order to frame the interaction order according to specific schemata of interpretation, this case study also points out the possibility of reframing the interaction order and redefining the Mogao Caves regarding the consents, disavowal, or contestations in the interactive dynamics between different types of tourists and guides. My field notes from my research at the Mogao Caves reveal at least three different kinds of interaction order, each with different tourism frames and embedded referential frameworks of meaning. The first one is guide-audience interactions in the frame of public education with reference to an academic framework of meaning; the second one is interaction among patriot citizens in the frame of mass forum with reference to a nationalist framework; and the third one is interactions among pilgrims and spirituality in a frame of religion and rituals with reference to a framework of spirituality and sacredness. The findings lead to the conclusion that the meaning of this grotto site should not be treated as something predetermined and static as it appears in official publications but as something constantly framed and reframed during encounters between tourists and on-site actors.

CHAPTER II

Notes

1. An earlier version of this case study has been published as, "Tourism Frames in Heritage Sites: A Case Study of Tourism in the Mogao Caves, China," in *Recreation and Society in Africa, Asia and Latin America, North America*, 2012, vol. 3, no. 1. Available at: <http://gir.uoguelph. ca/index.php/rasaala/article/view/2217/2712>. Date accessed: 24 Jan. 2013.

2. Further discussions on Goffman's notion of the "interaction order" of face-to-face interaction are beyond the scope of this case study. Readers interested in this subject can refer to Drew and Wootton (1988).

3. According to the Dunhuang Academy, in the Mogao Caves there are around 2400 statues and 45,000 square meters of murals. http://enweb. dha.ac.cn/timeline/

4. This is a quote from a guide I interviewed during my field research.

5. These are two quotes from conversations with domestic tourists. The quotes were translated from Mandarin by the author.

6. Falun Gong is a new religious movement that emerged in China in 1990s. The estimated number of its practitioners was in the tens of millions in the late 1990s. After the crackdown of practitioners' protesting in Beijing in 1999, the Chinese government officially declared Falun Gong as a heretical organization and forbid its activities and practices. For details on this subject, see Palmer (2007).

Chapter 12

Archaeology and Tourism: Lessons from the Zimbabwean Experience

Ancila Nhamo

The Zimbabwean Experience

The engagement between archaeology and tourism in Zimbabwe began even before the initial colonization of the country by the British in 1890. The stories and speculations about Great Zimbabwe and its builders began in the 16th century when Portuguese traders visited the site and wrote about it (McCall-Theal 1900). These accounts led renowned explorers such as Karl Mauch to come to southern Africa to search for the sites (Bernhard 1971; Burke 1969). The controversies that surrounded Great Zimbabwe meant that archaeological sites in the country were centers of research early on during colonialism. The country was colonized in 1890, but by early 1900 there were already several books and other writings produced about the archaeological sites in the country, mainly on the stone-walled buildings of the Zimbabwe culture (e.g., Bent 1802, 1892; Buckland 1891; du Toit

Tourism and Archaeology: Sustainable Meeting Grounds, edited by Cameron Walker and Neil Carr, 211–222. ©2013 Left Coast Press, Inc. All rights reserved.

1897; Geare 1906; Randall-MacIver 1906a, 1906b). From this time onward, the archaeological exploration became more rigorous and systematic, and by the 1930s, several archaeological expeditions and resultant publications had been published (e.g., Caton-Tompson 1931; Jones N. 1926). By the early 1900s, archaeological sites, and especially Great Zimbabwe, were attracting such significant numbers of visitors that the colonial government started initiating their development as tourist attractions (Collett 1990:3). However, sustained visits to archaeological sites came later, with active promotion of archaeological sites beginning in the 1940s.

During much of the colonial era, however, tourism was the preserve of white people in Zimbabwe, when both international and domestic visitors were mostly white. Consequently, the tourist attractions were developed according to the tastes of this market, and archaeological sites were targeted because the tourism industry had shown interest in them. Archaeology, as an epistemological discipline, was known only among the white population, although research publications and popular writings about archaeology in the country helped to elevate public interest levels.

The increase in research and tourist interests triggered the need to protect the archaeological sites. Legal measures to protect the archaeological heritage were first instituted in 1902 with the passing of the *Ancient Monuments Protection Ordinance* (Chiwaura 2005:18). The introduction of heritage institutions began with instituting the Monuments Commission in 1936 (Chiwaura 2005), which resulted in many archaeological sites being declared as national monuments in order to protect them. National monuments were also presented as tourist attractions. Many of them were demarcated and protected with fences and the erection of placards to inform the public of the access rules, which were restricted to those who had been granted permission, and those were mostly white visitors. Much of the areas around the national monuments were set aside as protected recreational parks and gardens where tourists would enjoy archaeology and the pristine natural environment. In and around the capital city, Harare, for example, many surviving archaeological sites lie within these parks and gardens. The same patterns applied to sites in rural areas where many elderly people remember the times when mainly white people visited them. They would also go on expeditions to look for archaeological sites or visit those that were reported by the district commissioners. Numerous archaeological sites also existed within white commercial areas that were co-protected by the property owners who welcomed visitors. Some property owners actually started making money off of these sites by developing them and providing tourist services such as coffee shops (NMMZ Annual Report 1985/86).

The above arrangements worked well during the colonial period mainly because of a very strict policing system that would deter people, especially blacks, from breaking the access rules. There were also enough funds to state-sponsor much of the protection of the archaeological sites while allowing only a few people access to them. Although the visitors paid fees to access some of these archaeological sites, many of them were looked after through donations from well-wishers and government funding of the heritage institutions that administered the archaeological heritage. However, this proved to be unsustainable after the attainment of independence. The arrangement was affected by changes in state priorities coupled with an increased demand for social service, which meant that the available resources were then being channeled toward providing basic services to the majority rather the minority. This put a strain on the national resources, and there was a huge reduction in the budget available to these areas (Collett 1990). It became difficult for the newly renamed institution, the National Museum and Monuments of Zimbabwe (NMMZ), to maintain the pristine environments that were surrounding the archaeological sites and especially the national monuments (Collett 1990). The result of this situation was that many archaeological sites that were tourist attractions were no longer monitored diligently by NMMZ. The organization's conservation monitoring policy stipulates that national monuments are supposed to be visited three times annually (Chipunza 2005); however, the lack of resources meant that some sites would go for three or more years without any visit from the NMMZ officials (NMMZ Annual Report 1998/99). This laxed policing did not go unnoticed by the locals who took advantage, looted the fences, and vandalized the places in some cases. Even though the restriction of access was still institutionalized in the NMMZ Act Chapter 25.1, 1981 (formerly 313, 1972), the lack of policing meant that no perpetrators were brought to book. For example, increasing incidents of vandalism at archaeological sites were reported since 1992, although no arrests were ever made (NMMZ Annual Report 1992/93). There was vandalism twice at Domboshava National Monument, near Harare, but none of the perpetrators were ever apprehended (Chirikure and Pwiti 2008; NMMZ Annual Report 1994/95).

Nevertheless, it was not just the lack of financial resources that threatened the survival of tourism at many archaeological sites. The need for other services such as housing and farmlands put pressure on the archaeological heritage in other ways as well (Pwiti and Ndoro 1999). In towns, there was an increasing demand for houses to accommodate people who had migrated from rural areas in search of employment. This resulted in high-density residential buildings being constructed around some of the recreational parks and gardens that contained archaeological sites. The expansion of industrial areas also affected some of the archaeological sites, and without the monitoring by NMMZ some of them, including national monuments, were actually destroyed. In rural areas, villages also expanded into previously restricted areas in order to accommodate the growing populace. All of this affected the presentability of the archaeological sites as tourist attractions, and many of these, such as the Rhodia rock art site in the eastern part of Harare, were later de-listed from the national monuments register since they had lost the qualities that originally led to their listing (NMMZ Annual Report 1998/99).

The situation was exacerbated by the fact that the country's independence was won after a protracted armed struggle that pitted whites against blacks. The white visitors felt unsafe in the black neighborhoods and this further resulted in the abandonment of many archaeological attractions as reflected by the fall in visitorship from 1980 to 1985 (NMMZ Annual Report 1985/86). However, many attractions that were found in commercial areas, national parks, and other protected nature reserves continued to be attractive, although not at the same scale as before.

The liberation struggle had also affected the country's tourism appeal, and in all these protected areas archaeological sites were competing with other attractions. The 1980s saw a growth of nature-based tourism the world over (Valentine 1992), and Zimbabwe and other countries in southern Africa became known for tourism connected to wildlife, especially the big five: buffalo, elephant, rhino-ceros, leopard, and lion (Shumba et al. 1998). This meant that natural attractions took precedence over archaeological resources in most national parks, and this is a situation that still prevails (Bonyongwa 2011). Thus, archaeological sites played second fiddle to natural attractions. In Zimbabwe, this scenario was exacerbated by the political bickering over the control of archaeological sites in national parks and recreational areas between state institutions that are also responsible for the natural environment and for cultural heritage, such as Zimbabwe Parks and Wildlife Authority (ZPWA) and NMMZ. The fact that they belong to separate government ministries has led to a lack of resolution on this matter (Bonyongwa 2011; Mudenda 2008), which has further resulted in an unwillingness on the part of ZPWA to develop archaeological sites within their areas for tourism out of concern that NMMZ would claim jurisdiction over them. However, ZPWA has no skilled workforce of their own to manage and promote archaeological sites within their properties. The ZPWA, for example, owns 13% of the land in Zimbabwe (Shumba et al. 1998), and within this area, there are thousands of archaeological sites, many of which remain under-utilized for tourism purposes (Bonyongwa 2011).

Apart from all this, the other challenge that bedeviled the development of sustainable tourism usage of archaeological sites in the post independence era has to do with the lack of interest from black Zimbabweans. There is a lack of relevance for archaeology among the local black communities, and Collett (1990) has noted it as a problem that persists today (Bonyongwa 2011). The colonial period portrayed archaeology as an elitist discipline that was the preserve of whites. The country had no trained black archaeologists at the time of independence, the first one coming in 1986 (NMMZ Annual Report 1986/87). Although there are now a number of universities offering degrees in archaeology, the majority of the populace have little knowledge about the subject beyond Great Zimbabwe. Archaeology is studied at the university level by a few students, but beyond this, general access to archaeological books and knowledge is limited (Pwiti 1994). Those materials that are accessible are written in very technical language, which is not palatable to laypeople on the street even though Zimbabwe has high literacy levels (Katsamudanga 2009). This situation is further aggravated by a lack of money to buy books, and the majority of libraries in the country depend on donations, where archaeology books are not a high priority. This has made it more difficult to promote and sustain archaeological sites as tourist resources especially for the domestic market (Bonyongwa 2011).

A lack of knowledge also influences policy, and policy makers who should provide a supportive environment have no knowledge of archaeology. In the same vein, institutions that market tourism in Zimbabwe, such as tour operators and tourism organizations, have very little knowledge of archaeology; therefore, they tend to undersell it (Bonyongwa 2011). Today, the effects of all the above-mentioned challenges are that many of these archaeological sites are no longer included in the tourism packages that market the tourism attractions in the country. Archaeology has lost much of its luster as a tourism draw card, and very few archaeological sites have been developed as attractions since they lack basic tourist amenities and services. Often, they are difficult to access due to poor road maintenance. Even those that have these services lack the marketing component, so they are not as successful as natural attractions such as game reserves.

In spite of all the problems that are associated with archaeological sites, some have managed to survive into the independence era as tourist attractions. These include rock art sites such as Domboshava and those in Matopo Hills: Silozwani, Nswatugi, and Pomongwe among others. Some stonewall sites have also continued to attract interest, and apart from Great Zimbabwe, other sites include Khami, Naletale, Dhlodhlo, and Regina (Collett 1990). However, there are other challenges as well, and most significantly, there have been continuous fights between the local communities for control of the tourist revenues (Chakanyuka 2007; Chirikure and Pwiti 2008; Chirikure et al. 2010; Pwiti and Mvenge 1996). The conflicts emanated from the fact that the local community members wanted to benefit from the revenue that came from tourism to the archaeological sites in their areas. On the other hand, the state institutions, such as NMMZ, were operating with colonial-era legislations that did not allow for the sharing of benefits with the locals. This resulted in frictions between the two parties, especially in the 1980s and 1990s. The problems also resulted from the fact that many of the archaeological sites were sacred places to the local communities before they were annexed by the colonial state. With independence, the local communities expected these sacred sites to be returned to them to administer (Fontein 2006; Garlake 1982; Pwiti 1996). However, this was never done, and friction has ensued.

By the late 1990s, NMMZ began to change its policy. It started the process of incorporating a community participation approach where local communities were allowed to do business, such as selling souvenirs, within and around archaeological attractions. Local communities were eventually incorporated as stakeholders with a say in the management of the heritage and archaeological sites (Chakanyuka 2007; Chauke 2003; Mataga 2003). At present, some archaeological sites have been reclaimed as sacred shrines by certain communities and individuals (Chakanyuka 2007; Mataga 2003). The control of these places has changed with some sites becoming entirely under the control of locals in communities with NMMZ playing a peripheral role. In the Nharira Hills, for example, heritage officials' access to archaeological sites, with some included on the national monuments register, is restricted by the traditional spirit medium who claims ancestral ownership of the place. However, most of the sites, especially those with some degree of tourism potential, are still under the control of NMMZ with communities participating in only certain aspects. This has proven to have its own challenges that have been documented elsewhere (Chirikure et al. 2010). Some of the archaeological sites that are under the control of local communities have been vandalized due to a lack of knowledge and over-enthusiastic community members (Nhamo et al. forthcoming).

Notably, the greatest challenge to the sustainability of archaeological tourism came from the political and economic meltdown of Zimbabwe during the last decade. Archaeological sites, even those that had managed to retain visitors, have experienced a huge decline during the first decade of the 21st century. The economic situation began deteriorating in the last part of the 1990s, but tourism officials continued with the belief that it could actually save the economy (Mabugu 2002). This was not to be, since the political instability that followed in the early 2000s meant that the tourism sector, as a whole, nose-dived. Several countries including the United Kingdom, Japan, and the United States issued travel warnings to their citizens (Manwa 2007), which resulted in a plummeting of international visitors to Zimbabwe. In 1997, international visitors had passed 1 million per annum, but by 2001, there was already a 40% decline (Mabugu 2002). This downward trend continued throughout the decade and hit rock bottom in 2008 with most tourist businesses operating below 10% of their capacity. Even attractions that used to be popular started getting very few visitors. The instability had scared away international visitors while locals could no longer afford the luxury of visiting tourist places. The lack of fuel and other supplies exacerbated this situation throughout the decade, and there were not enough food supplies and other utilities for domestic use let alone for luxury trips to visit archaeological sites. For archaeology, the economic situation led to the shrinkage of both financial and human resources to maintain the sites, and there was also a brain drain as skilled people fled the country. The economic meltdown led to high rates of unemployment, at one time as high as 80% (Manwa 2007). This negatively affected archaeological sites, even those with a potential for tourism. Unemployment led people to look for ways to make a living, and quarrying began in the surrounding granite outcrops that were for sale, despite the existence of more than 200 rock art sites recorded in the Harare residential suburbs, such as Epworth, Highfield, and Glen Nora. Although there has been no systematic documentation of the surviving sites, several have been decimated through small-scale quarrying activities.

Nevertheless, it was not just the drop in tourism numbers that affected tourism at archaeological sites; rather, the agrarian revolution that initiated the political turmoil also had an impact on the whole nation. The archaeological sites that were in commercial areas and other reserved areas were taken over by new owners. Many of the people who took over the control of these areas had no knowledge of the importance of these places; therefore, most suffered damage through agricultural activities, while some were vandalized for no apparent reason. The new owners regarded these sites as useless because visitors were no longer coming, and they could no longer generate any revenue. The violence that accompanied the agrarian revolution also meant that visitors, especially whites, no longer felt safe venturing into the countryside. In some cases, they were not allowed to venture into formerly white-owned areas by the new farmers for fear that they might be seen as white farmers who were coming back to reclaim their farms.

Lessons from the Past?

In the last few years, Zimbabwe has been trying to revive its tourism sector. The Zimbabwe Tourism Authority (ZTA), the body that looks into marketing the tourism potential of the country, has taken various initiatives to improve tourism arrivals (Karambakuwa et al. 2011). It has invited and sponsored tourism buyers from all over the world. It has invited and hosted international celebrities, such as the Brazilian national soccer team in order to dispel the negative publicity that the country had accrued. Some international celebrities, such as singers Akon, Joe Thomas, and Sizzla Kanlonji were invited to become the country's tourism brand ambassadors.

The harsh economic conditions of the past decade have also increased the awareness of the populace in general, of the need to generate revenue rather than rely on donor-funded projects that can dry up when politics go wrong. They are therefore keen to venture into tourism activities to generate income, and this has heightened the need to develop economic resources. Further, since 2009, with the institution of a unified government, such initiatives have led to a greater political and economic stability. There has been an increase in tourism arrivals (Karambakuwa et al. 2011), and next year Zimbabwe will co-host the United Nations World Tourism Organization General Assembly with Zambia. It is hoped that this will improve the tourism flow into the country. At present, tourism is one of the fastest growing sectors of the Zimbabwean economy (Karambakuwa et al. 2011). All of these circumstances add to the urgency for developing archaeological sites as tourist attractions. To accomplish this, NMMZ, local communities, and individuals have been trying to revive tourist visits to archaeological sites.

There are a few lessons that these initiatives must take from the past experiences in Zimbabwe. First and foremost, the survival of archaeological sites greatly depends upon raising awareness of their relevance to the communities that live with them and to the nation at large. The experience of Zimbabwe shows that archaeological sites cannot survive without providing some tangible benefits to the communities around them, as well as to the country at large. Tourism is one way of making archaeological sites relevant; however, the experience at those sites that were used as attractions has shown that this is not without its own problems. The equitable sharing of the benefits with all stakeholders is an issue that has to be anticipated and dealt with, and it is a global issue that international institutions such as UNESCO are currently grappling with (Chirikure and Pwiti 2008; Chirikure et al. 2010).

Experience from the colonial era has also shown that archaeological-heritage-as-a-tourism-product should not be the preserve of only a few. It is precarious, because, if the circumstance changes, archaeological heritage becomes redundant as with the situation at most sites after independence where the utilization of archaeological sites by the locals went down due to the elitism (among other factors) that was associated with them. If archaeological sites are to be utilized for tourism, they have to be made accessible and marketed to everyone who wishes to enjoy them. This will result in an increase in their appreciation and relevance and thereby justify the continued preservation by the heritage institutions and the public.

Related to the issue of broader marketing, the slowdown in international tourism arrivals that was witnessed in the last decade provides another lesson to be learned, and targeting international visitors is a volatile strategy since their visits are influenced by factors that are usually beyond the control of heritage and tourism institutions.

Political instability, whether real or perceived, will lead to a decline in visitors, and consequently, to less attractive archaeological sites. It is, therefore, paramount to establish a strong relationship with the more predictable domestic tourism as well. In the last decade, many archaeological sites became "white elephants" because locals, or domestic tourists, did not know anything about them. Manwa's (2007) research revealed that of the few tourists that were visiting cultural sites in 2004, 90% were Zimbabwean; and this shows domestic tourists will still utilize archaeological sites even in times when foreigners perceive the country as politically unstable. Therefore, there is a need to target this market; although, its success also hinges on a healthy economy in order to sustain the extra expenses for tourism.

Furthermore, restricting the usage of archaeological sites for tourism purposes is not sustainable. The Zimbabwean experience has shown that the success of tourism is unpredictable, and even domestic tourists will not be spared economic meltdowns resulting in the erosion of their disposable incomes. In Africa, where political and economic stability cannot be guaranteed, it is imperative for archaeological sites to establish relevance beyond the ability to generate money in order to ensure their preservation when tourism falters. Therefore, social benefits need to be emphasized together with the economic benefits. The sacredness of archaeological sites should be maintained wherever possible, and the preservation of other values such as the intangible aspects of archaeological sites has also proved to be important (Manyanga 1999, 2003; Mataga 2003). These intangibles will most likely be appreciated by tourists, add to the attractiveness of the archaeological sites, and will help to ensure their relevance for the surrounding communities. Other ties that archaeological sites have with members of local communities should also be preserved. For example, the importance of archaeological sites in the generation of knowledge about the ancestors of present communities can also be stressed. All of this will ensure that the archaeological sites remain relevant even when foreign tourists cease to visit, as they did in the last decade.

There are also some current challenges that have to be overcome before the sustainable use of archaeological sites for tourism can be attained. The disjunction between institutions responsible for cultural heritage, natural heritage, and tourism makes it more difficult to develop archaeological sites as sustainable tourism resources. As has been mentioned earlier, there is friction between NMMZ and ZPWA, and this is a problem because archaeological sites in national parks and recreation areas have a high potential to be tourism attractions, especially since they are already part of developed attractions. It has already been established that many of the archaeological sites in Zimbabwe are difficult to develop as stand-alone attractions (Collett 1990); thus, those that can complement other attractions have a better chance of success.

There is also little active coordination between NMMZ and tourism organizations. Although the director of NMMZ is a member of the ZTA board of directors, the Authority has very little information on archaeological sites in the country apart from Great Zimbabwe (Bonyongwa 2011). Other tourism organizations have also proven to lack basic knowledge about archaeological sites, so this situation needs to be rectified if archaeological sites are to be integrated into the tourism sector. There is also a need to improve the quality of the service at archaeological sites and provide acceptable tourist amenities.

The NMMZ must improve their tourism service arm by employing knowledgeable tour guides and providing information about archaeological sites to tour operators, tourism organizations, and the public (Collett 1990; Manwa 2007). The country must create policies that bring together professionals from different disciplines such as archaeology, heritage management, and tourism to work toward the sustainable utilization of the archaeological resources.

As experience has shown, the use of archaeological sites for tourism is usually complicated by many challenges; however, tourism provides an opportunity to utilize archaeological heritage for national development, and thus both heritage and tourism professionals must find ways to overcome these challenges. A sustainable approach to this utilization should ensure the survival of archaeological sites since they are nonrenewable.

Chapter 13

Meet the Flintstones: Contestable Cultural Heritage of the *Pica-Piedras* in a Phurépecha Community in Mexico

Tricia Gabany-Guerrero and Narcizo Guerrero-Murillo

Introduction and Case Study Background

The study area is located within central-west Mexico in the state of Michoacán, a zone of rare freshwater lakes, rivers, and over 40,000 volcanic cones (Hasenaka and Carmichael 1985).[1] The Late Postclassic Phurépecha Empire developed in this ecologically diverse region as the virtually impenetrable western rival of the Mexica, or Aztec Empire (Williams and Novella 1994). High in the *Meseta*

Tourism and Archaeology: Sustainable Meeting Grounds, edited by Cameron Walker and Neil Carr, 223–233. ©2013 Left Coast Press, Inc. All rights reserved.

Figure 13.1   San Juan Parangaricutiro Church buried in lava.

Phurépecha (western highlands), the *Comunidad Indígena of Nuevo Parangaricutiro* (CINSJP) is located about 200km west of Morelia.

This community is perhaps best known for the church tower located in old San Juan that still stands after the eruption of the Parícutin volcano (1943), which buried the town and its best agricultural lands (Luhr 1993). Thousands of national and international tourists visit the buried church (Figure 13.1) and Parícutin volcano every year; cultural and ecological tourism represent important sources of income not only for the CINSJP but for the neighboring community of Angahuan (Guerrero-Murillo 2000). The CINSJP reconstituted itself in 1981 to form the largest communal lumber industry in the Americas, basing its claim on the *Titulos Reales* granted by the King of Spain in 1715 (Gabany-Guerrero 1999).

While working with tribal councils has formed an ideal model for cultural heritage tourism and community archaeology in a variety of nation-state/indigenous nation contexts (Colwell-Chanthaphonh and Ferguson 2006; David, et al. 2004; Fawcett Jr. 2012; Ferguson 2001; Marshall 2002), engagement with complex civil-religious authorities in indigenous communities in Mexico has a somewhat more contested history. Perhaps because the federal authority over Mexican cultural heritage is so clear in the *Ley Federal de Monumentos* (*Poder Legislativo 1986*), the rights of the indigenous communities over cultural heritage resources are absolutely subsumed under the institution of the National Institute of Anthropology and History (INAH), which manages all excavations and museums. In 1993, INAH formed a partnership with the General Office of Popular Culture to develop a new program for community museums, but both funding and bureaucratic procedures have stymied the creation of more than a handful of community/government projects, such as the community museum program established in Oaxaca, Mexico (Erikson 1996). In addition, local participation in the educational aspects of archaeology has not been encouraged at primary or secondary schools outside of very specific urban exceptions (Mexico City, D. F.). This policy has left little space for local-level collaborative and cooperative engagement in archaeological research, cultural heritage preservation, and tourism.

The case study described here provides a new explanation for how indigenous community authority systems function in conjunction with (and sometimes parallel to but different from) the nation-state with respect to questions of cultural heritage management. We believe that by understanding how *usos y costumbres* (customary laws) are integrated with civil-religious hierarchies, new possibilities for collaboration are unveiled.

By opening up this discussion, of course, there may be cases where indigenous communities decide not to engage in collaborative relationships, based on their own historical experiences with "outsiders" and autonomous determination. Our comment on this is that regardless of the nation-state, the role of anthropologists and archaeologists must be to respect the particular indigenous community's role in determining how its heritage will be preserved. Remaining buried, hidden, and untouched are also ways of preserving the past that while not ideal for researchers, may do what is needed to retain sacred spaces in contested ground or circumstances. The White Mountain Apache model (Welch 2009) for cultural resource management is an excellent example of how policies were developed to serve the interests of the autochthonous nation, as well as to provide opportunities for research. Our suggestion is that adaptation of this model within the historical context of Mexican indigenous communities would be advantageous. The question is whether the Mexican nation-state and researchers (both national and international) are prepared for the adjustments that would impact long-standing practices.

Our research and field experience indicate that new policies, at the intersections of cultural heritage, archaeology, and tourism in Mexico would lead to a resurgence of interest in the multicultural heritage of Mexico, discourage looting, intercept the multinational underground trade in cultural heritage artifacts at the local level, encourage the establishment of local educational programs, promote local-shared control over cultural heritage through community museums, and fund local control over tourism.

Through our case study in the multicultural, but ancestrally dominant Phurépecha community of *Nuevo Parangaricutiro*, we examine specific practices by civil-religious authorities, which have defied the imposition of federal, imperial, and local authorities in order to preserve and protect their cultural heritage resources while generating more sources of income for the local community.[2]

Case Study

Mexico has a long trajectory of cultural heritage management issues from the Porfiriato's recognition of a "glorious indigenous past," while simultaneously demoralizing the indigenous present (Warman 1980), to *indigenista* strategies that attempt to modernize indigenous communities by deconstructing and reconstructing their leadership into acceptable modernist formulations (Aragón Andrade 2007; Díaz Polanco 2009). Each of these strategies intended the subordination of leadership to the nation-state through the eventual dismantling of indigenous leadership, albeit under different rationales. These complex relationships of domination are fraught with incomplete processes that are contested and reformulated within the contexts of specific historical moments.

Recent studies of *usos y costumbres* in Mexico (Kyle and Yaworsky 2008; Sierra 1995; Silva 2008) provide a venue for re-examining how power is articulated within communities and between indigenous community leadership and representatives of state authority (at local, state, and national levels). Overlapping power domains illustrate how customary law has coexisted with state law from colonial to contemporary periods. By examining cultural heritage within the context of customary law *and* civil-religious hierarchies – the "tortillas and beans" of 20th century anthropological studies in Mexico – (Carrasco 1961; Wolf 1956), this study integrates previous attempts to understand how indigenous communities function with contemporary cultural heritage studies. Here we conceptualize how Phurépecha leadership is crucial for understanding how cultural heritage is a vital part of understanding cultural identity within the specific context of history. Friedman (1992) emphasizes that those hegemonic processes within which people construct their identities are neither deterministic nor new, and that the human condition consists of social arenas in which variable power dynamics influence how identities are constructed.

If one is engaged in "negotiating culture," that is, involved in the construal and interpretation of ethnographic or historical realities, then one is bound on a collision course with others for whom such realities are definitive. Culture is supremely negotiable for professional culture experts, but for those whose identity depends upon a particular configuration, this is not the case. Identity is not negotiable. Otherwise it has no existence (Friedman 1992:140).

The *cabildo* is the culmination of the civil-religious hierarchy that implements customary law in this Phurépecha community.[3] Ritual activities and customary laws are managed by the Phurépecha *Comunidad Indígena Cabildo* (Franco Mendoza 1997), which was established as the ruling body when Spanish colonial rule was implemented in the region (estimated at 1520–1525). The *cabildo* officers were an official part of the Spanish religious-political rule in the *República de Indios*, in varying degrees depending on culture, geography, and historical context (Taylor 1996). The *cabildo* has resisted many state and religious institutional attempts at deconstruction in a multitude of indigenous communities (Bornemann 1999; Earle 2007; Kyle and Yaworsky 2008; Sierra 1995; Silva 2008).

In San Juan Parangaricutiro, Phurépecha officials of the pre-Hispanic Tarascan Empire appear to have been directly transferred into the Spanish civil-religious hierarchy of the *cabildo* (Gabany-Guerrero 1999). While noted in a few cases in Michoacán, Bornemann (1999:613) supports this interpretation in the case of Tepeaca (Central Mexico):

Todos los cargos de los oficiales de república estaban cubiertos por aquellos quienes ostentaron cargos de gobierno en la época prehispánica. [All of the appointments of the officials of the republic (Indian) were covered by those who held similar appointments under the Pre-Hispanic government. (Gabany-Guerrero, translation]

Even in the 21st century, two of the *cabildo* members are known by their Phurépecha titles in *Nuevo San Juan Parangaricutiro: quengue* (*mayordomo*-steward) and *carari* (*escribano*-scribe) (Gabany-Guerrero 1999). The *sacristán*, while not formally a member of the *cabildo*, forms a critical link among the Catholic priests, the *cabildo*, and the Phurépecha community. As a layperson, the *sacristán* was the legal caretaker of church property (as of 1681), and keys were one of the important symbols of his role (Taylor 1996:332–333). The respect shared between the *cabildo* and the *sacristán* provides a formidable relationship to protect the religious and cultural resources of the community. Jointly, the *cabildo* and *sacristán* hold legal rights to manage specific communally-held lands (such as the Hospital of the Virgin of the Nueva Concepción) that lie within the communal lands of the *Comunidad Indígena de Nuevo Parangaricutiro*, as well as moral authority over all the behavior of community members. Taylor (1996:326) noted the critical role of the *fiscal* (a member of the *cabildo*) in "corporal punishment for the *cura*" (priest) for matters beyond what would be considered the domain of the Roman Catholic Church. In these matters of cultural morality, we make the assumption that Phurépecha values were also included in the milieu of the *fiscal* role of enforcer.[4]

The Old Temple

Within the CINSJP, both ancient and new management structures operate. *Comunidad Indígena* elders categorize cultural heritage sites as sacred spaces that embody usufruct natural (agricultural and forestry) and cultural resource rights. Cultural heritage sites are part of the reproduction of belief systems that are curated by elders with specific responsibilities for conservation and consecrated (sacred) uses.

The cultural heritage site of *Templo Viejo* has remained under the custodial stewardship of the lineage of the *sacristán* for generations. As part of our field research, we asked about how long the *sacristán's* lineage had held usufruct rights over the communally owned parcels, but no one could remember. Sometimes communal lands are "bought and sold" within the community itself, but after consulting with the *Representante Comunal* first about permission to visit the property, and then with the *sacristán* because he controlled the usufruct rights, we found that this particular site was considered differently from a typical farming, orchard, or lumber property. The *sacristán* held the keys to the double-gated parcel, an unusual practice in what used to be open orchard and pasture land. Small mounds of rock-studded grass with mini-plots of blue corn (four stalks to a mound) pocketed the entrance to the parcel. We had asked permission from the *sacristán* to visit the cultural site to ask the question: Was this the site of a colonial period chapel, or was this site part of the Phurépecha Prehispanic heritage – or was it both?

Under the *sacristán's* supervision and the permission of INAH (the national agency responsible for archaeological research), the research team[5] entered this parcel as part of a general superficial survey of the zone near an established rock art heritage location (Gabany-Guerrero 2004). *Templo Viejo's* monumental architecture included a massive circular pyramid embedded in the edge of a natural mountainside, a possible sunken plaza with stone walls and a cave underpinning the cultural site. When research team members discussed these preliminary findings with the *sacristán*, he suggested to us and a member of the *cabildo* who accompanied us, that, "well, yes indeed, we did find stones with images on the faces and thought about what they might mean. But, someone came from *Mexico* [Mexico City] a long time ago, like forty years ago, and took the stones with images. We don't know who they were." [Gabany-Guerrero, translation of field interview]

In the ensuing years, the *sacristán* explained that he had decided to fence the property, for a number of reasons. A growing number of thieves who might steal avocados he had planted between the structures had made it necessary, he explained, and also because he "didn't want people just nosing around this place and there were a lot of 'new' people in town now." He invited the research team to return to stay in the cabin he had just built to do fieldwork and explained that he was happy to see that we also thought that this was an important place.

This experience with the *sacristán* illustrated what we had heard in field conversations in the Phurépecha highlands. Outsiders were known for entering sacred places and removing cultural heritage without engaging the elders or *Comunidad Indígena* in the process of studying their cultural heritage. Archaeologists, tourists, and private collectors had operated in a manner that was considered disrespectful to *cabildo* elders, communal property holders, and the *Comunidad Indígena* leadership. The devaluing of Phurépecha cultural heritage has permeated outsiders' views (Malmström 1995).

Fred, Wilma, and Bambam

The view from outside is also reflected in Catholic Church practices within the community of *Nuevo Parangaricutiro*. For approximately 52 years, one cura ruled over the town and its parishioners (Moheno 1985), taking them from the old town of San Juan Parangaricutiro to the establishment of the new settlement after the birth of the Paricutin volcano. When interviewed in 1993 (Gabany-Guerrero 1999), the cura discussed his personal and professional views about how the Phurépecha language had "dragged the community down" and how he saw it as his personal mission to "rid the *indios* of their language." This attitude was turned into practice by the redefinition of what it meant to be Phurépecha in *Nuevo San Juan Parangaricutiro*. Families of status (whether *mestizo* or Phurépecha) sent their children to the private Catholic school where speaking Phurépecha was not permitted. Rituals in the church were expressly prohibited from including Phurépecha terms. Phurépecha terms were permitted only at the hospital of the Virgen of the Concepción where *cabildo* members conducted their meetings in their native language.

The cura's transformation of the town was, in a sense, completed by the creation of a series of monumental gardens around the newly installed replica of the former church. The cura had visited Disneyland in the late 1960s and decided to create a Catholic and *michoacano* version of the park with the appropriate coin-operated religious music boxes beside each religious memento. The immaculately maintained gardens (by local gardeners) around the church were so successful in drawing patronage from both the tourists and the town that the cura decided to create an even greater attraction, a zoo. The zoo was constructed only a few blocks from the church on top of *mal país* from an ancient eruption. The zoo contained(s) among its treasured collection a lion, peacocks, eagles, local fauna, exotic birds, a llama, and a special exhibit of The Flintstones (Figure 13.2). Lifesize plaster

Figure 13.2   The Flintstone display at the *Nuevo Parangaricutiro* Zoo.

figures of Fred, Wilma, and Bambam were flanked by the culture of the *pica-piedras*, the stone-age people.

The pica-piedras display included large basalt stones, which formed the characteristic structures illustrated in the cartoon. The connection between the pica-piedras and Phurépecha cultural heritage was created by an event that was narrated by a *Phurépecha ejido* (landowner). When a superficial survey was conducted in the fields around the town, we interviewed the *ejiditario* regarding the history surrounding *El Cerrito de la Campana*. At this cultural heritage site, a twenty-meter-high round earthen mound rises out of a corn field. The *ejiditario* explained that a series of large flat basalt slabs (locally called *lajas*) were located at the base of the earthen mound. Not knowing what to do with the lajas, but understanding that they were important, he

Figure 13.3 The laja from a cultural heritage site cemented into the Flintstone display.

believed that they should be donated to the Church where he hoped that they would be preserved. The *ejiditario* stated that he was told by the cura that the only logical place for the lajas, because they belonged to the "previous people, the pica-piedras," was the zoo. He was instructed to take the lajas up to the Flintstones display in the zoo where they were cemented into the display (Figure 13.3).

The Phurépecha past was frozen in another time, not real or human time but a time relegated to cartoon characters that were hapless, kind of funny, not dangerous, but also not serious. Real history, Christian history, was brought to Michoacán by the Spaniards (Arbenz 1933). Other previous forms were no better than the pica-piedras that were displayed in the zoo.

The repercussions of repeatedly viewing ancestral cultural objects as caricatures in a cartoon has lasting effects. The Flintstones constantly suggest the silliness of past histories, and the necessity for a dismantling of Phurépecha heritage in order to create a new form of history that does not rely on Phurépecha language, symbolism, or metaphors to create identity. The principle form of resistance to the constant dismantling of a culture involves the civil-religious hierarchy that enforces customary law with respect to cultural heritage. The Flintstone case, as noted above, lies outside the domain of these practices because the zoo operated solely under the explicit authority of the cura. No appeal could be made, but it might be in the future of contested domains, where identity *is* non-negotiable.

Notes

1. Throughout Mexico, the name Phurépecha is now used to refer to the people given the misnomer of Tarasco/Tarascue during the colonial period. Several Mexican authors continue to use these terms only when referring to the pre-Hispanic or colonial period populations. The majority of academic authors in the US persist in using the term Tarascan, despite the disjuncture with contemporary Phurépecha communities. The discussion is not without contention as noted by Márquez Joaquín (2007).
2. Here we wish to acknowledge the collaborative work of the research team that includes Dr. Steven Hackenberger, Dr. Lisa Ely from Central Washington University, and Dr. James Chatters (AMECSPELL OUT), the successive *Representantes de Bienes Comunales de La Comunidad de San Juan Nuevo Parangaricutiro, El Cabildo de San Juan Nuevo Parangaricutiro, El Sacristán del Sanctuario del Señor de los Milagros, La Casa de la Cultura de Nuevo Parangaricutiro, Presidentes del Municipio de Nuevo Parangaricutiro, Ejiditarios de San Francisco Uruapan, El Consejo Nacional de Arqueología del Instituto Nacional de Antropología e Historia,* and the communal landholders who have graciously given permission for studies on their lands. In addition, the researchers would like to thank the graduate students who have contributed their time and energy to fieldwork and the primary and secondary school teachers of *Nuevo Parangaricutiro* for engaging their students by visiting the research sites and bringing the past into a discussion of what it means to be Phurépecha and San Juaneco. The authors are solely responsible for the interpretations made in this article.
3. In this case study, we are careful to acknowledge that the historical and ethnic experience of *San Juan Parangaricutiro and Nuevo San Juan Parangaricutiro* may not be generalizable for other Phurépecha Highland communities.
4. Understanding the complex relationships in the enforcement of cultural morality may also provide clues to how other organizations can asume these functions and integrate into the civil-religious hierarchy of contemporary Michoacán.
5. Here we include Dr. Steven Hackenberger and Dr. Lisa Ely.

Chapter 14

Conclusion: Manifesting Sustainable Meeting Grounds

Cameron Walker and Neil Carr

Why have we placed such an emphasis on establishing the foundations of a dialogue among the disciplines of archaeology and tourism? We are convinced that the sharing of ideas and data among disciplines will enhance our overall appreciation of any number of issues associated with archaeological tourism and improve our prospects for coming up with sustainable solutions for cultural, environmental, and preservation dilemmas. Among fierce competition for funding and public support, it is imperative to confirm archaeology's relevance for the past, present, and the future. We have placed emphasis on the concept of sustainability in order to emphasize how crucial we see this for the future of archaeology and archaeological tourism. In this final chapter, we distinguish some of the main themes that arise when archaeological sites are promoted for tourism, and we reflect on the variety of case-study discussions of particular aspects as they arise

Tourism and Archaeology: Sustainable Meeting Grounds, edited by Cameron Walker and Neil Carr, 235–251. ©2013 Left Coast Press, Inc. All rights reserved.

in real-world scenarios. Communication, cooperation, values, and timing are all at work here but there are also loftier, mutual goals to preserve, conserve, educate, entertain, and cooperate with local communities. Much is made of the necessity of incorporating the support of local communities, although the real world all too often falls short in achieving anything close to ideal.

Ask just about anyone who works within the disciplines of humanities and social science, including anthropology and tourism studies, and they will attest to the problems associated with communication between disciplines. Even if the jargon and specialized languages are shared, other key differences all too often get in the way of achieving mutual goals. This is certainly the case with archaeologists and tourism scholars who have approached the phenomenon of archaeological (and heritage) tourism. It may be that, until now, there have been so few conversations between archaeologists and tourism scholars because both are relatively young disciplines, with professional archaeology arriving just after World War II in the United States and the study of tourism emerging as a discipline in the 1960s.

Yet another reason for miscommunication, as discussed variously in the three conceptual chapters, may relate to the beginnings of the profession of academic archaeology as it emerged from an earlier tradition of (usually) elite treasure-hunters. Tourism studies grew out of travel encounters between elite Europeans and other peoples of different classes, ethnicities, worldviews, and lifestyles. Both disciplines have endeavored to rise above the legacies of ethnocentrism, treasure-hunting, and colonialism; but cultural attitudes are ever slow to change, and so the shadowy associations have tended to linger into the 21st century.

Shady Milieus and Colonialism

Even now, when most people think of archaeology, the adventurous images of Indiana Jones and Lara Croft are likely to come to mind, and today's professional archaeologists have been known to lament the persistent image of archaeologist-adventurer as their doppelganger. Images of colonialism occur to social scientists everywhere they look and can also be found within the pages of this book, with descriptions of Western archaeologists and tourists imposing their own colonialist brands, even if it is done in a less obvious way.

Scholars often search out specific approaches to study another culture, and these approaches are not inherently colonial. Yet, colonialist themes all too often emerge. Indeed, this very book manifests quite a few colonialist elements, not only in the preponderance of emphasis on North American and European sites, but also in the concentration of the authors' nationalities. Finding authors who could appropriately discuss the issues we felt were crucial proved to be more difficult than we would have predicted. For instance, most of the authors are native English speakers; communication was nevertheless complicated by the assorted scholarly approaches that predominate in England, Canada, the United States, Australia, and New Zealand. It seems that while some placed more weight on theory, others were more interested in the applied aspects and practical methodology. We were trying something new, and it was more problematic than we had anticipated in the approach, the emphasis, and the focus – all of it. Ideally, we might have covered case studies from all of the major continents and authored by scholars from many different nations, but ultimately, we had to rely upon people whose research areas fit well with the goals of this book and who were willing to take it on; this something that is an inherent hurdle for all edited work. Reliability is crucial for a successful collaborative project, and ultimately, we came to adopt a more fluid approach for this volume. Despite any and all perceived shortcomings, we are gratified and confident that our authors have produced a strong, multivocal discussion, which will pave the way for further dialogue in the future that can go beyond, while being based upon, this book.

A Bird's-Eye View of Archaeology

During the Age of Exploration in the 19th century, wealthy individuals, known as antiquarians, from Western Europe and the United States were the first to do the work that eventually became the profession of archaeology. For quite a while, a few wealthy explorers avidly collected antiquities and possessed both the intellectual proclivities and the bank accounts to personally finance their own expeditions. German millionaire Heinrich Schliemann epitomized the antiquarian when he discovered the legendary site of Troy at modern-day Hissarlik, Turkey. Yet another antiquarian, Englishman Arthur Evans, maintained a lifelong passion to unearth the palace of Knossos on the island of

Figure 14.1   Crowds waiting to see the throne room at Knossos.

Crete (Palyvou 2003; Scarre and Fagan 2003:17–18). (Figure 14.1)
These wealthy elites are called "premodern" by Castañeda, who has
expanded the category to include museums, curators, collectors,
colonial and governmental administrators, and collector-patrons who
had an end goal to appropriate and exploit "those nations, cultures,
and peoples located in peripheries subordinated within global geo-
politics."

With such an undisciplined, yet romantic back-story, it is no
wonder that the imagery of the dashing archaeologist persists in
the public imagination. This quixotic past is undeniably linked
to the looting of antiquities and tends to elicit a prickly, self-protective
response among modern archaeologists, especially in the United States.
It may be something that has been observed in the reactions of some
archaeologists to the site Vindolanda as mentioned in the case study
by Birley. It may also be that the prickliness is aroused by being compared to practitioners from almost a century ago. At the same time,
failing to engage more fully with an interested public has meant that,
in the past, archaeologists have tended to overlook the potential
advantages that come with an enthusiastic public audience. As the
prolific news stories, television documentaries, and adventure films

attest, the public maintains a keen interest in the human past and wants to learn more about it. And, as archaeologists come to realize the significant opportunities for financial and political support that accompanies an interested public, archaeological interpretation and preservation is gradually becoming more integrated into research strategies. While progress is being made in the field of CRM (Cultural Resource Management), or contract archaeology, in many regions of the United States, this distinction does not exist in many parts of the world. This book demonstrates that there is great potential for finding a meeting ground for shared interests, goals, and concerns, and that we would all benefit from continuing to have dialogues between archaeologists and tourism scholars.

All three conceptual chapters and each of the nine case studies verify that archaeological methods and objectives have become more stringent over time; nevertheless in the public imagination, adventurers remain in pursuit of the most elusive ancient mysteries. It is a colorful, exciting image that is perpetually reinforced in films and television, and it is not hard to see why the public might prefer a dashing Indiana Jones over a rumpled archaeologist. However, by adhering to strict ethical standards and loudly decrying any and all unprofessional attitudes and methodologies, archaeologists are also refuting perceived connections with that antiquarian past. It seems somewhat ironic then, when archaeologists themselves are occasionally accused of being elitist when the strident advocacy comes across as condescending to the public.

In the case of Sir Arthur Evans, his personal wealth allowed him to build fairly elaborate architectural reconstructions at Knossos on the island of Crete (Figure 14.2) (Palyvou 2003:221–229). Evans made known that the reconstructions were expressly meant for the tourists who were already arriving to see Knossos firsthand. Evans was certain that his reconstructions would assist the visitors' imaginations, who would be awed by the sophisticated grandeur of the earliest civilization in Europe. Evans' reconstructed architecture still sits among the excavated walls and floors of later Mycenaean, Greek, and Roman occupations, and as Evans had predicted, the reconstructions remain popular with tourists today.

Knossos is now something of an anachronism since reconstructions are generally reviled by archaeologists as acts of hubris all too reminiscent of colonialist times. The experience of Evans has, in some

Figure 14.2 Evans' architectural reconstruction at Knossos.

ways, been mirrored in the attempt by the Trust at Vindolanda to provide a partial reconstruction of a Roman fort, especially since the standards for consolidation/reconstruction are more clearly defined.

Today, visitors to Knossos are given very few details about the different periods of occupation, and too often they leave the site utterly misinformed about the Minoans and their palatial architecture. Even in the contested world of archaeological/heritage tourism, Knossos remains unique in that the reconstructions seem to more accurately reflect the late 18th through early 19th centuries British upper-class ideals of luxury and elegance than anything truly Minoan (Duke 2007; Palyvou 2003). In one vivid scenario written by Castañeda, Evans is imagined at work like a potter at his wheel, reshaping Knossos into his own idiosyncratic image. Likewise, Wallace and Hannam suggest that tour guides at Knossos are trained to establish a strong link between the Bronze Age Minoans and later Western civilizations in order to confirm a cultural primacy for the site and for Greece. Among Minoan scholars, however, this long-held Western point of view has been steadily eroding as more recent research reveals a much more complex and nuanced picture than was previously understood. Even so, as Wallace and Hannam correctly point out, it is very hard to redirect an interpretation once it has become ingrained in the popular literature, and it is especially difficult when the new understandings are antithetical or unflattering to the ingrained story that has been told for generations. At times, as with the archetypal Minoans, it takes a paradigm shift that is frustratingly tricky to achieve at anything quicker than a snail's pace.

Antiquarians, as wealthy tourists, were also associated with a singularly privileged style of tourism, the European Grand Tour, as the ultimate elite tourism experience from the late 1600s until the mid 1800s. However, antiquarians were also likely to travel to less hospitable locales in Africa, Latin America, and the Middle East where they often endured tremendous hardships brought on by disease, hostile locals, and perilous travel conditions. It could be dangerous, but if the quest succeeded, they became a part of history.

People were traveling much earlier than the Grand Tour, of course, and there are many notable instances where ancient travelers collected artifacts as souvenirs along the way. As one example, the Aztecs frequently traveled to the long-abandoned city of Teotihuacán (which they named as "the City Where the Gods Began"), at least in part to collect artifacts to bring back and place in the most sacred of Aztec temples at Tenochtitlan (Scarre and Fagan 2003:461). Antiquarians shared the penchant for removing artifacts from the spectacular ruins they explored, although at least a few antiquarians also took care to document their excavation work with field notes, illustrations, and photographs. As Castañeda reminds us, they also did tremendous damage to most of those archaeological sites for the dual purposes of museum collecting and making their mark on history. At a time when the primary objective was to find rare and precious artifacts and indulge in a bit of self-aggrandizement, antiquarian-adventurers certainly recognized the inherent value of the artifacts, if not with the sites themselves.

All too often, the local inhabitants could only watch as the remnants of their cultural heritage were whisked away to be placed in the museums of other, wealthier nations. Gradually, governments and local communities began to resist the plunder of their heritage by passing laws that required excavation permits, and directed where excavated artifacts were to be warehoused. Provenance, or the chain of custody record for an artifact, has steadily become more challenging as proprietary attitudes toward artifacts have been integrated into political, religious, and social causes. Late nineteenth-century American, Clarence B. Moore, exemplified the antiquarian approach by maintaining a paddle-wheel steamboat named Gopher, with a fully staffed crew and an onboard photography darkroom, for cruising the rivers of the southeastern United States in order to locate and excavate the sites of the Mississippian Mound Builders (Knight 1998; Milanich 2000; Pearson et al. 2000). After a while, however, local Alabama residents grew frustrated that Moore was shipping the artifacts back to the Peabody Museum at Harvard University; they worked for many years to enact laws and purchase the land around the site of Moundville in an effort to control who excavated there and ensure that the artifacts remained within the state of Alabama (Knight 1998; Milanich 2000; Pearson et al. 2000).

Heritage Struggles

The struggle for control over heritage is a theme shared by all of the case studies but may be most illustrative in Tate-Libby's description of an ongoing contemporary struggle on the island of Hawai'i between those who want to open up a *kīpuka* (an untouched oasis of vegetation in the middle of a lava flow) for tourism development and those who want to preserve it as a pristine example of Old Hawaiian culture. Now at an impasse, this particular piece of land signifies the Native Hawaiian ambition to control sites with cultural significance, including the burial grounds of their ancestors, but there is sure to be more debate in the future.

Another case study perspective, provided by Pinter, offers a clear-eyed and cautionary perspective on the somewhat different challenges for the small town of Springerville, Arizona. Managing the nearby Casa Malpais National Historic Landmark, unlike the beach at Punalu'u, is not vulnerable to developmental pressures because it is Arizona State Trust Land, and yet there are other calculations that have brought persistent challenges. In this scenario, Pinter points out that a small community will too often mistakenly assume that their resource will, by itself, attract substantial tourism business. All too often, this leads to a disappointing outcome, and Pinter suggests that it makes more sense for such a resource to be included as part of a regional tourism development plan, especially when the site is located well-off the popular tourism track. Pinter carefully lays out a number of factors to take into account, including: a discerning evaluation of a site as a tourism resource; identification of the key factors involved with preservation, interpretation, education, and sustainability; determination of the level of community engagement; and establishment of a wide range of partners.

In the case of Casa Malpais, the complex negotiation process involved numerous stakeholders, among them the archaeological community, state officials, Hopi and Zuni scholars and representatives, and those responsible for the economic goals of the region. With time and hard work, the town was able to create an integrated interpretive and education program featuring its own museum and visitor center, but it recognizes that changes and updates are inevitable to maintain public interest.

Cultural sensitivity vs. embeddedness, the chapter discussion between Tim Wallace and Kevin Hannam, has the potential to be a fairly divisive topic. In this case, however, it may be that the many-shared concerns of the two authors suggest a maturing academic awareness of the problems associated with introducing significant numbers of tourists to archaeological/heritage sites and neighboring communities. Oftentimes, the local communities are primarily indigenous, as illustrated by the dominant Maya presence in the region of Guatemala where Tim Wallace operates an annual ethnographic field school. Wallace and Hannam acknowledge that while archaeologists may be regarded as "interpreters-in-chief" of a site, they are also constrained to work within the sociopolitical environment of the region. These "constraints" oblige archaeologists and tourism officials to work together when the goal is to transform an archaeological site into a successful tourism destination.

Most archaeologists eventually move on to another project, leaving site management to an official agency of some sort, but responsible archaeologists will always attempt to disseminate the results of their work. Inevitably, archaeology is a destructive, expensive, time- and labor-intensive process that cannot be sustained indefinitely. The responsible pattern has been to excavate for a couple of years, then do study seasons for three to five years in order to analyze, interpret and publish the results of the previous excavation work. These publications are usually found in academic journals and books, which seldom reach an interested public unless the subject is something so unique or special that it attracts the attention of the popular media. Arguably, there are a mere handful of archaeologists who are able to attract media attention on a regular basis, but until recently, the indisputably prominent has been the media savvy Dr. Zahi Hawass, former Secretary General of the Supreme Council of Antiquities for Egypt. Now, that has all changed since the overthrow of Egypt's government during the "Arab Spring" movement, and the prominence of Dr. Hawass has dimmed in the uncertainty of the current political climate.

Social, economic, and political situations greatly influence how archaeological sites are maintained in a particular country, as demonstrated by the powerful descriptions of the fate of many of the sites of Great Zimbabwe by Ancila Nhamo. What was once a thriving domestic tourism business became disrupted by economic and political instability. Tourism officials became convinced that tourists were more interested in the wildlife safaris than in the Zimbabwe ruins, so they failed to protect them, and many were destroyed over the years.

Social and political changes are also depicted in the case study by Ming-chun Ku, who discusses the prominent World Heritage Site of the Mogao Caves. Despite the rise of Chinese communism, these caves have been maintained as important cultural heritage attractions, even though any explicit worship of the Buddha images in the caves is discouraged.

The vast majority of the world's professional archaeologists have little or no training in marketing their research; and in fact, there is an assumption that popularizing an archaeological site actually diminishes its scientific validity. This is demonstrated in the case study of Vindolanda by Birley, and is a pattern also found in the broader world of anthropology where popularizing research may also diminish its academic merit. Conversely, the political, economic, and social benefits that derive from public interest have only recently been recognized, but if the public identifies with the social and informational value of an archaeological site, then they are more likely to support maintaining the site. This is an issue that is at the heart of the debate by Castañeda.

The pressure of public scrutiny has the potential to induce politicians and government agencies to do the things that will sustain a site, even if it is only as an economic resource.

Sometimes these efforts go awry, as related in the case study of the Phurépecha in the Mexican state of Michoacan. Random efforts to relate the stone-age occupants of the region to the Flintstones cartoon may seem odd, but there is also an implicit attitude that tourists are not as interested in this indigenous society as they are in others in Mexico, such as the Maya.

To convey the cultural components that determine a site's significance, Wallace and Hannam use the term, embeddedness, while suggesting that in order to maintain their credibility, archaeologists are compelled to incorporate the embedded values of nearby communities. Arguably, this realization may be gaining ground among anthropologists, archaeologists, and local communities; although, Wallace and Hannam contend that the tourism industry has long sought to understand both the culture of tourists and the tourism culture itself for somewhat different reasons. The authors might be hard pressed to corroborate the strength of this claim, since tourism development has always been based upon the principles of capitalism, which makes it questionable whether much meaningful attention is ever paid to the culture of locals, for example. Certainly, there are archaeologists who continue to ignore the values embedded within local communities, but they do so at their own political peril in today's fast-changing world.

Interpretation and Entertainment

It is increasingly common for local, often indigenous, communities to participate in ceremonies with dancing and singing when tourists are present. Sometimes the ceremonies are performed by and for the locals themselves, in spite of the presence of tourists, but more often, the ceremonies have become part of a program that is performed by the locals specifically for tourists. On such occasions, the more sanguine view is that tourism helps to promote cultural continuity by encouraging locals to maintain ceremonial traditions, especially the ones that tourists find most appealing. A more cynical contention is that staging ceremonies for entertainment purposes forever distorts their cultural meanings and changes them in unpredictable ways (see Smith [1989] and Smith and Brent [2001] for a more detailed discussion of these interpretations of the impacts of tourism on culture).

From an anthropological perspective, culture is continually changing, so the question then becomes: who is instigating the culture change, and is the impetus for change coming from within, or has it been imposed from outside the culture?

Tourism's influence on cultural traditions was also discussed by Hughes, Little, and Ballantyne in their dialogue on the perceptions of visitors about the authenticity of performances staged primarily for tourism. This subject has been broached by other scholars in some interesting ways, notably by Edward Bruner (2004) for instance, who briefly served as a tour guide to investigate how the Balinese and other Indonesians respond to tourism. He concluded that while the Balinese perform some of their dances solely for tourists, their artistic flourishes often show up later as new forms of cultural expression. In this way, the dances (or ceremonies) are created or adapted for tourism purposes but are eventually absorbed and sustained as new cultural traditions. This process speaks to the discussion by Castañeda about the inheritance of the past, but Bruner also noted that tourists were not all that concerned about whether or not a dance was authentic (in the anthropological sense) or was created out of an already established cultural tradition. What they wanted was to be entertained.

Hughes, Little, and Ballantyne raise some compelling questions about whether tourists expect or even recognize a high degree of authenticity while they are being entertained. Alternatively, it might just as well be asked: are they more entertained by highly authentic experiences? Ultimately, the authors question whether entertainment and authenticity can ever be mutually compatible, which is a question rich with promising possibilities for future research.

Public Interpretation of Archaeology

Hughes, Little, and Ballantyne engaged in an exchange of ideas about how to appropriately define education, and in particular, the qualities necessary for educating visitors at archaeological sites. Archaeologists, at least in the United States, tend to prefer the term "interpretation," in part because it conveys a point of view that has been decided in advance. Ordinarily, public interpretation tells a story set in a specific time and place, and it relies on a script that has been sanctioned by the academic or political ruling elite. As such, is situated within the intricate discussion of interpellation by Castañeda. In the United States, interpretation draws from contemporary political, economic, and social forces, including those of political correctness, which has resulted in a diminished influence for archaeologists. As other voices, such as Native American and special interest groups gain power, more archaeologists have had to turn to the subjects of interpretation, preservation, and sustainability as worthy research topics.

Archaeologists have tended to see their roles as translators between the past and the present, or "between different perspectives of the past and between the specific and the general" (Hodder 1991:15). For the most part, archaeologists now realize the need to add other voices to the mix, such as the voices of local descendants, when deciding how the story of a site or artifact is told to the public. Accordingly, public interpretation has become a more prominent undertaking in the archaeologist's portfolio.

But telling a story and telling a story well are not necessarily the same thing, and a story must compellingly relate the human experience. The writing skills required for an academic journal are somewhat different from publications with popular appeal, and this makes it somewhat easier to understand how archaeologists, tourism scholars, and members of the tourism industry might assign different values to a project that popularizes archaeology.

As an archaeologist with extensive applied and academic experience, Scott Hamilton describes his case study as a marriage of convenience. Beginning with a frank confession that he once thought of cultural or heritage tourism as secondary to the demands of his "real" research, he learned otherwise after he excavated the historical site of Red Rock House prior to a planned waterfront redevelopment for tourism. Hamilton describes his realization that the project was not all that effective in making many long-term contributions to heritage tourism, leading him to ask an essential question: is it ever enough to excavate (in itself a destructive process) a nonrenewable resource solely for tourism purposes? It is likely that most archaeologists and tourism scholars would answer this question with a resounding "no," but what about tourism developers? Does an archaeological site have inherent value because it is there, or is value assigned according to its perceived importance to some other situation or context?

For Hamilton, not only is tourism primarily an elite activity, but archaeological tourism persists as a form of entertainment. Yet without this entertainment, as noted by Castañeda, people will not visit or buy into the value of archaeology and the preservation of archaeological remains. Both realities are something that archaeologists, tourism venues, and public interpretation experts would do well to ponder when designing presentations about the past.

The Study of Tourism

As a legitimate study area, tourism has been steadily gaining ground, despite lingering biases in academia. Likewise, the subject of interpretive archaeology for the public has been steadily gaining an academic foothold within the field of archaeology, as demonstrated by the prominence of the Society for American Archaeology's Public Education Committee. A practical-minded Philip Kohl has pointed out that archaeologists might as well study public interpretation since they will inevitably become embroiled in marketing tourism anyway (2004:295).

Overall, tourism officials and site managers rather than archaeologists will be the ones who determine which stories are told about an archaeological site, at least in part because they may be better at marketing a site for commercial purposes. Effectively exposing the public to archaeological research is something of an art form in that some stories will be exaggerated while others will be omitted altogether, especially when they conflict with an officially established narrative. How this is done is in itself a contentious issue, as noted by Castañeda. Increasingly, more than one interpretation may be required at archaeological sites, especially where particularly momentous or controversial events once occurred (Little 2004).

The story of the Alamo in San Antonio, Texas, was briefly described by Wallace and Hannam as a historical example for how the roles of celebrated American heroes are featured most prominently in Alamo docent presentations. Typically, the perspective of the Mexican side of the conflict is not included in tour-guide spiels, even though their story is also quite compelling, and Hispanics now make up the majority of the local population in the San Antonio area (Walker 2008). The subject of slavery is played down since the Mexicans were fighting to end slavery and the American Alamo "heroes" wanted to preserve it. Even if history is indeed written by the victors, Wallace and Hannam suggest that the dominant story will be rewritten time and again to convey the current values of power, class, ethnicity, and gender.

Strategies that Encourage Sustainable Tourism

A highly successful model for sustainable tourism planning is found in two different perspectives regarding the management of the World Heritage Site of Hadrian's Wall in England. Hadrian's Wall became a tourist attraction at least 500 years ago and has drawn visitors ever since. A key tool for maintaining public enthusiasm means regularly publicizing new finds and issuing special alerts to the media whenever spectacular finds (as defined by the media and general public rather than necessarily by archaeologists) are unearthed. Ever since Hadrian's Wall was listed as a World Heritage Site in 1987, the Vindolanda Trust has served as one of the site's overseers. A primary goal of the Trust is to continually refine their approach to design a sustainable tourism program, although Birley tellingly wonders whether tourism will ultimately end up saving or destroying the site. A very different perspective has been presented by Ku in her discussion of the Mogao Caves in China.

In choosing the locations for case studies, coeditor Neil Carr persuasively argued for including two separate perspectives of such a singular and extensive site, resulting in a second case study by Warnaby, Bennison, and Medway. The marketing of Hadrian's Wall expressly pronounces it the greatest Roman structure in all of Britain, and indeed the monument entails a complex construction of forts, gates, and turrets distributed across 70 miles. Since May, 2006, the site has been administered by the Hadrian's Wall Heritage Limited (HWHL), which oversees capital improvements to areas that will enhance the visitor experience and generate income locally. The authors stress that interpretation and access are important factors for providing a successful visitor experience as are sustainable programs. For these reasons, HWHL initially focused on improving local bus services to and from the site, and promoting the Hadrian's Wall National Trail for visitors to explore as part of a walking or cycling holiday. Hadrian's Wall exemplifies a particularly laudable effort to establish and maintain a number of sustainable meeting grounds for the interests of archaeology and the interests of tourism.

The interaction between archaeologists and visitors may be highly variable; as witnessed by Emilie Sibbesson's sharing of her archaeological perspective about the medieval castle and surrounding buildings of Dilston. Sibbesson suggests that local interest was initially stimulated by a certain fascination with the Jacobean Radcliffe family who once lived there but that the public is also intrigued by any archaeological research they might come across. Eventually, excavators recognized they needed a strategy for the time-consuming but rewarding site tours for the crowds who visited the site. After the excavation work came to an end, the crowds stopped coming, so researchers began to tackle restoration work on the castle and plan for the future, which included the design for a more formal site interpretation program. As such, this case study and the Vindolanda one by Birley encapsulates the need for sustainability of both tourism and archaeology at a site in a way that is mutually beneficial.

As these chapter discussions and case studies confirm, even the best of intentions and the highest levels of planning do not guarantee a successful transformation of an archaeological site into a tourism destination. Geographic location, local enthusiasm, and other factors addressed in the case studies only allow for a certain degree of adaptation.

Final Thoughts

The goal of this edited volume was to initiate an interdisciplinary conversation about some of the most controversial topics challenge the fields of tourism and archaeology. To begin building a bridge between the parallel worlds of archaeology and tourism studies, we brought together a group of representative authors from each discipline to participate in an exchange of ideas. Unfortunately, timing and logistics have required putting this volume together with the cooperation of scholars whose research was such that they could fully participate in a timely manner and meant that we were not able to adequately address preferences for greater geographic and ethnic diversity.

A predominance of sites in the English-speaking world is regrettable but it is hoped that more such cross-disciplinary discussions will emerge in the literature because academics of both archaeology and tourism studies need to communicate more fully about the many shared goals and issues. As such, it must be stressed that this book should be read as a beginning of a dialogue that facilitates a greater understanding of the intersections of tourism and archaeology rather than as an end in itself.

There is potential for finding effective solutions for the numerous socioeconomic and environmental problems related to archaeological tourism. Human beings have long demonstrated a tremendous capacity for innovation and problem-solving, and we have the potential to effectively repair, or at least mitigate, damage from tourism and/ or archaeology through a common purpose. Archaeological sites are non-renewable resources, while tourism seems destined to continually expand, at least within the context of the contemporary oil-fueled industrialized world. The ability to continually attract visitors to archaeological sites should not be taken for granted as effectively demonstrated by Nhamo's discussion of Great Zimbabwe and Gabany-Guerrero's experience with the Phurépecha of Michoacan.

As we come to identify the many meeting grounds of shared concerns and purposes, we (i.e., archaeologists, tourism scholars, and officials of the tourism industry) must build on the tools necessary to make archaeological tourism much more sustainable, especially since it will likely take all the shared knowledge we can muster to be successful. This effort requires that everyone talk to one another (rather than at one another) and engage all stakeholders in a sustainable venture that goes beyond the narrowly defined boundaries of tourism or archaeology and recognizes the broader geographical, social, cultural, and economic positions that encompasses both.

References

Abbink, J. G. 2004 Tourism and Its Discontents: Suri-Tourist Encounters in Ethiopia. In Tourists and Tourism, S. Gmelch, ed. Pp. 267–288. Long Grove, IL: Waveland Press.

ACHP [United States Advisory Council on Historic Preservation] N.d. Policy Statement: Archaeology, Heritage Tourism, and Education. Released August 15, 2008. http://www.achp.gov/ArchPolicy.pdf.

AIA [Archaeological Institute of America, Archaeology Magazine, and the Adventure Travel Trade Association] N.d. A Guide to Best Practices for Archaeological Tourism. accessed August 8, 2013. http://www.archaeological.org/webinfo.php?page=10482.

Alberge, D. 2005 New Enemy Menaces Hadrian's Wall. The Times, April 11, p. 3.

Alter, R. 1973 The Masada Complex. Commentary, 56(1):9–54.

Althusser, L. 2009 Reflections on an Archaeological Ethnography of "Looting" in Kozani, Greece, Archaeological Ethnographies, Y. Hamilakis and A. Anagnostopoulos, eds. Public Archaeology, vol. 8, nos. 2–3.

Althusser, L., ed. 1971 Ideology and Ideological State Apparatuses. Lenin and Philosophy and Other Essays, Pp. 127–186. London: New Left Books.

Anderson, B. 2001 Imagined Communities, Revised and Extended Edition. London: Verso.

Antoniadou, I. 2009 Reflections on an Archaeological Ethnography of "Looting" in Kozani, Greece. Archaeological Ethnographies, Y. Hamilakis and A. Anagnostopoulos, eds. Public Archaeology, vol. 8, nos. 2–3.

Appadurai, A. 1981 The Past as a Scarce Resource. Man (N.S.) 16(2):201–219.

Aragón Andrade, O. 2007 Indigenismo, movimientos y derechos indígenas en México:La reforma del artículo cuarto Constitucional de 1992. Morelia, Michoacán, México: División de Estudios de Posgrado de la Facultad de Derecho y Ciencias Sociales: Instituto de Investigaciones Históricas: Universidad Michoacana de San Nicolás de Hidalgo.

Arbenz, C. 1933 Die Adjektive auf -imos, ein Beitragf zur griechischen Wortbildung. Tubingen: Druck von H. Laupp, Jr.

Archaeological Institute of America Sustainable Preservation Initiative. Accessed June, 2012. http://www.archaeological.org/ sitepreservation/spi.

Ardren, T. 2004 Where are the Maya in Ancient Maya Archaeological Tourism? Advertising and the Appropriation of Culture. In Marketing Heritage: Archaeology and Consumption of the Past, Y. Rowan and U. Baram, eds. Pp. 103–113. Walnut Creek, CA: AltaMira Press.

_____ 2002 Conversations about the Production of Archaeological Knowledge and Community Museums at Chunchucmil and Kochol, Yucatán, México. World Archaeology, vol.1 34(2):379–400.

Arizona Archaeological Society N.d. Arizona Archaeology Advisory Commission. Accessed December, 2008. http://www.azarchsoc. org/index.html.

_____ 1997 Presenting the Past to the Public: Guidelines for the Development of Archaeological Parks in Arizona. Arizona State Parks Board. Phoenix: Arizona State Land Department.

_____1995 Certificate of Purchase No. 53–99454, Exhibit A, Additional Conditions. Phoenix: Arizona State Land Department.

Arthurs, D. N.d. The Rediscovery of Red Rock House A 19th Century Fur Trade Post in Northern Ontario. Unpublished MS. Thunder Bay: Ontario Ministry of Citizenship and Culture.

Ashworth, G. 2011 Preservation, Conservation and Heritage: Approaches to the Past in the Present through the Built Environment. Asian Anthropology 10:1–102.

_____ 1997 Conservation as Preservation or as Heritage. Built Environment 23(2):92–102.

REFERENCES

ASI 2004 Archaeological Survey of India, Activities. Ministry of Tourism and Culture, New Delhi. Accessed March 4, 2004. http://asi.nic.in/activities.html.

Atalay, S. 2010 We Don't Talk About Catalhoyuk, We Live It: Sustainable Archaeological Practice Through Community-based Participatory Research. World Archaeology 42(2):418–429.

Austen, P. and C. Young 2002 Hadrian's Wall World Heritage Site Management Plan 2002–2007. Hadrian's Wall World Heritage Site Management Plan Committee. Hexham: English Heritage on Behalf of Hadrian's Wall World Heritage Site Management Plan Committee.

Austen, P. and C. Young 2002 Hadrian's Wall World Heritage Site Management Plan 2002–2007. Hadrian's Wall World, Hexham: Heritage Site Management Plan Committee (for English Heritage).

Bakhtin, M. 1981 Discourse in the Novel. In The Dialogic Imagination, M. Holquist, ed. Austin: University of Texas Press.

Ballantyne, R., A. Crabtree, S. Ham, K. Hughes, and B. Weiler 2000 Tour Guiding: Developing Effective Communication and Interpretation Techniques. Brisbane: Queensland University of Technology.

Ballantyne, R., J. Packer, and K. Hughes 2008 Environmental Awareness, Interests and Motives of Botanic Gardens Visitors: Implications for Interpretive Practice. Tourism Management 29(3):439–444.

Ballantyne, R., J. Packer, K. Hughes, and L. Dierking 2007 Conservation Learning in Wildlife Tourism Settings: Lessons from Research in Zoos and Aquariums. Environmental Education Research 13(3):367–383.

Barrera, Jr., W. and R. Hommon 1972 Salvage Archaeology at Wailauninole, Ka'u, Hawai'i. Report (72)1. Honolulu: Department of Anthropology, Bishop Museum.

Baudrillard, J. 1995 Simulacra and Simulation. Ann Arbor: University of Michigan Press.

——— 1989 America. London: Verso.

Bawaya, M. 2005 Maya Archaeologists Turn to the Living to Help Save the Dead. Science 309(5739):1317–1318.

Beckwith, M. 1940 Hawaiian Mythology. New Haven: Yale University Press.

Beeho, A. and R. Prentice 1997 Conceptualizing the Experiences of Heritage Tourists: A Case Study of New Lanark World Heritage Village. Tourism Management 18(2):75–87.

Ben-Yehuda, N. 2002 Sacrificing Truth: Archaeology and the Myth of Masada. Amherst: Prometheus/Humanity Books.

_____ 1995 The Masada Myth: Collective Memory and Myth-making in Israel. Madison: University of Wisconsin Press.

Benjamin, W. 1968 The Work of Art in the Age of Mechanical Reproduction. In Illuminations, Arendt Hannah ed. Harry Zohn trans. Pp. 217–251. New York: Harcourt Brace and Jovanovich.

Bennett, T. 1995 Birth of the Museum. London: Routledge.

Bent, J. 1892 The Ruins of Mashonaland, and Explorations in the Country. Proceedings of the Royal Geographical Society and Monthly Record of Geography, vol. 14, no. 5, Pp. 273–298.

_____ 1802 The Ruined Cities of Mashonaland: Being a Record of Excavation and Exploration in 1891. London: Longmans, Green and Co.

Berger, D. 2006 The Development of Mexico's Tourism Industry Pyramids by Day, Martinis by Night. New York: Palgrave MacMillan.

Berlyne 1962 New Directions in Motivation Theory. In *Anthropology and Human Behavior*, T. Gladwin and W. C. Sturtevant, eds. Pp. 150–173. Washington DC: Anthropological Society of Washington.

Bernhard, F. 1971 Karl Mauch: African Explorer. Cape Town: Struik.

Bernstein, B. 1992 Collaborative Strategies for the Preservation of North American Indian Material Culture. Journal of the American Institute for Conservation 31(1):23–29.

Betancourt, P. 2002 Who Was in Charge of the Palaces? In Monuments of Minos Rethinking the Minoan Palaces, J. Driesen, I. Schoep, and R. Laffineur, eds. Aegeum 23, Annales d'Archeologie Egeenne de l'Universite de Liege et UT-PASSAP.

Bidwell, P. 1999 Hadrian's Wall 1989–1999. In The Cumberland and Westmorland Antiquarian and Archaeological Society and the Society of Antiquaries of Newcastle upon Tyne, Carlisle.

Binks, G., J. Dykes, and P. Dagnall 1988 Visitors Welcome: A Manual on the Presentation and Interpretation of Archaeological Excavations. London: English Heritage: HMSO.

Birley, E. 1961 Research on Hadrian's Wall. Kendal.

Birley, A. and Blake, J. 2007. *Vindolanda Excavations 2005–2006*. Vindolanda Trust Publications: Bardon Mill.

Birley, R. 1998 The Fort at the Rock: Magna and Carvoran on Hadrian's Wall. Haltwhistle: Roman Army Museum Publications.

———— 1995 The Making of Modern Vindolanda: The Life and Work of Anthony Hedley 1777–1835. Haltwhistle: Roman Army Museum Publications.

———— 1977 Vindolanda, a Roman Frontier Post on Hadrian's Wall. London: Thames & Hudson.

Bok, D. 2004 Universities in the Marketplace. Princeton: Princeton University Press.

Bonyongwa, R. 2011 Rock Art Tourism in Zimbabwe: Challenges and Possibilities. M.A. thesis, History Department, University of Zimbabwe.

Bornemann, M. 1999 El Gobierno de Los Indios en La Nueva España, Siglo XVI. Señores o Cabildos. Revista de Indias 59(217): 599–617.

Boswell, R. and D. O'Kane 2011 Introduction: Heritage Management and Tourism in Africa. Journal of Contemporary African Studies, 29(4):361–369.

Breathnach, T. (2006) Looking for the real me: Locating the self in heritage tourism. Journal of Heritage Tourism, 1(2): 100–120.

Breeze, D. and B. Dobson 2000 Hadrian's Wall, 4th edition. London: Penguin Books.

Breglia, L. 2006 Monumental Ambivalence. Austin: University of Texas Press.

Brink, J. 2008 Imagining Head-Smashed-In: Aboriginal Buffalo Hunting on the Northern Plains. Edmonton: Athabasca University Press.

British Archaeology 2005 New Body to Promote Endangered Roman Wall. British Archaeology, vol. 82, May/June. Accessed January 8, 2005. http://www/britarch.ac.uk/ba/ba82/news.shtml.

Brodie, N. 2001 Illicit Antiquities. London: Routledge.

Brodie, N., M. Morag, C. Luke, and K. Tubb, eds. 2006 Archaeology, Cultural Heritage, and the Antiquities Trade. Gainesville: University Press of Florida.

Broodbank, C. 2004 Minoanization. Proceedings of the Cambridge Philological Society 50:46–91.

Bruce, J. 1867 The Roman Wall, 3rd edition. London.

Bruner, E. 2005 Culture on Tour: Ethnographies of Travel. Chicago: University of Chicago Press.

Bruner, E. 2004 Tourism in a Balinese Borderzone. In Tourists and Tourism, S. Gmelch, ed. Pp. 127–156. Long Grove, IL: Waveland Press.

Bruner, E. and P. Gorfain 2005 (1984) Dialogic Narration and the Paradoxes of Masada. In Culture on Tour: Ethnographies of Travel, E. Bruner, ed. Pp.169–188. Chicago: University of Chicago Press.

Buckland, A. 1891 Ruins in South Central Africa. Living Age 190: 62–64.

Buntinx, G. and I. Karp 2007 Museum Frictions. Durham: Duke University Press.

Burke, E. E., ed. 1969 The Journals of Carl Mauch His Travels in the Transvaal and Rhodesia 1869–1872. Salisbury: National Archives of Rhodesia.

Burke, R., ed. 2006 Work Hours and Work Addiction. In Research Companion to Working Time and Work Addiction, Pp. 3–35. Cheltenham: Edward Elgar.

Camarena, C. and T. Morales 2007 Community Museums and Global Connections: The Union of Community Museums of Oaxaca. In Museum Frictions: Public Cultures/Global Transformations, G. Buntinx, G. Rassool, C. Kratz, L. Szwaja, T. Ybarra-Frausto, B. Kirshenblatt-Gimblett, and I. Karp, eds. Pp. 322–346. Durham: Duke University Press.

Camden, W. 1722 Britannia, E. Gibson, ed. London.

Campbell, M. 1988 The Witness and the Other World. Ithaca: Cornell University Press.

Campbell, S. 1976 Fort William: Living and Working at the Post. Fort William Archaeological Project, Ontario. Toronto: Ministry of Culture and Recreation.

Carrasco, P. 1961 The Civil-Religious Hierarchy in Mesoamerican Communities: Pre-Spanish Background and Colonial Development. American Anthropologist 63(3):483–497.

Castañeda, Q. E. N.d. Situating Activism in Archaeology: The Activist Imperative, Soul-Loss and "Making History." In Trans-forming Archaeology, Sonya Atalay, Lee Rains Clauss, Randall H. McGuire, and John R. Welch, eds. Walnut Creek, California: Left Coast Press, in press.

Castañeda, Q. E. 2012 The Neo-Liberal Imperative of Tourism: Rights and Legitimization in the UNWTO Global Code of Ethics. Practicing Anthropology, 34(3):47–51.

———— 2010 Constructing the Past, Making History. The Imperative for Ethnographic Archaeology. Paper presented at the Annual Meeting of the Society for American Archaeology, St. Louis, April 10.

———— 2009a Conjunctivitis: Notes on Historical Ethnography, Paradigms, and Social Contexts of Archaeology. In Prophet, Pariah, and Pioneer: Walter W. Taylor and American Archaeology, A. Maca, J. Reyman, and W. Folan, eds. Pp. 333–356. Boulder: University Press of Colorado.

———— 2009b Heritage and Indigeneity. In Cultural Tourism in Latin America, M. Baud and A. Ypeji, eds. Pp. 263–296. Leiden and Boston: Brill.

———— 2009c Notes on the Work of Heritage in the Age of Archaeological Reproduction. In Archaeologies and Ethnographies, L. Mortensen and J. Hollowell, eds. Pp. 109–119. Gainesville: University Press of Florida.

———— 2009d The "Past" as Transcultural Space: Using Ethnographic Installation in the Study of Archaeology. Yannis Hamilakis and Aris Anagnostopoulos, guest editors, special double issue of Public Archaeology 8(2–3):262–282.

———— 2008 The "Ethnographic Turn" in Archaeology: Research Positioning and Reflexivity in Ethnographic Archaeologies. In Ethnographic Archaeologies: Reflections on Stakeholders and Archaeological Practices, Q. E. Castañeda and C. Matthews, eds. Pp. 25–62. Lanham, MD: AltaMira Press.

———— 2006 Ethnography in the Forest: An Analysis of Ethics in the Morality of Anthropology. Cultural Anthropology 21(1):121–145.

———— 2004 "We Are Not Indigenous!" An Introduction to the Maya Identity of Yucatán. The Journal of Latin American Anthropology 9(1):36–63.

Castañeda, Q. E. 2003 Stocking's Historiography of Influence: Boas, Gamio, and Redfield at the Cross "Road to Light." Critique of Anthro-pology 23(3):235–262.

Castañeda, Q. E. 1997 On the Correct Training of Indios in the Handcraft Market at Chichen Itzá: Tactics, Tactility of Gender, Class, Race and State. Journal of Latin American Anthropology 2(2):106–143.

_____ 1996 In the Museum of Maya Culture: Touring Chichén Itzá. Minneapolis: University of Minnesota Press.

Castañeda, Q. E. and C. N. Matthews 2008 Ethnography and the Social Construction of Archaeology. In Ethnographic Archaeo-logies, Q. E. Castañeda and C. N. Matthews, eds. Pp. 1–24. Lanham, MD: AltaMira Press.

Castillo Cocom, J. A. 2002 Privilege and Ethics in Archeology. Paper. "Towards a More Ethical Mayanist Archaeology." M. Cohodas et al., organizers. Held at University of British Columbia, Vancouver.

Castillo Cocom, J. A. and Q. E. Castañeda, eds. 2004 Estrategias Identitarias. SEP, UPN, and Merida: OSEA.

_____ 2002 Deciphering the Archaeology Glyph: The Experience is Fiction. Paper Presented at the American Anthropology Association Meetings, New Orleans, November 22.

Castillo Cocom, J., and Q. E. Castañeda, eds. 2008 The "Past" as Transcultural Space: Using Ethnographic Installation in the Study of Archaeology. Public Archaeology 8(2–3):262–282

_____ 2004 Estrategias Identitarias. SEP, UPN, and Merida: OSEA.

_____ 2002 Deciphering the Archaeology Glyph: The Experience is Fiction. Paper Presented at the American Anthropology Association Meetings, New Orleans, November 22.

Center for Desert Archaeology N.d. About the Center. Electronic Document. Accessed January, 2009. http://www.cdarc.org/pages/who/.

_____ 2008a Celebrate! Preservation Archaeology News, Spring 2008.

_____ 2008b Draft Feasibility Study for the Little Colorado River Valley National Heritage Area. Tucson: Center for Desert Archaeology.

Center for Desert Archaeology 2005 Feasibility Study for the Santa Cruz River Valley National Heritage Area. Center for Tucson: Center for Desert Archaeology.

Chakanyuka, C. 2007 Implications of "Fast Track" Land Resettlement Programme on Cultural Heritage in Zimbabwe. M.A. thesis, History Department, University of Zimbabwe.

Chambers, E. 2006 Heritage Matters: Heritage, Culture, History, and Chesapeake Bay. College Park, MD: Maryland Sea Grant Program.

———— 2000 Native Tours: The Anthropology of Travel and Tourism. Prospect Heights, IL: Waveland Press.

Caton-Thompson, G. 1931 The Zimbabwe Culture: Ruins and Reactions. Oxford: Clarendon Press.

Chang, S. 1999 JiuShiChunQiu – DunHuangWuShiNian (Ninety Springs and Autumns – Fifty Years in Dunhuang). Lanzhou: Gansu Culture.

Chauke, C. 2003 Community Participation in Heritage Management. M.A. thesis, History Department, University of Zimbabwe.

Chhabra, D. 2007 Exploring Market Influences on Curator Perceptions of Authenticity. Journal of Heritage Tourism 2(2):110–119.

Chhabra, D., R. Healy, and E. Sills 2003 Staged Authenticity and Heritage Tourism. Annals of Tourism Research 30(3):702–719.

Ching, L. and Stephens, R. 1994. Powerstones: Letters to a Goddess. self published.

Chipunza, K. 2005 Protection of Immovable Culture Heritage in Zimbabwe: An Evaluation. In Legal Frameworks for the Protection of Immovable Cultural Heritage in Africa, W. Ndoro and G. Pwiti, eds. Pp. 42–45. Rome: ICCROM.

Chirikure, S., M. Manyanga, W. Ndoro, and G. Pwiti 2010 Unfulfilled Promises: Community Participation at Some of Africa's World Heritage Sites. International Journal of Heritage Studies 16(1–2):30–44.

Chirikure, S. and G. Pwiti 2008 Community Involvement in Archaeology and Cultural Heritage Management: An Assessment from Case Studies in Southern Africa and Elsewhere. Current Anthropology 49(3):467–484.

Chiwaura, H. 2005 The Development of Formal Legislation and the Recognition of Traditional Customary Law in Zimbabwe's

Heritage. In Legal Frameworks for the Protection of Immovable Cultural Heritage in Africa, Pp. 18–21. W. Ndoro and G. Pwiti, eds. Rome: ICCROM.

Clancy, M. 2001 Exporting Paradise Tourism and Development in Mexico. Amsterdam: Pergamon.

Clark, J. 2002 Hawaii Place Names: Shores, Beaches, and Surf Sites. Honolulu: University of Hawaii Press.

_____ 1985 Beaches of the Big Island. Honolulu: University of Hawaii Press.

Cloutier, J. 1976 Fort William: Food-related Artifacts. Fort William Archaeological Project, Ontario. Toronto: Ministry of Culture and Recreation.

Coan, Rev. T. 1868 Letter (to J. D. Dana) dated Hilo, April 7, 1868. In Recent Eruptions of Mauna Loa and Kilauea, Hawaii, J. D. Dand, ed. American Journal of Science and Arts 2(47):89–98.

Cobos, R. 2006 The Relationship between Tula and Chichén Itzá: Influences or Interactions? In Lifeways in the Northern Maya Lowlands, J. Mathews and B. Morrison, eds. Pp. 173–183. Tucson: University of Arizona Press.

Coe, M. 2002 Mexico from the Olmecs to the Aztecs, 5th edition. New York: Thames and Hudson.

Cohen, E. 1988 Authenticity and Commoditization in Tourism. Annals of Tourism Research 15:371–386.

_____ 1978 The Impact of Tourism on the Physical Environment. Annals of Tourism Research 5:215–237.

Coll, R., S. Tofield, B. Vyle, and R. Bolstad 2003 Free-choice Learning at a Metropolitan Zoo. Paper presented at the Annual Meeting of the National Association for Research in Science Teaching, Philadelphia, PA, March 23–26.

Collett, D. 1990 The Master Plan for the Conservation and Resource Development of the Archaeological Heritage. Harare, NMMZ.

Collingwood Bruce. 1867. The Roman Wall, an historical and topographical description of the Barrier of the Lower Isthmus, extending from the Tyne to the Solway. John Russell Smith: London.

Colwell-Chanthaphonh, C. and T. Ferguson 2008 Collaboration in Archaeological Practice: Engaging Descendant Communities. Walnut Creek, CA: AltaMira Press.

———— 2006 Memory Pieces and Footprints: Multivocality and the Meanings of Ancient Times and Ancestral Places among the Zuni and Hopi. American Anthropologist 108(1):148–162.

Cooper, C., D. Fletcher, D. Gilbert, D. Wanhill, and R. Shepherd 1998 Tourism: Principles and Practice, 2nd edition. Harlow: Longman.

Cordy, R. 2000 Exalted Sits the Chief: The Ancient History of Hawai'i Island. Honolulu: Mutual Publishing.

Corsane, G., ed. 2005 Issues in Heritage, Museums and Galleries: An Introductory Reader. London: Routledge.

Crisp, J. 2005 Sleuthing the Alamo: Davy Crockett's Last Stand and Other Mysteries of the Texas Revolution. New York: Oxford University Press.

Crozier, S.N. and W. Barrera. 1974. Archaeological Survey and Excavations at Punalu'u, Island of Hawai'i. Honolulu: Bernice P. Bishop Museum.

Cultural Information Service 1981 A Viewer's Guide to Masada. An ABC Novel for Television. New York: Cultural Information Service.

Danson, E. 1957 An Archaeological Survey of West Central New Mexico and East Central Arizona. Papers of the Peabody Museum of Archaeology and Ethnology 44(1). Cambridge: Harvard University.

David, B., I. McNiven, L. Manas, J. Manas, S. Savage, J. Crouch, G. Neliman and L. Brady 2004 Goba of Mua: Archaeology Working with Oral Tradition. Antiquity 78(299):158–172.

Davidson, R. 1998 Travel and Tourism in Europe, 2nd edition. Harlow: Longman.

De Chernatony, L. and McDonald, M. (1998), Creating Powerful Brands in Consumer, Services and Industrial Markets, 2nd ed., Butterworth-Heinemann, Oxford.

Destination Viking 2005 Welcome to Destination Viking. [online]. Norway. Accessed March 6, 2005. http://www.destinationviking.com.main.htm.

Díaz Polanco, H. 2009 La Diversidad Cultural y la Autonomía en México. México, D. F.: Nostra Ediciones.

Dickens, C. 1995 Hard Times. New York: Penguin.

Dickinson, F. 2001 Tracking a Legend: A North Country Legacy of Jacobite Times. Newcastle Upon Tyne: Cresset Books.

Diekmann, A. and K. Hannam 2012 Tourism Mobilities in India's Slum Spaces. Annals of Tourism Research 39(3):1316–1336.

Donato, E. 1979. The Museum's Furnace. In J.V. Harrari, ed., Textual Strategies, Pp. 213–238. Ithaca: Cornell University Press.

Drennan, R. and S. Mora, eds. 2002 Archaeological Research and Heritage Preservation in the Americas. Washington, DC: Society for American Archaeology.

Drew, P. and A. Wootton, eds. 1988 Erving Goffman: Exploring the Interaction Order. Cambridge: Polity Press.

Driessen, J., I. Schoep, and R. Laffineur, eds. 2004 Monuments of Minos Rethinking the Minoan Palaces. Aegeum 23. Proceedings of the International Workshop "Crete of the Hundred Palaces?" held at Université Catholique de Louvain, Louvain-la-Neuve, vol. 1, Pp. 14–15, December 2001.

Du Toit, S. 1897 Rhodesia, Past and Present. London: Heinemann.

Dudley, D. 1970 Roman Society. Harmondsworth: Penguin Books.

Duke, P. 2007 Tourist's Gaze, the Cretan's Glance: Archaeology and Tourism on a Greek Island. Walnut Creek, CA: Left Coast Press.

Dunlap, J. and S. Kellert 1989 Informal Learning at the Zoo: A Study of Attitude and Knowledge Impacts. Philadelphia: Zoological Society of Philadelphia.

Earle, R. 2007 The Return of the Native: Indians and Myth-making in Spanish America, 1810–1930. Durham: Duke University Press.

Eastern White Mountains Heritage Program N.d. White Mountains Interpretive and Heritage Center: The Vision. Accessed December 2008. http://www.lcmarketingdesign.com/Portfolio/HeritageCenter.pdf.

Eco, U. 1990 Travels in Hyperreality. New York, NY. Mariner Books.

Edgell, Sr., D. 2006 Managing Sustainable Tourism: A Legacy for the Future. London: Routledge.

Erikson, P. 1996 "So My Children Can Stay in the Pueblo:" Indigenous Community Museums and Selfdetermination in Oaxaca. Mexico. Museum Anthropology 20(1):37–46.

Evans, A. 1921 The Palace of Minos: vol. 1. London: Macmillan.

Evans, S. 2008 Ancient Mexico and Central America: Archaeology and Culture History, 2nd edition. New York: Thames and Hudson.

Fagan, B. 2005 Archaeology. New York: Prentice Hall.

Falk, J., ed. 2001 Free-Choice Science Education: How We Learn Science Outside of School. New York: Teacher's College Press, Columbia University.

Falk, J. and L. Dierking 2000 Learning from Museums: Visitor Experiences and the Making of Meaning. Walnut Creek, CA: AltaMira Press.

Fawcett, Jr., W. 2012 Bridging the Divide: Indigenous Communities and Archaeology into the 21st Century. American Indian Culture & Research Journal 36(2):166–168.

Feifer, M. 1985 Tourism in History: From Imperial Rome to the Present. New York: Stein and Day.

Ferguson, T. 2001 Applied Anthropology in the Management of Native American Cultural Resources: Archaeology, Ethnography, and History of Traditional Cultural Places. NAPA Bulletin 20(1):15–17.

Fonia, R. 2002 (1857) Memorial Museum, Residency, Lucknow. Lucknow: Archaeological Survey of India.

Fontein, J. 2006 The Silence of Great Zimbabwe: Contested Landscapes and the Power of Heritage. Harare: Weaver Press.

Ford, A. 1999 Environment, Land Use, and Sustainable Development: The El Pilar Archaeological Reserve. Maya Flora and Fauna in Belize and Guatemala 20(37):31–50.

Fornander, A. 1878 An Account of the Polynesian Race, its Origins and Migrations and the Ancient History of the Hawaiian People to the Times of Kamehameha I, 3 vols. London: Trubner.

Forster, R. 2002 (1881) The History of Corbridge. Paisley: Try Malden Ltd.

Franklin, A. & Crang, M. 2001. The trouble with tourism and travel theory. Tourist Studies 1(1): 5–22

Franco Mendoza, M. 1997 La Ley y la Costumbre en la Cañada de los Once Pueblos. Zamora, Michoacán: El Colegio de Michoacán.

Friedman, J. 1992 Myth, History, and Political Identity. Cultural Anthropology 7(2):194–210.

Fuchs, L. 1961 Hawaii Pono: "Hawaii the Excellent" An Ethnic and Political History. Honolulu: Bess Press.

Fyall, A. and B. Garrod 1998 Heritage Tourism: At What Price? Managing Leisure 3:213–228.

Gabany-Guerrero, T. 1999 Deciphering the Symbolic Heritage of the Tarascan Empire Interpreting the Political Economy of the Hospital of Parangaricutiro, Michoacán, México. Ph.D. dissertation, Dept. of Anthropology, State University of New York at Albany.
_____ 2004 Cliff Paintings of Parangaricutiro, Michoacán, Mexico. Report Submitted to the Foundation for Mesoamerican Studies.

Gabbert, W. 2004 Of Friends and Foes: The Caste War and Ethnicity in Yucatán. The Journal of Latin American Anthropology 9(1):90–118.

Gann, D. 2007 Casa Malpais: Preservation and Access. Arizona Insight April 2007:11. Phoenix: Arizona Humanities Council.

Gann, E. 1981 Masada. New York: Jove.

Garlake, P. 1982 Prehistory and Ideology in Zimbabwe. Africa 52(3):1–19.

Garrod B. and A. Fyall. 2000. Managing Heritage Tourism. Annals of Tourism Research 27(3):682–708.

Gazin-Schwartz, A. 2004 Mementos of the Past: Material Culture of Tourism at Stonehenge and Avebury. In Marketing Heritage: Archaeology and the Consumption of the Past, Y. Rowan and U. Baram, eds. Pp. 93–102. Walnut Creek, CA: AltaMira Press.

Geare, R. 1906 Recently Discovered Ruins in Rhodesia. Scientific American 94(11):231–232.

Geertz, C. 1997 Cultural Tourism: Tradition, Identity and Heritage Construction. In Tourism and Heritage Management, W. Nuryanti, ed. Pp. 14–24. Yogyakarta: Gadja Mada University Press.

Genoways, H. and M. Andrei, eds. 2008 Museum Origins. Walnut Creek, CA: Left Coast Press.

Gere, C. 2009 Knossos and the Prophets of Modernism. Chicago: University of Chicago Press.

Giecco, F., F. Dickinson, F. Wooler, P. Crompton and J. Reeves 2003 The Dilston Castle Project. Unpublished Archaeological Report. www.nparchaeology.co.uk.

Gilmore, J. and B. Pine 2007 Authenticity: What Consumers Really Want. Boston: Harvard Business School Press.

Glover, J., D. Rissolo, J. Mathews, and C. A. Furman 2012 El Proyecto Costa Escondida: Arqueologia y Compromiso Comunitario a lo Largo de la Costa Norte de Quintana Roo. Chungara, Revista de Antropología Chilena 44(3):511–522.

Glover, N. 2008 Co-produced Histories: Mapping the Uses and Narratives of History in the Tourist Age. The Public Historian 30(1):105–124.

Gmelch, S., ed. 2004 Tourists and Tourism. Long Grove, IL: Waveland Press.

Goffman, E. 1974 Frame Analysis: An Essay on the Organization of Experience. Cambridge: Harvard University Press.

———— 1983 The Interaction Order. American Sociological Review 48:1–17.

Goldberg, A. 1983 Identity and Experience in Haitian Voodoo Shows. Annals of Tourism Research 10(4):479–495.

Gooch, L. 1995 The Desperate Faction? The Jacobites of North-East England 1688–1745. University of Hull Press: Hull.

Gosden, C. 2001 Postcolonial Archaeology: Issues of Culture, Identity, and Knowledge. In Archaeological Theory Today, I. Hodder, ed. Pp. 241–61. Boston, MA: Polity Press.

Gössling, S., C. Hall, and D. Weaver, eds. 2008 Sustainable Tourism Futures: Perspectives on Systems, Restructuring and Innovations. London: Routledge.

Graburn, N. 1989 Tourism: The Sacred Journey. In Hosts and Guests the Anthropology of Tourism, 2nd edition, V. Smith, ed. Pp. 21–36. Philadelphia: University of Pennsylvania Press.

Graham, B., G. Ashworth, and J. Tunbridge 2000 A Geography of Heritage. London: Arnold.

Granovetter, M. 1985 Economic Action and Social Structure: The Problem of Embeddedness. American Journal of Sociology 91(3): 481–510.

Granovetter, M. 1990 The Old and the New Economic Sociology. In Beyond the Marketplace, R. Friedland and A. Robertson, eds. New York: Aldine.

Greene, J. 1999 Preserving Which Past for Whose Future? The Dilemma of Cultural Resource Management in Case Studies from Tunisia, Cyprus and Jordan. Conservation and Management of Archaeological Sites 3(1–2):43–60.

Greene, L. 1923 Hawaiian Stories and Wise Sayings. Poughkeepsie, N.Y.: Vassar College.

Greenwood, D. 2004 Culture by the Pound: An Anthropological Perspective on Tourism as Cultural Commoditization. In Tourists and Tourism, S. Gmelch, eds. Pp. 157–170. Long Grove, IL: Waveland Press.

Guillemin, G. 1965 Iximche 1964. Antropología e Historia de Guatemala 17:41–42.

Guerrero-Murillo, N. 2000 The Indian Community of the 21st Century: Sustainable Resource Management in San Juan Nuevo Parangaricutiro, Michoacán, México. M.S. thesis, Central Washington University: Natural Resources Management.

Guttmann-Bond, E. 2010 Sustainability Out of the Past: How Archaeology Can Save the Planet. World Archaeology 42(3):355–366.

Hadrian's Wall Heritage Ltd. 2007a Hadrian's Wall Heritage Limited Strategic Plan March 2007. Accessed November 13, 2008. http://www.hadrians-wall.org/ResourceManager/Documents/HWHL_Strategic_Plan_March_2007.pdf.

Hadrian's Wall Heritage Ltd. 2007b Annual Review 2006–2007: Bringing History and Landscape to Life. Hexham: HWHL.

Hadrian's Wall Heritage Ltd. 2007c Hadrian's Wall Heritage Marketing Strategy 2007–2010. Hexham: HWHL Hadrian's Wall Heritage Ltd.

Hadrian's Wall Heritage Ltd 2008 Annual Review: Bringing History and Landscape to Life 2007–2008. Hexham: HWHL

Halewood, C. and K. Hannam 2001 Viking Heritage Tourism: Authenticity and Commodification. Annals of Tourism Research 28(3):565–580.

Hall, C. 2007 Introduction to Tourism in Australia: Development, Issues and Change, 5th edition. Pearson Education: French's Forest.

_____ 1998 Introduction to Tourism: Development, Dimensions and Issues, 3rd edition. Melbourne: Longman.

Hall, C. M. 2005 Reconsidering the geography of tourism and contemporary mobility. Geographical Research 43(2):125–139

Hall, C. M. & Lew, A. 2009. *Understanding and Managing Tourism Impacts: An Integrated Approach*. Routledge, Abingdon.

Hall, D. 2003 Tourism and Sustainable Community Development. London: Routledge.

Halverson, C. 1992 Turtles and Tourists: Excavations at the Nestor Falls Site (DgKl-3)1989 and 1990. Conservation Archaeology Report, Northwestern Region Report 16. Kenora: Ontario Ministry of Culture and Communications.

REFERENCES

Ham, S. 1992 Environmental Interpretation: A Practical Guide for People with Big Ideas and Small Budgets. Golden, CO: North American Press.

Hamilakis, Y. 2009 The Nation and Its Ruins. Oxford: Oxford University Press.

Hamilakis, Y. and A. Anagnostopoulos, eds. 2009 Archaeological Ethnography, Special Double Issue. Public Archaeology 8(2–3).

Hamilakis, Y. and P. Duke, eds. 2008 Archaeology and Capitalism: From Ethics to Politics. Walnut Creek, CA: Left Coast Press.

Hamilton, S. 2000 Dynamics of Social Complexity in Early Nineteenth-Century British Fur-Trade Posts. International Journal of Historical Archaeology 4(3):217–273.

_____ 1981 The Archaeology of The Wenesaga Rapids. Archaeology Research Report Ontario, Toronto: Ministry of Culture and Recreation 17:1–203.

Hamilton, S. and C. Richie 1985 Rediscovering Red Rock House: The 1984 Test Excavations. North Central Region Report 18, Thunder Bay, Ontario: Ontario Ministry of Citizenship and Culture.

Hamilton, S., A. Gliddon, and B. Hamilton 1986 Rediscovering Red Rock House: The 1985 Test Excavations. North Central Region Report 21, Thunder Bay, Ontario: Ontario Ministry of Citizenship and Culture.

Hamilton, S., T. Fisher, and J. Taylor-Hollings 2003 An Overview of the Culture and History of the Chapleau Cree First Nation: Cultural Heritage Themes. Unpublished report prepared for Chapleau Cree First Nation.

Hamilton, S., T. Fisher, and M. Diab 2000 Cultural Heritage Themes and Aboriginal Tourism Development in the Wawakapewin Region, Northwestern Ontario. Unpublished report prepared for Wawa-kapewin First Nation and the Shibogama Tribal Association.

Handler, R. 2008 A Dangerously Elusive Method: Disciplines, Histories and the Limits of Reflexivity. In Ethnographic Archaeologies: Reflections on Stakeholders and Archaeological Practices, Q.E. Castañeda and C. Matthews, eds. Pp. 95–118. Lanham, MD: AltaMira Press.

Handler, R. and E. Gable 1997 The New History in an Old Museum: Creating the Past at the Colonial Williamsburg. Durham: Duke University Press.

Handy, E. and M. Pukui 1998 The Polynesian Family System in Kaū, Hawai'i. Honolulu: Mutual Publishing LLC.

Handy, E., M. Pukui, and K. Livermore 1934 Outline of Hawaiian Physical Therapeutics. Honolulu: The Museum.

Hannam, K. 2006 Contested Discourses of War and Heritage at the British Residency, Lucknow, India. International Journal of Tourism Research 8(3):199–212.

Hannam, K. and C. Halewood 2006 European Viking Festivals: An Expression of Identity. Journal of Heritage Tourism 1(1):17–31.

Hansen, J. and G. McGowan 1998 Breaking Ground, Breaking Silence: The Story of New York's African Burial Ground. Henry Holt and Co: New York.

Harris, R., P. Williams and T. Griffin, eds. 2002 Sustainable Tourism. London: Butterworth-Heinemann.

Harris, Charles H. III and Louis R. Sadler. 2003 The Archaeologist was a Spy. Albuquerque: University of New México Press.

Hasenaka, T. and I. Carmichael 1985 The Cinder Cones of Michoacan-Guanajuato, Central Mexico: Their Age, Volume and Distribution, and Magma Discharge Rate. Journal of Volcanology & Geothermal Research 25(1–2):105–124.

Herbert, D. 1995 Heritage as Informal Education. Heritage, Tourism and Society, D. Herbert. London: Pinter.

Herbert, D. 1995. Preface. D. Herbert. (ed). Heritage, Tourism and Society. London: Pinter. Pp. xi–xii.

Herbert, D. 1995b. Heritage places, leisure and tourism. D. Herbert. (ed). *Heritage, tourism and society*. London: Pinter. 1–20.

Hess, M. 2004 'Spatial' Relationships? Towards a Reconceptualisation of Embeddedness. Progress in Human Geography 28(2): 165–186.

Himpele, J. and Q. E. Castañeda 1997 Incidents of Travel in Chichén Itzá. Documentary Educational: Watertown, MA Resources.

Hingley, R. and C. Nesbitt N.d. Hadrian's Wall: A Wall for All Times. British Archaeology Issue 102, Sept/Oct. accessed November 3, 2008. http://www.britarch.ac.uk/ba/ba102/feat2.html.

Historic Landmarks Program N.d. Casa Malpais Site. Accessed December 2008.

http://tps.cr.nps.gov/nhl/detail.cfm?ResourceId=709&ResourceType =Site.

Hodder, I. 2010 Cultural Heritage Rights: From Ownership and Descent to Justice and Well-being. Anthropological Quarterly 83(4):861–882.

———— 2003 Ethics and Archaeology: The Attempt at Çatalhöyük. Near Eastern Archaeology, 65(3):174–181.

———— 1991 Interpretive Archaeology and its Role. American Antiquity 56(1):7–18.

Hohmann, J. 1990a Master Stabilization and Development Plan for the Casa Malpais National Historic Landmark Site. Studies in Western Archaeology No. 3. Phoenix: Louis Berger and Associates.

Holden, A. 2008. Environment and Tourism (2nd ed). Routledge, Abingdon.

Hollowell, J. and G. Nicholas 2009 Using Ethnographic Methods to Articulate Community-Based Conceptions of Cultural Heritage Management. Archaeological Ethnographies. Public Archaeology 8(2–3).

Holtorf, C. 2006 Archaeology Is a Brand! The Meaning of Archaeology in Contemporary Popular Culture. Walnut Creek, CA: Left Coast Press Inc.

———— 2005 From Stonehenge to Las Vegas: Archaeology as Popular Culture. Walnut Creek, CA: AltaMira Press.

Holzer, D., D. Scott, and R. Bixler 1998 Socialisation Influences on Adult Zoo Visitation. Journal of Applied Recreation Research 23(1):43–62.

Honey, M. 2008 Ecotourism and Sustainable Development, 2nd edition: Who Owns Paradise? Washington, DC: Island Press.

Hooper-Greenhill, E. 1992 Museums and the Shaping of Knowledge. London: Routledge.

Horne, D. 1984 The Great Museum. London: Pluto Press.

Hunter-Blair, P. 1963 Roman Britain and Early England 55B.C.–A.D.871. New York and London: W. W. & Co. Inc.

ICOMOS N.d. ICOMOS Charter for the Interpretation and Presentation of Cultural Heritage Sites, ratified by the 16th General Assembly of ICOMOS. http://www.international.icomos.org/quebec2008/charters/interpretation/pdf/GA16_Charter_Interpretation_20081004_FR+EN.pdf.

Ii, J. 1959 Fragments of Hawai'i an History, translated by M.K. Pukui, D. Barrere, ed. Honolulu: Bishop Museum Press.

Jaume B. Granquesa and Marc Morell 2007 Transversal Indicators and Qualitative Observatories of Heritage Tourism in Cultural Tourism Globall and Local Perspectives edited by Greg Richards. Binghamton, NY: The Haworth Hospitality Press.

Johnson, N. 1999 Framing the Past: Time, Space and the Politics of Heritage Tourism in Ireland. Political Geography 18:187–207.

Jones, A. 1999 Archaeological Reconstruction and Education at the Jorvik Viking Centre and Archaeological Resource Centre, York, UK. In The Constructed Past: Experimental Archaeology, Education and the Public, P. Stone and P. Planel, eds. Pp. 258–268. London: Routledge.

Jones, L. 1995 Twin City Tales. Boulder: University Press Colorado.

Jones, N. 1926 The Stone Age in Rhodesia. London: Oxford University Press.

Jordanova, L. 1989 Objects of Knowledge: A Historical Perspective on Museums. In The New Museology, P. Vergo, ed. Pp. 22–40. London: Reaktion Books.

Ka 'Ohana o Ka Lae. 1987 Ka'u Oral Pele: Goddess of Hawai'i's Volcanoes Histories: Interviews with Residents of Ka'u island of Hawaii. Na Maka o ka 'Aina: Na'alehu

Kane, H. 1987 The Kawainui Press: Captain Cook.

Karambakuwa R., T. Shonhiwa, L. Murombo, J. Mauchi, N. Gopo, W. Denhere, F. Tafirei, A. Chingarande, and V. Mudavanhu 2011 The Impact of Zimbabwe Tourism Authority Initiatives on Tourist Arrivals in Zimbabwe (2008–2009). Journal of Sustainable Development in Africa 13(6):68–77.

Karp, I., C. Kratz, L. Szwaja, and T. Ybarro-Frausto, eds. 2006 Museum Frictions: Public Cultures/Global Transformations. Durham: Duke University Press.

Katsamudanga, S. 2009 Consuming the Past: Public Perception Towards the Discipline of Archaeology in Zimbabwe. Paper presented at the SANORD 2nd International Conference on Inclusion and Exclusion in Higher Education, Rhodes University, Grahamstown, South Africa.

Ka'û Preservation N.d. Protecting Hawai'i 's Largest Wilderness Area. Accessed January 15, 2007. http://www.Ka'ûpreservation.org/.

Kaxil Kiuic N.d. Kaxil Kiuic Helen Moyers Biocultural Reserve. Accessed September, 2010. http://www.kiuic.org.

Keen, J. 1999 The Ancient Technology Centre, Cranbourne, UK: A Reconstruction Site Built for Education. In The Constructed Past: Experimental Archaeology, Education and the Public, P. Stone, and P. Planel, eds. Pp. 229–244. London: Routledge.

Kehoe, A. 1998 The Land of Prehistory. New York: Routledge.

Keitumetse, S. 2011 Sustainable Development and Cultural Heritage Management in Botswana: Towards Sustainable Communities. Sustainable Development 19(1):49–59.

Kelly, J. 2006 Ke 'ika ia Punalu'u: Ka'u Residents Want More Respect for a Beloved Place. Hawaii Island Journal vol. XXX, 5(2):3.

Kelly, M. 1980 Majestic Ka`u: Mo`olelo of Nine Ahupua`a. Department of Anthropology, Honolulu: Bernice P. Bishop Museum Press.

Kersting, J. N.d. [c.2003]. The PIT Experience: Life Lessons and So Much More. USDA Forest Service Passport in Time. Accessed November 11, 2008. http://www.passportintime.com/.

Kidd, K. 1949 The Excavation of Ste. Marie I. Toronto: University of Toronto Press.

Kidder, A. 1930 Division of Historical Research. Carnegie Yearbook No. 29 (1929–1929). Washington: C.I.W.

King, S. and R. Roth N.d. Broken Trust: Greed, Mismanagement & Political Manipulation at America's Largest Charitable Trust / S. King & R. Roth. Honolulu: University of Hawai'i Press. Accessed 2006. http://www.loc.gov/catdir/toc/ecip063/2005032815.html.

King, T. 2008 Cultural Resource Laws and Practice. Lanham, MD: AltaMira Press.

King, T. and M. Lyneis 1978 Preservation: A Developing Focus of American Archaeology. American Anthropologist 80(4):873–893.

Kirshenblatt-Gimblett, B. 1998 Destination Culture. Berkeley: University of California Press.

Klimko, O. 1998 Nationalism and the Growth of Fur Trade Archaeology in Western Canada. In Bringing Back the Past: Historical Perspectives on Canadian Archaeology, P. Smith and D. Mitchell, eds. Pp. 203–213. Mercury Series Archaeological Survey of Canada, Paper 158, Canadian Museum of Civilization: Hull.

Kluckhohn, C. eds. 1940 The Conceptual Structure in Middle American Studies. In The Maya and their Neighbors, Hay, Clarence L., Ralph L. Linton, Samual K. Lothrop, and Harry L. Shapiro, eds. Pp. 41–51. New York.

Knight, Jr., V. 1998 The Moundville Excavations of Clarence Bloomfield Moore. Alabama Heritage (48):6–17.

Knudson, D., T. Cable, and L. Beck 1995 Interpretation of Cultural and Natural Resources. State College, PA.: Venture Publishing.

Kohl, P. 2004 Making the Past Profitable in an Age of Globalization and National Ownership: Contradictions and Considerations. In Marketing Heritage Archaeology and Consumption of the Past, Y. Rowan and U. Baram, eds. Pp. 295–301. Walnut Creek, CA: AltaMira Press.

Kohl, P. and C. Fawcett 1996 Nationalism, Politics and the Practice of Archaeology. Cambridge: Cambridge University Press.

Ku, M. 2011 Actors and the Multiple Imaginaries on the Tourist Sites: A Case Study of the Mogao Caves, Dunhuang, China. Journal of Tourism and Cultural Change 9(3):217–225.

———— 2008 WenWu Zhi Yong? – ShiChang ZhuanXing Zhong Zhi ZhongGuo WenWu TiZhi De XingGou Yu ZhuanBian (The Use of Relics: Transformation of China's Cultural-Relic Institutions) Taiwan Sociology 16:149–192.

Kwas, M. 2000 On Site and Open to the Public: Education at Archaeological Parks. In The Archaeology Education Handbook, K. Smardz and S. Smith, eds. Pp. 340–351. Walnut Creek, CA: AltaMira Press.

Kyle, C. and W. Yaworsky 2008 Mexican Justice: Codified Law, Patronage, and the Regulation of Social Affairs in Guerrero, Mexico. Journal of Anthropological Research 64(1):67–90.

Lavine, S. 1991 Exhibiting Cultures. Washington, DC: Smithsonian Press.

Layton, R. and J. Thomas 2003 The Destruction and Conservation of Cultural Property. World Archaeological Bulletin 18:29–72.

Lazrus, P. 2006 Supporting and Promoting the Idea of a Shared Cultural Patrimony. In Archaeology, Cultural Heritage, and the Antiquities Trade, N. Brodie, M. Morag, C. Luke, and K. Tubb, eds. Pp. 270–283. Gainesvilles: University Press of Florida.

Leone, M. 2008 The Foundations of Archaeology. In Ethnographic Archaeologies: Reflections on Stakeholders and Archaeological Practices, Q. E. Castañeda and C. Matthews, eds. Pp. 119–138. Walnut Creek, CA: AltaMira Press.

Light, D. 1995 Heritage as Informal Education. In Heritage, Tourism and Society, D. Herbert, ed. Pp. 117–145. London: Mansell.

Lilley, I. 1999 Native Title and the Transformation of Archaeology. The Postcolonial World. Sydney: University of Sydney Press.

Lind, A. 2004 Immigration to Hawai'i. Social Process in Hawai'i: A Reader. 3rd edition, P. Manicus, ed. Honolulu: University of Hawai'i Press.

Little, Barbara J. 2002 Archaeology as a Shared Vision. Pp. 3–19 in Public Benefits of Archaeology, Barbara J. Little, editor. University Press of Florida, Gainesville.

Little, B. 2007 Historical Archaeology: Why the Past Matters. Walnut Creek, CA: Left Coast Press.

———— 2004 Is the Medium the Message? The Art of Interpreting Archaeology in U.S. National Parks. In Marketing Heritage Archaeology and Consumption of the Past, Y. Rowan and U. Baram, eds. Pp. 269–286. Walnut Creek, CA: Left Coast Press.

Little, B. and F. McManamon 2005 Archaeology and Tourism in and around America's National Parks. The SAA Archaeological Record 5(3):12–14, 60.

Lovata, T. 2007 Inauthentic Archaeologies: Public Uses and Abuses of the Past. S. Clift and P. Grabowski, eds. Walnut Creek, CA: Left Coast Press Inc.

Lowenthal, D. 1981 Our Past Before Us: Why Do We Save it? London: T. Smith.

Luhr, J. 1993 Paricutin; The Volcano Born in a Mexican Cornfield. Phoenix: Geoscience Press.

Mabugu R. 2002 Short-term Effects of Policy Reform on Tourism and the Macroeconomy in Zimbabwe: Applied CGE Analysis. Development Southern Africa 19(3):419–430.

Maca, Allan L. 2010 Then and Now: W. W. Taylor and American Archaeology. In Prophet, Pariah, and Pioneer: Walter W. Taylor and American Archaeology, Allan L. Maca, Jonathan E. Reyman and William J. Folan, eds. Pp. 3–56. Boulder: University Press of Colorado.

Maca, A., J. Reyman, and W. Folan, eds. 2009 Prophet, Pariah, and Pioneer: Walter W. Taylor and American Archaeology. Boulder: University Press of Colorado.

MacCannell, D. 1976 The Tourist: A New Theory of the Leisure Class. New York: Schocken.

Malcolm-Davies, J. 2004 Borrowed Robes: The Educational Value of Costumed Interpretation at Historic Sites. International Journal of Heritage Studies 10 (3):277–293.

Malmström, V. 1995 Geographical Origins of the Tarascans. Geographical Review 85(1):31–40.

Malpais Foundation 1999 Minutes of the September 29, 1993 Meeting. Town of Springerville, Arizona.

_____ 1995 Minutes of the February 3, 1995 Meeting. Town of Springerville, Arizona.

_____ 1993 Minutes of the April 9, 1999 meeting. Town of Springerville, Arizona.

Manwa, H. 2007 Is Zimbabwe Ready to Venture into the Cultural Tourism Market? Development Southern Africa 24(3):465–474.

Manyanga, M. 1999 The Antagonism of Living Realities: Archaeology and Religion: The Case of Manyanga (Ntaba zi ka Mambo) National Monument. Zimbabwea 6:10–14.

Manyanga, M. 2003 Intangible Cultural Heritage and the Empowerment of Local Communities: Manyanga (Ntaba Zi Ka Mambo) Revisited. Paper presented at the 13th ICOMOS General Assembly, Victoria Falls, Zimbabwe. http://www.icomos.org/victoriafalls2003/papers/C 3–5%2 0–%20Munyaradzi.pdf.

Marshall, Y. 2002 What is Community Archaeology? World Archaeology 34(2):211–219.

Martin, P., J. Rinaldo, and W. Longacre 1961 Mineral Creek Site and Hooper Ranch Pueblo, Eastern Arizona. Fieldiana: Anthropology 52.

Mason, R., M. MacLean, and M. de la Torre 2003 Hadrian's Wall World Heritage Site English Heritage: A Case Study. Los Angeles: The Getty Conservation Institute.

Mataga, J. 2003 Managing Intangible Heritage of Monuments and Sites in Zimbabwe: A Case Study of NMMZ. Unpublished MA thesis, History Department, University of Zimbabwe.

Matthews, C. 2008 The Location of Archaeology. In Ethnographic Archaeologies: Reflections on Stakeholders and Archaeological Practices, Q. E. Castañeda and C. Matthews, eds. Pp. 157–182. Walnut Creek, CA: AltaMira Press.

McCall-Theal, G. 1900 Records of South-eastern Africa III. Cape Town: Cape Colony Printers.

McDavid, C. 2004 From Traditional Archaeology to Public Archaeology to Community Action: The Levi Jordan Plantation Project. In Places in Mind: Public Archaeology as Applied Anthropology, P. Shackel and E. Chambers, eds. Pp. 35–56. New York: Routledge.

McDavid, C. and D. Babson, eds. 1997 In the Realm of Politics: Prospects for Public Participation in African-American and Plantation Archaeology. Historical Archaeology 31(3):1–152.

McGuire, R. 2008 Archaeology as Political Action. Berkeley: University of California Press.

McIntosh, A. and R. Prentice 1999 Affirming Authenticity: Consuming Cultural Heritage. Annals of Tourism Research 26(3):589–612.

McKercher, B. 2011 The Collective Effect of National Culture and Tourist Culture on Tourist Behavior. Journal of Travel & Tourism Marketing, Feb/Mar 28(2):145–164.

McKercher, B. and H. Du Cros 2002 Cultural Tourism the Partnership Between Tourism and Cultural Heritage Managment New York and London: The Hayworth Press, Inc.

McKillop, H. 2004 The Ancient Maya: New Perspectives. New York: W. W. Norton and Co. Inc.

McLeod, K. 1984 Excavation at the Mather-Walls House in Keewatin, Ontario. Conservation Archaeology Report Northwestern Region Report 4, Kenora: Ontario Ministry of Citizenship and Culture.

McMorran, C. 2008 Understanding the 'Heritage' in Heritage Tourism: Ideological Tool or Economic Tool for a Japanese Hot Springs Resort? Tourism Geographies 10(3):334–354.

Meadows, D. H., D. L. Meadows, J. Randers and W. Behrens 1972 The Limits of Growth. London: Pan.

Menon, K. 2003 The Residency, Lucknow. New Delhi: Archaeological Survey of India.

Merriman, N. 1999 Beyond the Glass Case: The Past, the Heritage and the Public in Britain. London: Leicester University Press.

Meskell, L., ed. 2009 Cosmopolitan Archaeologies. Durham: Duke University Press.

Meskell, L. and P. Pels 2005 Embedding Ethics. Oxford and New York: Berg.

_____ 2005 Introduction: Embedding Ethics. In Embedding Ethics, L. Meskell and P. Pels, eds. Pp. 1–28. Oxford and New York: Berg.

Mezirow, J. 1991 Transformative Dimensions of Adult Learning. San Francisco: Jossey Bass.

Milanich, J. 2000 Prolific Pioneer or Mound Mauler? Archaeology, 53(4):568.

Miller, L. 2009 2012: A Y2K for the New Age. Newsweek, Issue May 18, 2009. Published May 2, 2009, http://www.newsweek.com/id/195688.

Miller, J. 1996 Shingwauk's Vision: A History of Native Residential Schools. Toronto: University of Toronto Press.

Milloy, J. 1999 The Canadian Government and the Residential School System, 1879 to 1986. Winnipeg: University of Manitoba Press.

Moffat A. 2008 The Wall: Rome's Greatest Frontier. 34(2):211–219. Edinburgh: Birlinn.

Moheno, C. 1985 Las Historias y Los Hombres de San Juan Zamora, Mich.: Colegio de Michoacán.

Molyneaux, B. and P. Stone 1994 The Presented Past. London: Routledge.

Moscardo, G. 1999 Making Visitors Mindful: Principles for Creating Sustainable Visitor Experiences through Effective Communication. Champaign, IL: Sagamore Publishing.

Moscardo, G., R. Ballantyne and K. Hughes 2007 Designing Interpretive Signs: Principles in Practice. Colorado: Fulcrum Publishing.

Moscardo, G. and P. Pearce 1986 Historic Theme Parks: An Australian Experience in Authenticity. Annals of Tourism Research 13:467–479.

Mowforth, M. 2003 Tourism and Sustainability: Development and New Tourism in the Third World. London: Routledge.

Mudenda, M. 2008 Management of a Transboundary World Heritage Site: The Case of Victoria Falls. Unpublished M.A. thesis, History Department, University of Zimbabwe.

Mueller, T. 2008 Herod: The Holy Land's Visionary Builder. National Geographic 214(6) [December]:34–59.

N.A. 1981 National Museums and Monuments of Zimbabwe Act Chapter 25.11, 1981.

N.A. 1972 National Museums and Monuments of Zimbabwe Act Chapter 313, 1972.

———— 1998–1999 National Museums and Monuments of Zimbabwe (NMMZ) Annual Reports.

———— 1994–1995 National Museums and Monuments of Zimbabwe (NMMZ) Annual Reports.

———— 1992–1993 National Museums and Monuments of Zimbabwe (NMMZ) Annual Reports.

National Historic Landmarks Program 2008 Casa Malpais Site. Electronic document, http://tps.cr.nps.gov/nhl/detail.cfm?ResourceId=709&ResourceType=Site, accessed December 2008.

National Park Service 2008 What is a National Heritage Area? http://www.nps.gov/history/heritageareas/FAQ/INDEX.HTM, accessed December 2008.

Neily, Robert 1987 Draft National Register of Historic Places Nomination Form, Casa Malpais National Historic Landmark. Manuscript on file, Arizona State Museum. Tucson: University of Arizona.

Nhamo, A., A. Jopela and S. Katsamudanga 2013 Tradition and Modernity: A Critical Review of Inclusion and Exclusion of Other Voices and Actors in Archaeological Heritage Management in Southern Africa. In One world, many knowledge: Regional experiences, regional links, Pp. 175–192. Cape Town: The Southern African Nordic Centre (SANORD)

Nicholas, G. and T. Andrews 2005 Hadrian's Wall New Organisation Structure. Proposals Presented to Steering Group, April 2005.

North West Development Agency/One NorthEast (NWDA/ONE).

———— 2004 Hadrian's Wall Major Study Report Summary, September, 2004.

North West Development Agency/One NorthEast (NWDA/ONE). 2005 Hadrian's Wall New Organisation Structure Proposals Presented to Steering Group.

———— 1997 At a Crossroads: Archaeology and First Peoples in Canada. Department of Archaeology, Simon Fraser University. North West Development Agency / One North East.

Orams, M. 1994. Towards a More Desirable Form of Ecotourism Tourism Management [0261-5177] 6(1):3–8.

Orser, C. Jr. 2004 Historical Archaeology, 2nd edition. Upper Saddle River, N. J.: Pearson, Prentice Hall

Orser, C. Jr., ed. 2002 Encyclopedia of Historical Archaeology. New York: Routledge.

Packard, V. 1962 The Waste Makers. Harmondsworth: Penguin.

Packer, J. 2006 Learning for Fun: The Unique Contribution of Educational Leisure Experience. Curator 49(3):329–344.

Palmer, D. 2007 Qigong Fever: Body, Science, and Utopia in China. New York: Columbia University Press.

Palyvou, C. 2003 Architecture and Archaeology: The Minoan Palaces in the Twenty-First Century. In Theory and Practice in Mediterranean Archaeology: Old World and New World Perspectives, J. Papadopoulos, and R. Leventhal, eds. Pp. 205–233. Los Angeles: The Cotsen Institute of Archaeology at UCLA.

Papadopoulos, J. and R. Leventhal, eds. 2003 Theory and Practice in Mediterranean Archaeology: Old World and New World Perspectives. Los Angeles: The Cotsen Institute of Archaeology at UCLA.

Patterson, T. 1999 The Political Economy of Archaeology in the USA. Annual Review of Archaeology 28:155–174.

———— 1994 Toward a Social History of Archaeology in the United States. Harcourt Brace College Publishers.

———— 1986 The Last Sixty years: Towards a Social History of Americanist Archaeology in the United States. American Anthropologist 88:7–26.

Pattullo, P. and O. Minelli 2009 The Ethical Travel Guide: Your Passport to Exciting Alternative Holidays, 2nd edition. London: Earthscan Publications Ltd.

Pearson, C., T. Birchett, and R. Weinstein 2000 An Aptly Named Steamboat: Clarence B. Moore's 'Gopher.' Southeastern Archaeology 19(1):82–87.

Pels, P. 1999 Professions of Duplexity: A Prehistory of Ethical Codes in Anthropology. Current Anthropology 40(3):101–136.

Pels, P. and O. Salemin, eds. 2000 Introduction: Locating the Colonial Subjects of Anthropology. In Colonial Subjects, P. Pels and O. Salemink, eds. Pp. 1–52. Ann-Arbor: University of Michigan.

Pinter, T. 2005 Heritage Tourism and Archaeology: Critical Issues. In Archaeology and Heritage Tourism, T. Pinter and M. Kwas, eds. The SAA Archaeological Record 5(3):9–11.

Poder Legislativo, Estados Unidos Mexicanos 1986 Ley Federal Sobre Monumentos y Zonas Arqueológicos, Artísticos e Históricos. Mexico, D.F.

Polanyi, K. 1944 The Great Transformation: The Political and Economic Origins of Our Time. Boston: Beacon Press.

Poria, Y., A. Reichel, and A. Biran 2005 Heritage Site Management: Motivations and Expectations. Annals of Tourism Research 33(1):162–178.

Pratt, M. 1992 Imperial Eyes. London: Routledge.

Preserve America 2008 Descriptive List of 2006 Preserve America Grants (Round 1). Electronic document, http://www. preserveamerica.gov/list-0309.html, accessed December 2008.

Price, R. and S. Price 1994 Equatoria. London: Routledge.

Pwiti, G. 1994 Archaeology, Prehistory and Education in Zimbabwe. In The Presented Past, P. Stone and P. Molyneaux, eds. Pp. 338–348. London: Routledge.

———— 1996 Let the Ancestors Rest in Peace? New Challenges for Cultural Heritage Management in Zimbabwe. Conservation and Management of Archaeological Sites 1(3):151–160.

Pwiti, G. and G. Mvenge 1996 Archaeologists, Tourists and Rain-makers: Problems in the Management in Rock Art Sites in Zimbabwe, a Case Study of Domboshava National Monument. In Aspects of African Archaeology, G. Pwiti and R. Soper, eds. Pp. 816–822. Harare: University of Zimbabwe Publications.

Pwiti, G. and W. Ndoro 1999 The Legacy of Colonialism: Perceptions of Cultural Heritage in Southern Africa with Specific Reference to Zimbabwe. African Archaeological Review 16(3):143–153.

Pyburn, K. A. 2008. Public Archaeology, Indiana Jones, and Honesty. In Archaeologies, K. Pybern, ed. vol. 4, issue 2, Pp. 201–204

Pyburn, K. Anne. 2009. The Future of Archaeology as Anthropology. Anthropology News 50:9(9–10).

Rajnovich, G. and C. Reid 1987 Rescuing Rat Portage Prehistory: Preliminary Report on the 1986 Excavations of the Ballynacree Site in Kenora. Conservation Archaeology Report Northwestern Region Report 11, Kenora: Ontario Ministry of Culture and Citizenship.

Ramesh, R. 2007 Protests Force India War Grave Visitors to End Tour. The Guardian, September, 27.

Randall-MacIver, D. 1906a The Rhodesia Ruins: Their Probable Origins and Significance. The Geographical Journal 27(4):325–336.

———— 1906b Medieval Rhodesia. London: MacMillan.

Reade, L. and N. Waran 1996 The Modern Zoo: How do People Perceive Zoo Animals? Applied Animal Behaviour Science 47:109–118.

Remy, J. 1868 Contributions of a Venerable Savage to the Ancient History of the Hawaiian Islands. Translated by William Brigham. Privately printed. Boston: Press of A. A. Kingman.

Renfrew, C. 2000 Loot, Legitimacy and Ownership: The Ethical Crisis in Archaeology. London: Duckworth.

Restall, M. 2004 Maya Ethnogenesis. The Journal of Latin American Anthropology 9(1):64–89.

Robertshaw, A. N.d. A Dry Shell of the Past: Living History and the Interpretation of Historic Houses. Accessed on September 11, 2003. http://www.heritage-interpretation.org.uk/j2c-shell.htm.

Robinson, R. and C. Clifford 2007 Primi, Secondi, Insalata: Augmenting Authenticity at Special Events via Foodservice Experiences. International Journal of Event Management Research 3(2), Special Edition:1–11.

Robinson, T. 2006 Work, Leisure and the Environment: The Vicious Circle of Overwork and Over Consumption. Cheltenham: Edward Elgard.

Rogers, E. 1963 Changing Settlement Patterns of the Cree-Ojibwa of Northern Ontario. Southwestern Journal of Anthropology 9(1):64–88.

Rogers, E. 1994 Northern Algonkians and the Hudson's Bay Company, 1821–1890. In Aboriginal Ontario: Historical Perspectives on the First Nations, E. Rogers and D. Smith, eds. Pp. 307–343. Ontario Historical Studies Series, Toronto: Dundurn Press.

Rogers, E. and D. Smith, eds. 1994 Aboriginal Ontario: Historical Perspectives on the First Nations. Ontario Historical Studies Series, Toronto: Dundurn Press.

Rough Guides 2007 Ethical Travel Guide (Rough Guide 25s). Rough Guides: New York.

Rowan, Y. and U. Baram, eds. 2004 Marketing Heritage: Archaeology and the Consumption of the Past. Walnut Creek, CA: AltaMira Press.

Russell, I. 2006. Images of the past: Archaeologies, Modernities, Crises and Poetics. I. Russell (ed). *Images, representations and heritage: Moving beyond modern approaches to archaeology.* Springer: New York. Pp. 1–38.

Ryan, C. and J. Saward 2004 The Zoo as Ecotourism Attraction – Visitor Reaction, Perceptions and Management Implications: The Case of Hamilton Zoo, New Zealand. Journal of Sustainable Tourism 12(3):245–266.

Rydell, R. 1993 World of Fairs: The Century-of-Progress Expositions. Chicago: University of Chicago Press.

SAA Salary Survey 2005 Salary Survey Conducted for the Society for American Archaeology, in Cooperation with the Society for Historical Archaeology. Compiled by Association Research, Inc.

Sabloff, J. 1999 Distinguished Lecture in Archaeology: Communication and the Future of American Archaeology. American Anthropologist 100(4):869–875.

Sandvikens, K. 2003 Viking Festival. [on-line], Arsunda, Sweden. http://www.sandviken.se/skweb.asp?S=3&B=151&P=1528, accessed on February 3, 2003.

Sawyer, R. 2002 A Discourse on Discourse: An Archaeological History of an Intellectual Concept. Cultural Studies 16(3):433–456.

Scarre, C. and B. Fagan 2003 Ancient Civilizations, 2nd edition. Upper Saddle River, N. J.: Prentice-Hall, Pearson Education, Inc.

Schele, L. and P. Mathews 1998 The Code of Kings: The Language of Seven Sacred Maya Temples and Tombs. New York: Scribner.

Screven, C. 1999 Information Design in Informal Settings: Museums and Other Public Spaces. In Information Design, R. Jacobson, ed. Pp. 131–192. Cambridge: The MIT Press.

Seton, A. 1962 Devil Water. London: Hodder & Stoughton.

Shackel, P. 2003 Memory in Black and White: Race, Commemoration, and the Post-Bellum Landscape. Walnut Creek, CA: AltaMira Press.

Shackley, M. 1996 Wildlife Tourism. London: Thompson Business Press.

Shanks, M. and C. Tilley 1987 Re-Constructing Archaeology. Cambridge: Cambridge University Press.

Shapira, A. 1992 Land and Power: The Zionists Resort to Violence. New York: Oxford University Press.

Sheller, M. & Urry, J. 2006. The new mobilities paradigm. Environment and Planning A. 38: 207–226.

Shumba, E., et al 1998 Biodiversity. The State of Zimbabwe's Environment, M. Chirenje, L. Sola and D. Paleczny eds., Pp. 269–310. Harare: Ministry of Mines, Environment, and Tourism.

Sierra, M. 1995 Indian Rights and Customary Law in Mexico: A Study of the Nahuas in the Siera dePuebla. Law & Society Review 29(2):227–254.

Silva, C. 2008 "No todo empezó en Cádiz": simbiosis política en Oaxaca entre Colonia y República. (Spanish). "Not Everything Began in Cádiz:" Political Symbiosis in Oaxaca Between Colonialism and Republicanism, 19:8–35.

Silverman, H. 2005 Two Museums, Two Visions: Representing Cultural Heritage in Cusco, Peru. The SAA Archaeological Record 5(3):29–32.

_____ 2002 Touring Ancient Times: The Present and Presented Past in Contemporary Peru. American Anthropologist 104(3):881–902.

Simpson, F. and H. Williams 2008 Evaluating Community Archaeology in the UK, Public Archaeology 7(2):69–90.

Slaughter, S. and L. Leslie 1999 Academic Capitalism Politics, Policies, and the Entrepreneurial University. Baltimore: The Johns Hopkins University Press.

Slick, K. 2002 Archaeology and the Tourism Train. In Public Benefits of Archaeology, B. Little, ed. Pp. 219–227. Gainesville: University of Florida Press.

Smith, L. 2006 Uses of Heritage. London: Routledge.

Smith, V., ed. 1989 Hosts and Guests the Anthropology of Tourism. Philadelphia: University of Pennsylvania Press.

Smith V. and M. Brent, eds. 2001 Hosts and Guests Revisited: Tourism Issues of the 21st Century. New York: Cognizant Communication Corp.

Sorensen, C. 1989 Theme Parks and Time Machines. In The New Museology, P. Vergo, ed. Pp. 60–73. London: Reaktion Books.

Stagl, J. 1995 A History of Curiosity: The Theory of Travel, 1550–1800. Chur, Switzerland: Harwood Academic Publishers.

State of Hawai'i Department of Land and Natural Resources 2007 Report to the Twenty-Fourth Legislature 2007, Regular Session from the South Kona-Ka'ū Coastal Conservation Task Force. Honolulu: State of Hawai'i.

State of Hawai'i Department of Land and Natural Resources (2006) 'Report to the Twenty-Fourth Legislature 2007 Regular Session From The South Kona – Ka'ū Coastal Conservation Task Force', Honolulu: State of Hawai'i .

Stokes, J.F.G. 1909. 'Heiau from Honu'apo to Punalu'u, Ka'ū', in Heiaus of Hawai'i, unpublished Ms, Honolulu: Bishop Museum Library.

Stone, P. and P. Planel 1999 Introduction. In The Constructed Past: Experimental Archaeology, Education and the Public, P. Stone, and P. Planel, eds. Pp. 1–14. London: Routledge.

Stone, P. and P. Planel, eds. 1999 The Constructed Past: Experimental Archaeology, Education and the Public. London: Routledge.

Swarbrooke, J. 1999 Sustainable Tourism Management. Wallingford: CABI.

Taylor, A. and A. Gliddon 1989 The Mountain Portage Archaeological Project. Conservation Archaeology Report North Central Region Report 28, Thunder Bay: Ontario Ministry of Culture and Communications.

Taylor, Sarah 2012 Maya Cosmopolitans: Everyday Life at the Interface of Archaeology, Heritage, and Tourism Development. State University of New York at Albany, ProQuest, UMI Dissertations Publishing.

Taylor, W. 1996 Magistrates of the Sacred: Priests and Parishioners in Eighteenth-century Mexico. Stanford, CA: Stanford University Press.

———— 1948 A Study of Archaeology. Menasha, WI: American Anthropological Association.

Taylor-Hollings, J. 2006a Stage Two Archaeological Research at the Kirkness and Stormer Lakes in the Whitefeather Forest Planning Area, Northwestern Ontario. Unpublished report prepared for the Ontario Parks Ontario Ministry of Natural Resources in partnership with Pikangikum First Nation and the Whitefeather Forest Research Cooperative.

———— 2006b Stage Two Archaeological Research at Roderick Lake in the Whitefeather Forest Planning Area, Northwestern Ontario. Unpublished report prepared for the Ontario Parks, Ontario

Ministry of Natural Resources in partnership with Pikangikum First Nation and the Whitefeather Forest Research Cooperative.

Taylor-Hollings, J. and S. Hamilton N.d. Archaeological Explorations in the Berens and Bloodvein River Systems: The Woodland Caribou Signature Site and Whitefeather Forest Planning Area of Northwestern Ontario. Unpublished public education atlas prepared for Pikangikum First Nation.

Tenorio-Trillo, M. 1996 Mexico at the World's Fairs. Berkeley: University of California Press.

Thompson, R. 1989 Cliff Dwellings and the Park Service: Archeological Tourism in the Southwest. In International Perspectives on Cultural Parks: Proceedings of the First World Conference, Mesa Verde National Park, CO, 1984, Pp. 219–224. Washington, DC: National Park Service.

Tilden, F. 1977 (1957) Interpreting Our Heritage, 3rd edition. Chapel Hill: University of North Carolina Press.

Timothy, D. 2011. *Cultural Heritage and Tourism: An Introduction.* Bristol: Channel View Publications.

Timothy and Boyd 2006 World Heritage Sites in the Americas. In Managing World Heritage Sites, Pp. 239–249. Leask, A., and A. Fyall, eds. Oxford and Burlinton, MA: Butterworth-Heinemann, an imprint of Elsevier Press.

Town of Springerville N.d. Springerville, Arizona: Gateway to Arizona's White Mountains. Accessed December 2008. http://www.springerville.com.

Trigger, B. 2006 A History of Archaeological Thought. London: Cambridge University Press.

_____ 1994 Alternative Archaeologies: Nationalist, Colonialist, Imperialist. Man 19:355–370.

_____ 1985 Writing the History of Archaeology. In Objects and Others, G. Stocking, ed. Pp. 218–235. Madison: University of Wisconsin Press.

Tully, G. 2007 Community Archaeology: General Methods and Standards of Practice. Public Archaeology 6(3):155–187.

Turner, L. and J. Ash 1976 The Golden Hordes: International Tourism and the Pleasure Periphery. New York: St. Martin's Press.

Turner, V. and E. Turner 1978 Image and Pilgrimage in Christian Culture. New York: Columbia University Press.

Urry, J. 1990 The Tourist Gaze. London: Sage Publications.

Vafadari, A. 2008 Visitor Management, the Development of Sustainable Cultural Tourism and Local Community Participation at Chogha Zanbil, Iran. Conservation and Management of Archaeological Sites 10(3):264–304.

Valentine, P. 1992 Review: Nature-based Tourism. In Special Interest Tourism, B. Weiler and C. Hall eds., Pp. 43–49. London: Belhaven Press.

Valeri, V. 1985. Kingship and Sacrifice: Ritual and Society in Ancient Hawai'i. Chicago: University of Chicago Press.

Veverka, J. N.d. Exhibit Evaluation for Children's Exhibits: The Kirby Science Center Experience. Accessed on April 30, 2008. http://www.heritageinterp.com.

Wagner, C. 2005 The Conscientious Tourist: Ethical Choices Influence Travelers' Vacation Planning. (Economics). The Futurist. September 1, vol. 39 issue:5:14(2). Thomson Gale.

Waitt, G. 2000 Consuming Heritage: Perceived Historical Authenticity. Annals of Tourism Research 27(4):835–862.

Wai-Yin, C. 2004 Heritage Preservation and Sustainability of China's Development. Sustainable Development 12(1):15–31.

Walker, C. 2009 Heritage or Heresy: Archaeology and Culture on the Maya Riviera. Tuscaloosa: The University of Alabama Press.

———— 2005 Archaeological Tourism: Looking for Answers along Mexico's Maya Riviera. NAPA Bulletin 23(1):60–76.

Walton, J., ed. 2005 Histories of Tourism. Multilingual Matters, Limited.

Warburton 1753 Vallum Romanum or, The History and Antiquities of the Roman Wall, Commonly Called the Picts Wall, in Cumberland and Northumberland, Built by Hadrian and Severus. London.

Warman, A. 1980 "We Come to Object": The Peasants of Morelos and the National State. Baltimore: Johns Hopkins University Press.

Washburn, J. 2005 University Inc. New York: Basic Books.

Watkins, J., K. Pyburn, and P. Cressey 2000 Community Relations: What the Practicing Archaeologist Needs to Know to Work Effectively with Local and/or Descendant Communities. In Teaching Archaeology in the 21st Century, S. Bender and G. Smith, eds. Pp. 73–82. Washington, DC: Society for American Archaeology.

Watson, J. 2001 Indigenous Archaeologies. Walnut Creek, CA: AltaMira Press.

Weaver, D. 2005 Sustainable Tourism. London: Butterworth-Heinemann.

Weaver, D. and M. Oppermann. 2000 Tourism Management. Brisbane: John Wiley & Sons.

Welch, J. 2009 Best Cultural Heritage Stewardship Practices by and for the White Mountain Apache Tribe. Conservation and Management of Archaeological Sites 11(2):148–160.

Welch, J., K. Hoerig, and R. Endfield, Jr. 2005 Enhancing Cultural Heritage Management and Research through Tourism on White Mountain Apache Tribe Trust Lands. The SAA Archaeological Record 5(3):15–19.

Whitworth, A. 2000 Hadrian's Wall: Some Aspects of its Post-Roman Influence on the Landscape, British Archaeological Report 296. Oxford: Archaeopress.

Wickens, E. 1997 Licensed for Thrills: Risk-taking and Tourism. In Tourism and Health: Risk, Research and Responses, S. Clift and P. Grabowski, eds. London: Pinter. Pp forthcoming.

Wilk, R. 1999 Whose Forest? Whose Land? Whose Ruins? Ethics and Conservation. Science and Engineering Ethics 5(3):367–374.

Willey, G. and J. Sabloff 1993 A History of American Archaeology. San Franciso: W. H. Freeman and Co.

Williams, E. and R. Novella, eds. 1994 Arqueología del Occidente de México: Nuevas Aportaciones. Zamora, Mich.: El Colegio de Michoacán.

Williams, A. & Hall, C. M. 2002. Tourism, migration, circulation and mobility: The contingencies of time and place. A. Williams & C. M. Hall (eds). *Tourism and migration: New relationships between production and consumption*. Kluwer Academic Publishers, Dordrecht. Pp. 1 – 52

Withey, L. 1998 Grand Tour and Cooks Tours: A History of Leisure Travel, 1750 to 1915. London: Aurum Press.

Wolf, E. 1956 Aspects of Group Relations in a Complex Society: Mexico. American Anthropologist 58(6):1065–1078.

World Monuments Fund N.d. Accessed June, 2012. www.wmf.org

World Tourism Organization 2006a Tourism Market Trends. Madrid: WTO.

_____ 2006b Tourism Highlights. Madrid: WTO.

Worsley, L. 2004 Changing Notions of Authenticity: Presenting a Castle over Four Centuries. International Journal of Heritage Studies 10(2):120–149.

WTO [World Tourism Organization] N.d. Global Code of Ethics for Tourism. Accessed October 13, 2008. http://www.unwto.org/code_ethics/eng/global.htm.

Wylie, A. 1999 Science, Conservation, and Stewardship: Evolving Codes of Conduct in Archeology. Science and Engineering Ethics 5(3):319–336.

Wylie, J. and J. Bauer 2008 The Changing Face of Heritage Tourism. Legacy, the Magazine of the National Association for Interpretation 19(1):30–37.

Yadin, Y. 1966 Masada: Herod's Fortress and the Zealots' Last Stand. New York: Random House.

Yadin, Y. and G. Gottlieb 1969 The Story of Masada by Yigael Yadin Retold for Young Readers. New York: Random House.

Young, C. 2006 Hadrian's Wall: Conservation and Archaeology through Two Centuries. In Romanitas: Essays on Roman Archaeology in Honour of Sheppard Frere on the Occasion of His Ninetieth Birthday, R. Wilson, ed. Pp. 203–210. Oxford: Oxbow Books.

Zemesky, R., W. Massy, and G. Wegner 2005 Remaking the American University. Newark: Rutgers University Press.

Zerubave, Y. 1980 Last Stand: On the Transformation of Symbols in Modern Israeli Culture. Ann Arbor: Ann Arbor University Microfilms.

Zimmerman, Larry. 2008. Real or Reconstructed People? In Q. E. Castañeda and C. N. Matthews, eds. Ethnographic Archaeologies, Pp. 183–204. Walnut Creek, CA: AltaMira Press.

Zukin, S. and P. DiMaggio, eds. 1990 Introduction to Structures of Capital. Cambridge: Cambridge University Press.

Index

About the Authors

Roy Ballantyne is a Research Professor in the School of Tourism at the University of Queensland in Brisbane, Australia. He has over 30 years experience in teaching and researching in tertiary institutions, and he has a well-established international reputation for his work in environmental/heritage interpretation, environmental education, and visitor research. He has published 83 papers in refereed journals and 58 other publications in the fields of visitor research, environmental education, and higher education.

David Bennison is part-time Professor of Retailing at Manchester Metropolitan University Business School. His interests primarily lie in the fields of retail locational planning and place marketing, and he has published extensively on these topics, and has undertaken consultancy work for a range of retailers, developers, and local authorities.

Andrew Birley is the Director of Excavations for the Vindolanda Trust and has worked along the line of Hadrian's Wall for the past 15 years excavating sites and publishing his research. Andrew is responsible for the excavation and volunteers program at Vindolanda. He is the third generation and the fifth family member to work at the site – work that started in the 1920s when his grandfather, Professor Eric Birley, set up the Department of Archaeology at the University of Durham.

Neil Carr is an Associate Professor in the Tourism Department at the University of Otago, New Zealand. He has held previous positions at the University of Queensland, Australia, and the University of

Hertfordshire, UK. Neil has published over 40 peer-reviewed papers in a variety of academic journals and edited books. In addition, he is the editor of the *Annals of Leisure Research* and is on the editorial board of four academic journals.

Quetzil E. Castañeda, founding Director of OSEA, the Open School of Ethnography and Anthropology, is currently a Research Associate in Anthropology and Visiting Assistant Professor in the Latin American and Caribbean Studies Program at Indiana University. His research is represented in publications such as *In the Museum of Maya Culture* (University of Minnesota, 1996), *Ethnographic Archaeologies* (Alta-Mira Press, 2008), and the award-winning ethnographic film, *Incidents of Travel in Chichén Itzá* (D.E.R. 1997).

Tricia Gabany-Guerrero is an Assistant Professor of Anthropology at California State University, Fullerton. She received her doctorate in anthropology from The University at Albany, State University of New York where she specialized in Mesoamerican anthropology. Her doctoral and post-doctoral research focused on the ethnohistorical and archaeological analyses of the Tarascan or Phurépecha people of Michoacán, Mexico.

Narcizo Guerrero-Murillo is an Environmental Conservationist at the Natural Resources Conservation Services of the United States Department of Agriculture in Riverside, California. He has an MS in Natural Resources Management from Central Washington University where his thesis focused on sustainable development in the Phurépecha community of San Juan Nuevo Parangaricutiro, Michoacán, Mexico. Of Phurépecha heritage himself, he works on biodiversity studies, community development, and environmental archaeology in Mexico as the President of the Mexican Environmental & Cultural Research Institute.

Scott Hamilton (MA University of Alberta, PhD Simon Fraser University) specializes in the archaeology of the northern Plains and subarctic of Canada and addresses both precontact aboriginal archaeology and the archaeology and ethnohistory of the fur trade. He divides his career between applied and academic research. His emphasis is on the integration of archaeology with aboriginal traditional knowledge and land use and occupancy studies.

Kevin Hannam is Professor of Tourism Mobilities at Leeds Metropolitan University, UK. He is founding coeditor of the journal *Mobilities* (with John Urry and Mimi Sheller). He is chair the ATLAS Backpacker Research Group, and he has published widely on aspects of culture, heritage, and ecotourism development in India and Scandinavia. He holds a PhD in geography from the University of Portsmouth.

Karen Hughes has been involved in tourism research for 20 years, covering a wide range of topics including tourist satisfaction with guided tours, encouraging responsible visitor behavior in national parks, visitor learning, visitors' use of and preferences for information centers, beach safety, wildlife tourism, and designing interpretive signs. She is currently a researcher with the University of Queensland's School of Tourism.

Ming-chun Ku is an Assistant Professor of Sociology at National Tsing Hua University in Taiwan. She has been working on China's heritage tourism in the Economic-Reform Era since her PhD dissertation research at the New School for Social Research. Her research interests include tourism, heritage, cultural politics, and cultural economy. She has conducted fieldwork on heritage tourism in Northwest and Southeast China, and creative/cultural industry parks in Taiwan and China.

Barbara J. Little is an Adjunct Professor of Anthropology at the University of Maryland. Recent publications include *Historical Archaeology: Why the Past Matters* (Left Coast Press, 2007), which was named an "Outstanding Academic Title" by *Choice* in 2008, and *Archaeology as a Tool of Civic Engagement* coedited with Paul A. Shackel (AltaMira Press, 2007). She also serves as Program Manager for the US National Park Service Cultural Resources Office of Outreach in Washington DC.

Jennifer Mathews is a Professor of Anthropology at Trinity University in San Antonio, Texas. She is the codirector of the Yalahau Regional Human Ecology Project in Quintana Roo, Mexico, and she has been conducting archaeological research there since 1993. Although her research has focused on the ancient Maya, more recently she has examined the historic period of the Yucatán Peninsula (1550–1950), as well as issues related to tourism and sustainability.

Dominic Medway is Professor of Marketing and Head of the Marketing, Operations Management and Service Systems Division at Manchester Business School. His principal research interests cover place marketing and retail marketing. His work is published in a range of academic journals such as *European Journal of Marketing, Environment and Planning A, Tourism Management, Journal of Business Research and Journal of Marketing Management.*

Ancila Nhamo is a Lecturer at the University of Zimbabwe and has a Masters degree in archaeology from the University of Bergen in Norway. She has recently submitted her PhD thesis at the University of Zimbabwe. Her interests are in archaeology and cultural heritage management, especially prehistoric rock art. She has published two books and several articles on rock art, as well as a number of articles on management and sustainable utilization of archaeological sites.

Teresa L. Pinter is the former Director of the Cultural Resources Division at Archaeological Consulting Services, Ltd., in Tempe, Arizona. As Deputy State Historic Preservation Officer at the Arizona SHPO, she assisted in the development of Casa Malpais Archaeological Park. She has collaborated with the Governor's Archaeology Advisory Commission on creating guidelines on the heritage tourism potential of archaeological resources, and has coordinated the Public Education Committee's Heritage Tourism Work Group for the Society for American Archaeology.

Emilie Sibbesson is a doctoral researcher and teaching assistant at the University of Southampton, UK. She specializes in everyday experiences of the transition from foraging to farming in prehistoric Britain. She is particularly interested in interdisciplinary studies and science communication. She is a member of the British Science Association, the Prehistoric Society, and the Institute for Archaeologists. She has excavated archaeological sites in the UK from the Channel Islands to the Outer Hebrides.

Julie Tate-Libby is an adjunct professor of anthropology and sociology at Wenatchee Valley College and Lower Columbia Community College in Washington State. She obtained her PhD from the University of Otago where she concentrated on the links between amenity migration and preservation movements in Hawai'i. Tate-Libby has published a number of articles on migration and place, as well as her current research on mountain worship in the Himalayas.

Cameron Walker is an Adjunct Professor in the Department of Anthropology at California State University, Fullerton, and is a member of World Heritage Tourism Research Network (a Global Collaboration Initiative) based at Mount St. Vincent University, Halifax, Nova Scotia. She also serves as California Network Coordinator for the Society for American Archaeology. Her interest in the intersection between archaeology, anthropology, and tourism are detailed in *Heritage or Heresy: Archaeology and Culture on the Maya Riviera* (University of Alabama Press, 2009).

Tim Wallace is an Associate Professor in the Department of Sociology and Anthropology at North Carolina State University, Raleigh, North Carolina. His primary interests are in heritage conservation, representation, and identity. His most recent research concerns tourism, heritage, and globalization in the communities around Lake Atitlan in the Guatemalan Highlands. He is currently the editor of the Society for Applied Anthropology Newsletter and president-elect of the National Association for the Practice of Anthropology.

Gary Warnaby is Professor of Marketing in the School of Materials, the University of Manchester. His research interests include the marketing of places and retailing. Results of this research have been published in academic journals including *Environment and Planning A, Journal of Marketing Management, European Journal of Marketing, Cities, Area, Marketing Theory, Journal of Business Research, Local Economy and the International Review of Retail, and Distribution and Consumer Research.*

green press

INITIATIVE

Left Coast Press, Inc. is committed to preserving ancient forests and natural resources. We elected to print this title on 30% post consumer recycled paper, processed chlorine free. As a result, for this printing, we have saved:

2 Trees (40' tall and 6-8" diameter)
1 Million BTUs of Total Energy
213 Pounds of Greenhouse Gases
1,151 Gallons of Wastewater
77 Pounds of Solid Waste

Left Coast Press, Inc. made this paper choice because our printer, Thomson-Shore, Inc., is a member of Green Press Initiative, a nonprofit program dedicated to supporting authors, publishers, and suppliers in their efforts to reduce their use of fiber obtained from endangered forests.

For more information, visit www.greenpressinitiative.org

Environmental impact estimates were made using the Environmental Defense Paper Calculator. For more information visit: www.papercalculator.org.